PHP Programming with PEAR

XML, Data, Dates, Web Services, and Web APIs

Maximize your PHP development productivity by mastering the PEAR packages for accessing and displaying data, handling dates, working with XML and Web Services, and accessing Web APIs

Stephan Schmidt

Carsten Lucke

Stoyan Stefanov

Aaron Wormus

BIRMINGHAM - MUMBAI

PHP Programming with PEAR

XML, Data, Dates, Web Services, and Web APIs

First published: September 2006

Production Reference: 1160906

Published by Packt Publishing Ltd.
32 Lincoln Road
Olton
Birmingham, B27 6PA, UK.

ISBN 1-904811-79-5

`www.packtpub.com`

Cover Image by `www.visionwt.com`

Credits

Authors

Stephan Schmidt

Carsten Lucke

Stoyan Stefanov

Aaron Wormus

Reviewers

Lukas Smith

Shu-Wai Chow

Arnaud Limbourg

Development Editor

Douglas Paterson

Assistant Development Editor

Nikhil Bangera

Technical Editor

Ashutosh Pande

Editorial Manager

Dipali Chittar

Indexer

Mithil Kulkarni

Proofreader

Chris Smith

Layouts and Illustrations

Shantanu Zagade

Cover Designer

Shantanu Zagade

About the Authors

Stephan Schmidt is working for 1&1 Internet, the world's largest web hosting provider in Karlsruhe. He is leading a team of PHP and Java programmers and focusses on the development of the websites and online ordering systems of 1&1. He has been an active contributor to the PHP open source scene since 2001, when he founded the PHP Application Tools website (`http://www.php-tools.net`) together with some friends, which today is one of the oldest PHP OSS projects. He has also been working on more than 15 PEAR packages (with a focus on XML and web services), as well as the id3 extension. Recently he started the XJConf project (`http://www.xjconf.net`) and also contributes to the Java community.

He is the author of the (German language) *PHP Design Patterns* (O'Reilly Verlag, ISBN 3-89721-442-3) as well as a co-author of several other books on PHP and has been writing articles for several magazines. He has also spoken at various open-source conferences around the globe.

He devotes his spare time to American super-hero comics and the golden 50s.

Carsten Lucke studied computer science at the University of Applied Sciences in Brandenburg, Germany. He is currently working as a software engineer for the software design and management AG (sd&m AG) in Munich, Germany.

In his spare time he writes articles for various magazines and contributes to the open-source community (especially PHP). He is the developer of a handful of PEAR/PECL packages, founder of the 3rdPEARty pear channel-server project (`3rdpearty.net`) and the `tool-garage.de` open-source and freeware project.

Stoyan Stefanov is a web developer from Montreal, Canada, Zend Certified Engineer, book author, and contributor to the international PHP community. His personal blog is at `http://www.phpied.com`.

I would like to thank Tom Kouri and the team at High-Touch Communications in Montreal; special thanks to Derek Fong for introducing me to PEAR and to Michael Caplan for always being up to speed with the latest PEAR development.

Aaron Wormus is a freelance consultant working out of Frankfurt Germany. With a background in client/server development and intranet infrastructure, Aaron uses the power of PHP and Open Source tools to implement customized back-end solutions for his clients.

As a writer, Aaron contributes regular articles for *PHPMagazine*, *PHPArchitect* and *PHPSolutions* magazines. The topics of his articles have included PEAR Packages, core PHP programming, and programming methodologies. Aaron is also an avid blogger, and keeps his personal blog flowing with technical posts, political rants, and regular updates on the state of the weird and wonderful thing that is the Internet.

When Aaron is not at his computer, you can probably find him chasing his two daughters around, or wandering around the floor of a technology conference on a caffeine-induced high.

About the Reviewers

Lukas Kahwe Smith has been developing PHP since 2000 and joined the PEAR repository in 2001. Since then he has developed and maintained several PEAR packages, most notably MDB2 and LiveUser and has influenced the organization of the project itself as a founding member of the PEAR Group steering committee and QA core team. Aside from several magazine publications he is a well known speaker at various international PHP conferences.

Shu-Wai Chow has worked in the field of computer programming and information technology for the past eight years. He started his career in Sacramento, California, spending four years as the webmaster for Educaid, a First Union company and another four years at Vision Service Plan as an application developer. Through the years, he has become proficient in Java, JSP, PHP, ColdFusion, ASP, LDAP, XSLT, and XSL-FO. Shu has also been the volunteer webmaster and a feline adoption counselor for several animal welfare organizations in Sacramento.

He is currently a software engineer at Antenna Software in Jersey City, New Jersey.

Born in the British Crown Colony of Hong Kong, Shu did most of his alleged growing up in Palo Alto, California. He studied Anthropology and Economics at California State University, Sacramento. He lives along the New Jersey coast with seven very demanding cats, three birds that are too smart for their own good, a cherished Fender Stratocaster, and a beloved, saint-like girlfriend.

Arnaud Limbourg has been developing in PHP for 4 years. He is involved in the PEAR project as an assurance quality member and co-maintainer of the LiveUser package. He currently works for a telecom company doing VoIP as a developer.

Table of Contents

Preface

PEAR is the PHP Extension and Application Repository, and is a framework and distribution system for reusable, high-quality PHP components, available in the form of "packages". The home of PEAR is `pear.php.net`, from where you can download and browse this extensive range of powerful packages. For most things that you would want to use in your day-to-day development work, you will likely find a PEAR class or package that meets your needs. In addition to the functionality offered by the packages, PEAR code follows strict coding guidelines, bringing a consistency to your PEAR development experience.

In this book, you will learn how to use a number of the most powerful PEAR packages to boost your PHP development productivity. By focusing on the packages for key development activities, this book gives you an in-depth guide to getting the most from these powerful coding resources.

What This Book Covers

Chapter 1 provides an introduction to the MDB2 database abstraction layer. You will see how to connect to the database, instantiate MDB2 objects, execute queries and fetch data. There are a number of features and SQL syntax that are implemented differently in the database systems that MDB2 supports. MDB2 does its best to wrap the differences and provide a single interface for accessing those features, so that the developer doesn't need to worry about the implementation in the underlying database system. You will see how to use this SQL abstraction feature to provide auto-increment fields, perform "replace" queries that will update the records that already exist or do an insert otherwise, and make use of prepared statements, a convenient and security-conscious method of writing to the database. You will also learn about MDB2 modules and how to extend MDB2 to provide custom fetch and result classes, iterators, and modules.

Now that you've got data from your database, you want to display it.

Chapter 2 covers a range of PEAR packages commonly used for presenting data in different formats. You will see how to use HTML_Table and HTML_Table_Matrix to create and format tables, generate and format an Excel spreadsheet with the Excel_Spreadsheet_Writer package, create a flexible, pageable "datagrid" with Structures_Datagrid, and generate PDF documents on the fly with File_PDF.

XML is another favorite format for working with data, and PEAR does not let you down with its XML support.

In *Chapter 3* we take an in-depth look at working with XML in PEAR. The chapter covers creating XML documents using the XML_Util, XML_FastCreate, XML_Serializer, and XML_XUL packages. The chapter also covers reading XML documents using a SAX-based parser and transforming PHP objects into XML (and back again!) with XML_Serializer and XML_Unserialize.

Chapter 4 introduces you to PEAR's support for web services and Web APIs. You will learn about consuming SOAP and XML-RPC web services, access the Google API, search blog entries with Services_Technorati, access the Amazon web service, access the Yahoo API, and learn how to offer web services, either XML-RPC or SOAP based. You will also get a taste of offering a REST-based service with XML_Serializer.

Chapter 5 covers PEAR's date and time functions using PEAR::Calendar and PEAR::Date. You will learn about the benefits these packages offer over the standard PHP date and time functions, and then see how to create, manipulate, and compare Date objects, work with Date_Span arithmetic, handle timezones, keep track of public holidays with Date_Holiday, and use the Calendar class to display an HTML calendar.

Conventions

In this book, you will find a number of styles of text that distinguish between different kinds of information. Here are some examples of these styles, and an explanation of their meaning.

There are three styles for code. Code words in text are shown as follows: "This class also provides a `setId()` method, which is called by the `Label` object when the artist is added to the list of signed artists."

A block of code will be set as follows:

```
function getDGInstance($type)
{
    if (class_exists($type))
```

```
    {
        $datagrid =& new $type;
        return $datagrid;
    } else
      {
        return false;
      }
}
```

When we wish to draw your attention to a particular part of a code block, the relevant lines or items will be made bold:

```
$driver        = Date_Holidays::factory($driverId, $year);
$internalNames = $driver->getInternalHolidayNames();
```

Any command-line input and output is written as follows:

```
$ pear-dh-compile-translationfile --help
```

New terms and **important words** are introduced in a bold-type font. Words that you see on the screen, in menus or dialog boxes for example, appear in our text like this: "clicking the **Next** button moves you to the next screen".

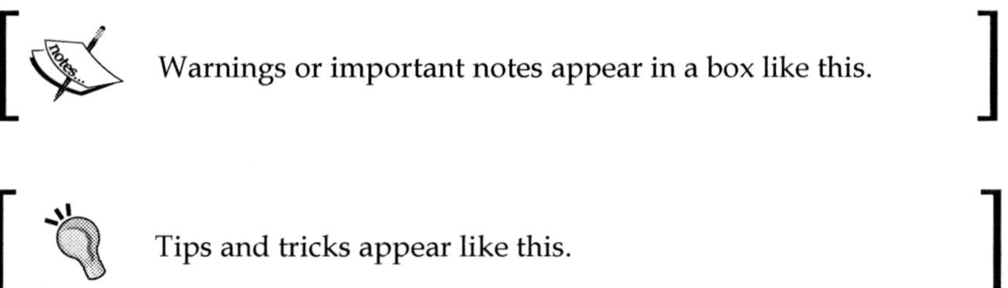

Warnings or important notes appear in a box like this.

Tips and tricks appear like this.

Reader Feedback

Feedback from our readers is always welcome. Let us know what you think about this book, what you liked or may have disliked. Reader feedback is important for us to develop titles that you really get the most out of.

To send us general feedback, simply drop an email to feedback@packtpub.com, making sure to mention the book title in the subject of your message.

If there is a book that you need and would like to see us publish, please send us a note in the **SUGGEST A TITLE** form on www.packtpub.com or email suggest@packtpub.com.

If there is a topic that you have expertise in and you are interested in either writing or contributing to a book, see our author guide on `www.packtpub.com/authors`.

Customer Support

Now that you are the proud owner of a Packt book, we have a number of things to help you to get the most from your purchase.

Downloading the Example Code for the Book

Visit `http://www.packtpub.com/support`, and select this book from the list of titles to download any example code or extra resources for this book. The files available for download will then be displayed.

The downloadable files contain instructions on how to use them.

Errata

Although we have taken every care to ensure the accuracy of our contents, mistakes do happen. If you find a mistake in one of our books—maybe a mistake in text or code—we would be grateful if you would report this to us. By doing this you can save other readers from frustration, and help to improve subsequent versions of this book. If you find any errata, report them by visiting `http://www.packtpub.com/support`, selecting your book, clicking on the **Submit Errata** link, and entering the details of your errata. Once your errata have been verified, your submission will be accepted and the errata added to the list of existing errata. The existing errata can be viewed by selecting your title from `http://www.packtpub.com/support`.

Questions

You can contact us at `questions@packtpub.com` if you are having a problem with some aspect of the book, and we will do our best to address it.

1
MDB2

The Web has matured and grown over the last decade and with it the need for more complex and dynamic sites. While storing information in a text file or simple database may have been suitable in the past, these days any serious application developer requires a firm knowledge of how to wield the relational database.

From the earliest versions of PHP, programmers have always been able to count on strong database support. However until the recent release of PDO there had been no standard way of interfacing with the multiple database drivers bundled with PHP. The lack of unified API has spawned several efforts to create database abstraction layers (DBAL). The primary goal of these efforts is to enable developers to write code that is not specific to the database back end being used, thereby enabling clients/users to deploy the application on whichever database platform they prefer.

The three most prominent full-featured database abstraction layers over the years have been AdoDB, PEAR::DB, and Metabase. In the last few years we have seen another very strong contender in the arena of database abstraction layers, and that is PEAR::MDB. This chapter is about MDB's second iteration—MDB2.

A Brief History of MDB2

It all started when Lukas Smith, a PEAR developer, submitted a few patches to the existing DBAL, Metabase. At some point he and the Metabase author started discussing bringing Metabase into PEAR as a new package. The goal of the new package was to merge the functionality of Metabase with the API of the existing and popular PEAR::DB into a feature-rich and well-performing database abstraction library, leveraging the PEAR infrastructure. Thus began the life of MDB2's predecessor PEAR::MDB.

After a few years of work on PEAR::MDB, it became apparent that the decision to keep a similar API to that of Metabase and PEAR::DB created some design issues, which hampered the growth of MDB into a full-featured DBAL. Since PEAR::MDB had reached a stable state in PEAR, it was not possible to fix these API issues without breaking backwards compatibility, which was not an option. The solution was to take the lessons learned during the development of Metabase and MDB and apply them to a new package that would contain a well-designed and modern API. The new package became MDB2.

Abstraction Layers

Before we get into the details of how MDB2 handles database abstraction, we should take a look at database abstraction theory and find out exactly what it means. There are several different facets to database abstraction, and we will go over them and specify what their requirements are.

Database Interface Abstraction

Database interface abstraction is the most important of all; it allows a programmer to access every database using the same method calls. This means that instantiating a database connection, sending a query, and retrieving the data will be identical, regardless of which database you are interfacing with.

SQL Abstraction

Most modern databases support a standard subset of SQL, so most SQL that you write will work regardless of which database back end you are using. However, many databases have introduced database-specific SQL lingo and functions, so it is possible that the SQL that you write for one database will not work on another. As an RDBMS (Relational DataBase Management System) matures, sometimes it implements features that are not compatible with older versions of the same database. So if an application developer wants to write SQL compliant with all versions of a specific database (or which can be used on multiple database back ends), one option is to stick to SQL they know is supported on all platforms. The better option though, is to use an abstraction layer that emulates the functionality when it's not available on the specific platform.

While there is no possible way to encapsulate every possible SQL function, MDB2 provides support for many of the most common features of SQL. These features include support for LIMIT queries, sub-selects, and prepared queries among others. Using the MDB2 SQL abstraction will guarantee that you'll be able to use this advanced functionality, even though it's not natively supported in the database you're using. Further in this chapter you'll learn more about the different SQL abstraction functions that MDB2 provides.

Datatype Abstraction

The third type of abstraction is the datatype abstraction. The need for this type of abstraction stems from the fact that different databases handle data types differently.

Speed Considerations

Now that you are salivating over all these great features that are bundled in MDB2, you should think about speed and performance issues. When using a database abstraction layer you need to understand that in many cases you will need to sacrifice performance speed for the wealth of functionality that the package offers. This is not specific to MDB2 or even database abstraction layers, but to abstraction layers or software virtualization systems in general.

Thankfully, unlike VMWare or Microsoft Virtual PC, which abstract each system call made, MDB2 only provides abstraction when a feature is not available in a specific back end. This means that performance will depend on the platform on which you are using MDB2. If you are very concerned about performance, you should run an opcode cache, or turn on a database-specific query caching mechanism in your particular database. Taking these steps in PHP itself or your database back end will make the overhead, which is inevitable in your database abstraction layer, much smaller.

MDB2 Package Design

The API design of MDB2 was created to ensure maximum flexibility. A modular approach was taken when handling both database back ends and specific advanced functionality. Each database -specific **driver** is packaged and maintained as an independent PEAR module. These driver packages have a life of their own, which means individual release cycles and stability levels. This system allows the maintainers of the database drivers to release their packages as often as they need to, without having to wait for a release of the main MDB2 package. This also allows the MDB2 package to advance in stability regardless of the state of the driver packages, the effect being that while the state of MDB2 is stable, some of its drivers may only be beta. Also, when a new database driver is released, it is tagged as alpha and the release process progresses according to PEAR standards.

The second type of modularity built into MDB2 is used for adding extended functionality to MDB2. Rather than include the functions into MDB2 itself or extend MDB2 with a new class that adds this functionality, you have the option to create a separate class and then load it into MDB2 using the `loadModule()` method. Once a module is loaded into MDB2, you will be able to access your methods as if they were built into MDB2. MDB2 uses this internally to keep the core components as fast as possible, and also makes it possible for the user to define and include their own classes into MDB2. You'll see the details of how to extend MDB2 later in this chapter.

Getting Started with MDB2

Let's discuss the necessary steps to install MDB2, to create an MDB2 object, and then set up some options to set the data fetch mode and finally disconnect from the database.

Installing MDB2

When installing MDB2, keep in mind that the MDB2 package does not include any database drivers, so these will need to be installed separately. MDB2 is stable, but as explained earlier, since the packages have different release cycles, the status of the package you plan to use may be beta, alpha, or still in development. This will need to be taken into consideration when installing a driver package.

The easiest way to install MDB2 is by using the PEAR installer:

```
> pear install MDB2
```

This command will install the core MDB2 classes, but none of the database drivers. To install the driver for the database you'll be using, type:

```
> pear install MDB2_Driver_mysql
```

This will install the driver for MySQL. If you wish to install the driver for SQLite, type:

```
> pear install MDB2_Driver_sqlite
```

The full list of currently available drivers is as follows:

- `fbsql`: FrontBase
- `ibase`: InterBase
- `mssql`: MS SQL Server
- `mysql`: MySQL
- `mysqli`: MySQL using the mysqli PHP extension; for more details, visit `http://php.net/mysqli`
- `oci8`: Oracle
- `pgsql`: PostgreSQL
- `querysim`: Querysim
- `sqlite`: SQLite

Connecting to the Database

To connect to your database after a successful installation, you need to set up the DSN (Data Source Name) first. The DSN can be a string or an array and it defines the parameters for your connection, such as the name of the database, the type of the RDBMS, the username and password to access the database, and so on.

DSN Array

If the DSN is defined as an array, it will look something like this:

```
$dsn = array ( 'phptype'  => 'mysql',
               'hostspec' => 'localhost:3306',
               'username' => 'user',
               'password' => 'pass',
               'database' => 'mdb2test'
             );
```

Here's a list of keys available to use in the DSN array:

- `phptype`: The name of the driver to be used, in other words, it defines the type of the RDBMS
- `hostspec`: (host specification) can look like `hostname:port` or it can be only the hostname while the port can be defined separately in a `port` array key
- `database`: The name of the actual database to connect to
- `dbsyntax`: If different than the `phptype`
- `protocol`: The protocol, for example TCP
- `socket`: Mentioned if connecting via a socket
- `mode`: Used for defining the mode when opening the database file

DSN String

A quicker and friendlier way (once you get used to it) to define the DSN is to use a string that looks similar to a URL. The basic syntax is:

```
phptype://username:password@hostspec/database
```

The example above becomes:

```
$dsn = 'mysql://user:pass@localhost:3306/mdb2test';
```

More details on the DSN and more DSN string examples are available in the PEAR manual at `http://pear.php.net/manual/en/package.database.mdb2.intro-dsn.php`.

Instantiating an MDB2 object

There are three methods to create an MDB2 object:

```
$mdb2 =& MDB2::connect($dsn);
$mdb2 =& MDB2::factory($dsn);
$mdb2 =& MDB2::singleton($dsn);
```

`connect()` will create an object and will connect to the database. `factory()` will create an object, but will not establish a connection until it's needed. `singleton()` is like `factory()` but it makes sure that only one MDB2 object exists with the same DSN. If the requested object exists, it's returned; otherwise a new one is created.

One scenario exists where you can "break" the singleton functionality by using `setDatabase()` to set the current database to a database different from the one specified in the DSN.

```
$dsn = 'mysql://root@localhost/mdb2test';
$mdb2_first =& MDB2::singleton($dsn);
$mdb2_first->setDatabase('another_db');
$mdb2_second =& MDB2::singleton($dsn);
```

In this case you'll have two different MDB2 instances.

All three methods will create an object of the database driver class. For example, when using the MySQL driver, the variable `$mdb2` defined above will be an instance of the `MDB2_Driver_mysql` class.

Options

MDB2 accepts quite a few options that can be set with the call to `connect()`, `factory()`, or `singleton()`, or they can be set later using the `setOption()` method (to set one option a time) or the `setOptions()` method (to set several options at once). For example:

```
$options = array ( 'persistent' => true,
                   'ssl' => true,
                 );
$mdb2 =& $MDB2::factory($dsn, $options);
```

or

```
$mdb2->setOption('portability', MDB2_PORTABILITY_NONE);
```

The full list of available options can be found in the package's API docs at: `http://pear.php.net/package/MDB2/docs/`. Let's take a look at two important ones right away.

Option "persistent"

This Boolean option defines whether or not a persistent connection should be established.

There is an informative article on `mysql.com` about the pros and cons of using persistent connections in MySQL; it's located at `http://www.mysql.com/news-and-events/newsletter/2002-11/a0000000086.html`.

The default value is `false`. If you want to override the default, you can set it when the object is created:

```
$options = array ( 'persistent' => true
                 );
$mdb2 =& MDB2::factory($dsn, $options);
```

Using `setOption()` you can define options after the object has been created:

```
$mdb2->setOption('persistent', true);
```

Option "portability"

MDB2 tries to address some inconsistencies in the way different DBMS implement certain features. You can define to which extent the database layer should worry about the portability of your scripts by setting the `portability` option.

The different portability options are defined as constants prefixed with `MDB2_PORTABILITY_*` and the default value is `MDB2_PORTABILITY_ALL`, meaning "do everything possible to ensure portability". The full list of portability constants and their meaning can be found at `http://pear.php.net/manual/en/package.database.mdb2.intro-portability.php`.

You can include several portability options or include all with some exceptions by using bitwise operations, exactly as you would do when setting error reporting in PHP. The following example will set the portability to all but lowercasing:

```
MDB2_PORTABILITY_ALL ^ MDB2_PORTABILITY_LOWERCASE
```

If you don't want use the full portability features of MDB2 but only trim white space in results and convert empty values to `null` strings:

```
MDB2_PORTABILITY_RTRIM | MDB2_PORTABILITY_EMPTY_TO_NULL
```

Probably the best thing to do is to leave the default `MDB2_PORTABILITY_ALL`; this way if you run into some problems with your application, you can double-check the database access part to ensure that the application is as portable as possible.

Setting Fetch Mode

One more setting you'd probably want to define upfront is the fetch mode, or the way results will be returned to you. You can have them as an enumerated list (default option), associative arrays, or objects. Here are examples of setting the fetch mode:

```
$mdb2->setFetchMode(MDB2_FETCHMODE_ORDERED);
$mdb2->setFetchMode(MDB2_FETCHMODE_ASSOC);
$mdb2->setFetchMode(MDB2_FETCHMODE_OBJECT);
```

Probably the friendliest and the most common fetch mode is the associative array, because it gives you the results as arrays where the keys are the names of the table columns. To illustrate the differences, consider the different ways of accessing the data in your result sets:

```
echo $result[0]; // ordered/enumerated array, default in MDB2
echo $result['name']; // associative array
echo $result->name; // object
```

There is one more fetch mode type, which is `MDB2_FETCHMODE_FLIPPED`. It's a bit exotic and its behavior is explained in the MDB2 API documentation as:

"For multi-dimensional results, normally the first level of arrays is the row number, and the second level indexed by column number or name. `MDB2_FETCHMODE_FLIPPED` switches this order, so the first level of arrays is the column name, and the second level the row number."

Disconnecting

If you want to explicitly disconnect from the database, you can call:

```
$mdb2->disconnect();
```

Even if you do not disconnect explicitly, MDB2 will do that for you in its destructor.

Using MDB2

Once you've connected to your database and have set some of the options and the fetch mode, you can start executing queries. For the purpose of the examples in this chapter, let's say you have a table called `people` that looks like this:

id	name	family	birth_date
1	Eddie	Vedder	1964-12-23
2	Mike	McCready	1966-04-05
3	Stone	Gossard	1966-07-20

A Quick Example

Here's a quick example, just to get a feeling of how MDB2 can be used. You'll learn the details in a bit, but take a moment to look at the code and see if you can figure it out yourself.

```
<?php
require_once 'MDB2.php';
// setup
$dsn = 'mysql://root:secret@localhost/mdb2test';
$options = array ('persistent' => true);
$mdb2 =& MDB2::factory($dsn, $options);
$mdb2->setFetchMode(MDB2_FETCHMODE_ASSOC);

// execute a query
$sql = 'SELECT * FROM people';
$result = $mdb2->query($sql);

// display first names
while ($row = $result->fetchRow())
{
    echo $row['name'], '<br />';
}

// release resources
$result->free();

// disable queries
$mdb2->setOption('disable_query', true);

// delete the third record
$id = 3;
$sql = 'DELETE FROM people WHERE id=%d';
$sql = sprintf($sql, $mdb2->quote($id, 'integer'));
echo '<hr />Affected rows: ';
echo $mdb2->exec($sql);

// close connection
$mdb2->disconnect();
?>
```

Executing Queries

To execute any query, you can use the `query()` or `exec()` methods. The `query()` method returns an `MBD2_Result` object on success, while `exec()` returns the number of rows affected by the query, if any. So `exec()` is more suitable for queries that modify data.

While you can basically perform any database operation with `query()`, there are other methods, discussed later, that are better suited for more specific common tasks.

Fetching Data

In the example above we had:

```
$sql = 'SELECT * FROM people';
$result = $mdb2->query($sql);
```

The variable `$result` will be an `MDB2_Result` object, or more specifically, it will be a database driver-dependent class that extends `MDB2_Result`, for example `MDB2_Result_mysql`. To navigate through the result set you can use the `fetchRow()` method in a loop.

```
while ($row = $result->fetchRow())
{
   echo $row['name'], '<br />';
}
```

Every time you call `fetchRow()`, it will move to the next record and will give you a *reference* to the data contained in it. Apart from `fetchRow()`, there are also other methods of the `fetch*()` family:

- `fetchAll()` will give you an array of all records at once.
- `fetchOne()` will return the value from first field of the current row if called without any parameters, or it can return any single field of any row. For example, `fetchOne(1,1)` will return **Mike**, the second column of the second row.
- `fetchCol($colnum)` will return all the rows in the column with number `$colnum`, or the first column if the `$colnum` parameter is not set.

Note that `fetchRow()` and `fetchOne()` will move the internal pointer to the current record, while `fetchAll()` and `fetchCol()` will move it to the end of the result set. So in the example above if you call `fetchOne(1)` twice, you'll get **Eddie** then **Mike**. You can also use `$result->nextResult()` to move the pointer to the next record in the result set or `$result->seek($rownum)` to move the pointer to any row specified by `$rownum`. If in doubt, `$result->rowCount()` will tell you where in the result set your pointer currently is.

You also have access to the number of rows and the number of columns in a result set:

```
$sql = 'SELECT * FROM people';
$result = $mdb2->query($sql);
echo $result->numCols(); // prints 4
echo $result->numRows(); // prints 3
```

Shortcuts for Retrieving Data

Often it is much more convenient to directly get the data as associative arrays (or your preferred fetch mode) and not worry about navigating the result set. MDB2 provides two sets of shortcut methods - `query*()` methods and `get*()` methods. They take just one method call to do the following:

1. Execute a query
2. Fetch the data returned
3. Free the resources taken by the result

query*() Shortcuts

You have at your disposal the methods `queryAll()`, `queryRow()`, `queryOne()`, and `queryCol()`, which correspond to the four `fetch*()` methods explained above. Here's an example to illustrate the difference between the `query*()` and the `fetch*()` methods:

```
// the SQL statement
$sql = 'SELECT * FROM people';
// one way of getting all the data
$result = $mdb2->query($sql);
$data = $result->fetchAll();
$result->free(); // not required, but a good habit
// the shortcut way
$data = $mdb2->queryAll($sql);
```

In both cases if you `print_r()` the contents in `$data` and use the associative array fetch mode, you'll get:

```
Array (  [0] => Array ( [id] => 1
                        [name] => Eddie
                        [family] => Vedder
                        [birth_date] => 1964-12-23
```

```
                              )
            [1] => Array ( [id] => 2
                           [name] => Mike
                           [family] => McCready
                           [birth_date] => 1966-04-05
                         )
        ...
        )
```

get*() Shortcuts

In addition to the `query*()` shortcuts, you have the `get*()` shortcuts, which behave in the same way, but also allow you to use parameters in your queries. Consider the following example:

```
$sql = 'SELECT * FROM people WHERE id=?';
$mdb2->loadModule('Extended');
$data = $mdb2->getRow($sql, null, array(1));
```

In this example the question mark in the statement is a placeholder that will be replaced by the value in the third parameter of `getRow()`.

You can also use named parameters, like this:

```
$sql = 'SELECT * FROM people WHERE id=:the_id';
$mdb2->loadModule('Extended');
$data = $mdb2->getRow( $sql,
                       null,
                       array('the_id' => 1)
                     );
```

Note that the `get*()` methods are in the Extended MDB2 module, which means that they are not available until you load that module using `$mdb2->loadModule('Extended')`.

Loading modules benefits from object overloading, which was not available before PHP5, so to get access to the methods of the Extended module in PHP4, you need to call them using:

```
$mdb2->extended->getAll($sql);
```

as opposed to:

```
$mdb2->getAll($sql);
```

getAssoc()

Another useful `get*()` method that doesn't have a directly corresponding `fetch*()` or `query*()` is `getAssoc()`. It returns results just like `getAll()`, but the keys in the result array are the values of the first column. In addition, if there are only two columns in the result set, since one of them is already used as an array index, the other one is returned as a string (as opposed to an array with just one element). A few examples to illustrate the differences between `getAll()` and `getAssoc()`:

```
$sql = 'SELECT id, name FROM people';
$mdb2->loadModule('Extended');
$data = $mdb2->getAll($sql);
```

`getAll()` will return an enumerated array and each element of the array is an associative array containing all the fields.

```
Array ( [0] => Array ( [id] => 1
                       [name] => Eddie
                     )
        [1] => Array ( [id] => 2
                       [name] => Mike
                     )
      ...
      )
```

If the same query is executed with `getAssoc()`, like `$data = $mdb2->getAssoc($sql);` the result is:

```
Array ( [1] => Eddie
        [2] => Mike
        [3] => Stone
      )
```

If your query returns more than two rows, each row will be an array, not a scalar. The code follows:

```
$sql  = 'SELECT id, name, family FROM people';
$mdb2->loadModule('Extended');
$data = $mdb2->getAssoc($sql);
```

And the result:

```
Array ( [1] => Array ( [name] => Eddie
                       [family] => Vedder
                     )
      ...
      )
```

Data Types

To address the issue of different database systems supporting different field types, MDB2 comes with its own portable set of data types. You can use MDB2's data types and have the package ensure portability across different RDBMS by mapping those types to ones that the underlying database understands.

The MDB2 data types and their default values are as follows:

```
$valid_types = array ( 'text'      => '',
                       'boolean'   => true,
                       'integer'   => 0,
                       'decimal'   => 0.0,
                       'float'     => 0.0,
                       'timestamp' => '1970-01-01 00:00:00',
                       'time'      => '00:00:00',
                       'date'      => '1970-01-01',
                       'clob'      => '',
                       'blob'      => '',
                     )
```

More detailed information on the data types is available in the `datatypes.html` document you can find in the `docs` folder of your PEAR installation. You can also find this document on the Web, in the PEAR CVS repository:

`http://cvs.php.net/viewcvs.cgi/pear/MDB2/docs/datatypes.html?view=co`

Setting Data Types

In all the data retrieval methods that you just saw (`query*()`, `fetch*()`, `get*()`) you can specify the type of the results you expect and MDB2 will convert the values to the expected data type. For example the `query()` method accepts an array of field data types as a second parameter.

```
$sql = 'SELECT * FROM people';
$types = array();
$result = $mdb2->query($sql, $types);
$row = $result->fetchRow();
var_dump($row);
```

Here the `$types` array was blank, so you'll get the default behavior (no data type conversion) and all the results will be strings. The output of this example is:

```
array(2)
{
    ["id"]   => string(1) "1"
    ["name"]=> string(5) "Eddie"
```

```
...
}
```

But you can specify that the first field in each record is of type `integer` and the second is `text` by setting the `$types` array like this:

```
$types = array('integer', 'text');
```

In this case you'll get:

```
array(2)
{
    ["id"]=>    int(1)
    ["name"]=>  string(5) "Eddie"
...
}
```

When setting the types, you can also use an associative array where the keys are the table fields. You can even skip some fields if you don't need to set the type for them. Some valid examples:

```
$types = array( 'id'   => 'integer',
                'name' => 'text'
              );
$types = array('name'=>'text');
$types = array('integer');
```

Setting Data Types when Fetching Results

If you didn't set the data types during a `query()` call, it's still not too late. Before you start fetching, you can set the types by calling the `setResultTypes()` method.

```
// execute query
$sql = 'SELECT * FROM people';
$result = $mdb2->query($sql);

// fetch first row without type conversion
$row = $result->fetchRow();
var_dump($row['id']);
// output is: string(1) "1"

// specify types
$types = array('integer');
$result->setResultTypes($types);

// all consecutive fetches will convert
// the first column as integer
```

```
$row = $result->fetchRow();
var_dump($row['id']);
// output is: int(2)
```

Setting Data Types for get*() and query*()

All the `get*()` and `query*()` methods that you saw earlier in this chapter accept data types as a second parameter, just like `query()` does.

You can set the data types parameter not only as an array `$types = array('integer')`, but also as a string `$types = 'integer'`. This is convenient when you work with methods that return one column only, such as `getOne()`, `queryOne()`, `getCol()`, and `queryCol()`, but you should be careful when using it for `*All()` and `*Row()` methods because the string type parameter will set the type for all the fields in the record set.

Quoting Values and Identifiers

The different RDBMS use different quoting styles (for example single quotes `'` as opposed to double quotes `"`) and also quote different data types inconsistently. For example, in MySQL you may (or may not) wrap integer values in quotes, but for other databases you may not be allowed to quote them at all. It's a good idea to leave the quoting job to the database abstraction layer, because it "knows" the different databases.

MDB2 provides the method `quote()` for quoting data and `quoteIdentifier()` to quote database, table, and field names. All the quotes MDB2 inserts will be the ones appropriate for the underlying RDBMS. An example:

```
$sql = 'UPDATE %s SET %s=%s WHERE id=%d';
$sql = sprintf( $sql,
                $mdb2->quoteIdentifier('people'),
                $mdb2->quoteIdentifier('name'),
                $mdb2->quote('Eddie'), // implicit data type
                $mdb2->quote(1, 'integer') // explicit type
              );
```

If you `echo $sql` in MySQL you'll get:

```
UPDATE `people` SET `name`='Eddie' WHERE id=1
```

In Oracle or SQLite the same code will return:

```
UPDATE "people" SET "name"='Eddie' WHERE id=1
```

As you can see in the example above, `quote()` accepts an optional second parameter that sets the type of data (MDB2 type) to be quoted. If you omit the second parameter, MDB2 will try to make a best guess for the data type.

Iterators

MDB2 benefits from the Standard PHP Library (`http://php.net/spl`), and implements the `Iterator` interface, allowing you to navigate through query results in a simpler manner:

```
foreach ($result as $row)
{
   var_dump($row);
}
```

For every iteration, `$row` will contain the next record as an array. This is equivalent to calling `fetchRow()` in a loop, like this:

```
while ($row = $result->fetchRow())
{
   var_dump($row);
}
```

In order to benefit from the `Iterator` implementation, you need to include the file `Iterator.php` from MDB2's directory by using the `loadFile()` method:

```
MDB2::loadFile('Iterator');
```

Then when you call `query()`, you pass the name of the `Iterator` class as a fourth parameter, like this:

```
$query = 'SELECT * FROM people';
$result = $mdb2->query($query, null, true, 'MDB2_BufferedIterator');
```

MDB2 comes with two `Iterator` classes:

- `MDB2_Iterator`: This implements SPL's `Iterator` and is suitable to work with unbuffered results.
- `MDB2_BufferedIterator`: This extends `MDB2_Iterator` and implements the `SeekableIterator` interface. When you work with buffered results (which is the default in MDB2), it's better to use `MDB2_BufferedIterator`, because it provides some more methods, like `count()` and `rewind()`.

Debugging

MDB2 allows you to keep a list of all queries executed in an instance, this way helping you debug your application. To enable the debugging, you need to set the `debug` option to a positive integer.

```
$mdb2->setOption('debug', 1);
```

Then you can get the collected debugging data at any point using:

```
$mdb2->getDebugOutput();
```

You can also set the option `log_line_break`, which specifies how the separate entries in the debug output will be delimited. The default delimiter is a line break `\n`.

Take a look at the following example that sets the `debug` option and the line separator, executes a few queries, and then draws an unordered list with the debug output.

```
$mdb2->setOption('debug', 1);
$mdb2->setOption('log_line_break', "\n\t");

$sql = 'SELECT * FROM people';
$result = $mdb2->query($sql);
$sql = 'SELECT * FROM people WHERE id = 1';
$result = $mdb2->query($sql);
$sql = 'SELECT name FROM people';
$result = $mdb2->query($sql);

$debug_array = explode("\n\t", trim($mdb2->getDebugOutput()));

echo '<ul><li>';
echo implode('</li><li>', $debug_array);
echo '</li></ul>';
```

This example will produce:

- **query(1): SELECT * FROM people**
- **query(1): SELECT * FROM people WHERE id = 1**
- **query(1): SELECT name FROM people**

It's a good idea to reset the debug level to 0 when your application is in production, so that you don't have the overhead of storing all executed queries in the debug log.

MDB2 SQL Abstraction

There are a number of features and items of SQL syntax that are implemented differently in the various database systems that MDB2 supports. MDB2 does its best to wrap the differences and provide a single interface for accessing those features, so that the developer doesn't need to worry about the implementation in the underlying database system.

Sequences

Auto-increment fields are a convenient way to define and update IDs as primary keys to your tables. The problem is that not all RDBMS support auto increments. To address this inconsistency, the concept of sequence tables is used in MDB2. The idea is that MDB2 will create and maintain a new table (without you having to worry about it) and will store and increment the last ID, which you can use later when inserting into in the main table.

Let's assume that the table `people`, which was used in this chapter's examples, is empty. Before you insert into this table, you need the next consecutive ID. For this purpose you call the method `nextId()` to give you the new ID, like this:

```
$my_new_id = $mdb2->nextId('people');
```

Now `$my_new_id` has the value `1`, and behind the scenes MDB2 will create a new table called `people_seq` with one field only, called `sequence`, and one row only, containing the value `1`. The next time you call `$mdb2->nextId('people')`, MDB2 will increment the value in `people_seq` and return `2` to you.

sequence
1

You're free to pass any identifier as a parameter when calling `nextId()`. MDB2 will append `_seq` to your identifier and create a new table with that name, if one doesn't already exist. Unless you have special needs, it helps code readability if you use an identifier that is the name of the main table you're inserting into.

While `sequence` is the default name of the field in the sequence table, it can be overwritten by setting the `seqcol_name` option, like this:

```
$mdb2->setOption('seqcol_name', 'id');
```

Additionally, the name of the sequence table can be customized by setting the `seqname_format` option. Its default value is `%s_seq`, where `%s` is replaced by the identifier you pass to `nextId()`.

Setting Limits

In MySQL you can limit the number of records returned by a query by using `LIMIT`. For example, the following query will give you only the first two records:

```
SELECT * FROM people LIMIT 0, 2;
```

`LIMIT` is MySQL-specific, so it may be missing from other database systems or implemented differently. To wrap all the differences and provide a common interface for limiting results, MDB2 offers the `setLimit()` method. An example:

```
$sql = 'SELECT * FROM people';
$mdb2->setLimit(2);
$result = $mdb2->query($sql);
```

If you want to define an offset (where to start when setting the limit), you specify the offset value as a second parameter:

```
$mdb2->setLimit(2, 1);
```

Note that `setLimit()` will affect only the next query; any query after that will behave as usual.

Another way to limit the results is by using the `limitQuery()` method from the Extended module. Instead of first setting the limit and then executing the query, you do it with one method call. To get two records starting from offset 1, write:

```
$mdb2->loadModule('Extended');
$sql = 'SELECT * FROM people';
$result = $mdb2->limitQuery($sql, null, 2, 1);
```

Using `limitQuery()` doesn't affect the queries executed after that and it returns an `MDB2_Result` object, just like `query()`.

Replace Queries

MySQL supports the `REPLACE` statement in addition to `UPDATE` and `INSERT`. `REPLACE` will update the records that already exist or perform an insert otherwise. Using `REPLACE` directly will create portability issues in your application, which is why MDB2 wraps this functionality in the `replace()` method. You call `replace()` by providing the name of the table and an array of data about the records.

```
$fields=array ( 'id' => array ( 'value' => 6,
                                'key'   => true
                              ),
                'name' => array ('value' => 'Stoyan'),
                'family' => array ('value' => 'Stefanov'),
```

```
                    'birth_date' => array ('value' => '1975-06-20')
                );
$mdb2->replace('people', $fields);
```

As you can see, the data to be written to the table was set using the `value` keys. It was also specified that the `id` is a key, so that (if using `REPLACE` directly is not an option) MDB2 can check if a record with this ID already exists. If you have a key that consists of several fields, set the `'key' => true` index for all of them. Other array elements you can use are:

- `type`: to specify the MDB2 data type
- `null`: (`true` or `false`) to specify whether the `null` value should be used, ignoring the content in the `value` key

The `replace()` method will return the number of affected rows, just like `exec()` does. Technically, the replace operation is an insert if the record doesn't exist or otherwise a delete and then an insert. Therefore the `replace()` method will return `1` if the record didn't exist previously or `2` if an existing record was updated.

Sub-Select Support

You can pass an SQL query string to the `subSelect()` method. In this case, if the database system supports sub-selects, the result will be the same query unchanged. If sub-selects are not supported though, the method will execute the query and return a comma-delimited list of the result values. It is important that the query you pass to `subSelect()` returns only one column of results. Example:

```
// sub-select query string
$sql_ss = 'SELECT id FROM people WHERE id = 1 OR id = 2';
// the main query
$sql = 'SELECT * FROM people WHERE id IN (%s)';
// call subSelect()
$subselect = $mdb2->subSelect($sql_ss);
// update and print the main query
echo $sql = sprintf($sql, $subselect);
// execute
$data = $mdb2->queryAll($sql);
```

If sub-selects are supported, the `echo` statement above will output:

```
SELECT * FROM people WHERE id IN
(SELECT id FROM people WHERE id = 1 OR id = 2)
```

Otherwise you'll get:

```
SELECT * FROM people WHERE id IN (1, 2)
```

Note that `subSelect()` is not a full sub-query replacement, it just emulates the so-called non-correlated sub-queries. This means that your sub-selects and your main query should be executable as stand-alone queries, so in your sub-query you cannot refer to results returned by the main query, and vice-versa.

Prepared Statements

Prepared statements are a convenient and security-conscious method of writing to the database. Again, not all database systems support prepared statements, so MDB2 emulates this functionality when it's not provided natively by the RDBMS. The idea is to have the following:

- A generic query with placeholders instead of real data that is passed to the `prepare()` method
- Some data about the records to be inserted, updated, or deleted
- A call to `execute()` the prepared statement

The generic query may use unnamed or named placeholders, for example:

```
$sql = 'INSERT INTO people VALUES (?, ?, ?, ?)';
```

or

```
$sql = 'INSERT INTO people VALUES
        (:id, :first_name, :last_name, :bdate)';
```

Then you call the `prepare()` method, which gives you an instance of the `MDB2_Statement_*` class corresponding to the current database driver you're using:

```
$statement = $mdb2->prepare($sql);
```

If you use unnamed parameters (the question marks), you need to have your data as an ordered array, like:

```
$data = array(
            $mdb2->nextId('people'), 'Matt', 'Cameron', '1962-11-28'
            );
```

And then you pass the data to the `execute()` method of the `MDB2_Statement` class:

```
$statement->execute($data);
```

Finally you release the resources taken:

```
$statement->free();
```

Named Parameters

If you use named parameters in your generic query, you have the convenience of using associative arrays when supplying data and not worrying about the order of the parameters as you would in the case of unnamed parameters. The following is a valid way to set data for a query with named parameters:

```
$data = array( 'first_name' => 'Jeff',
               'last_name' => 'Ament',
               'id' => $mdb2->nextId('people'),
               'bdate' => '1963-03-10'
             );
```

Binding Data

Another option for setting the data for a prepared statement is to use the `bindParam()` method. Here's an example:

```
// prepare the statement
$sql = 'INSERT INTO people VALUES
        (:id, :first_name, :last_name, :bdate)';
$statement = $mdb2->prepare($sql);

// figure out the data
$id = $mdb2->nextId('people');
$first_name = 'Kirk';
$last_name = 'Hammett';
$bdate = '1962-11-18';

// bind the data
$statement->bindParam('id', $id);
$statement->bindParam('first_name', $first_name);
$statement->bindParam('last_name', $last_name);
$statement->bindParam('bdate', $bdate);

// execute and free
$statement->execute();
$statement->free();
```

One thing to note about `bindParam()` is that it takes a reference to the variable containing the data. If you're inserting several new records, therefore calling `execute()` multiple times, you don't have to call `bindParam()` for every `execute()`. Just calling it once and then changing the data variables is enough (in this case `$id`, `$first_name`, `$last_name`, and `$bdate`). But if you want to store the actual value when binding, you can use the method `bindValue()` instead of `bindParam()`.

Another way to supply data before executing a prepared statement is to use the bindParamArray() method, which allows you to bind all parameters at once. In the code from the previous example you can replace the four calls to bindParam() with one call to bindParamArray():

```
$array_to_bind = array('id' => $id,
                       'first_name' => $first_name,
                       'last_name' => $last_name,
                       'bdate' => $bdate
                      );
$statement->bindParamArray($array_to_bind);
```

Execute Multiple

Once you have prepared a statement, you can insert multiple rows in one shot by using executeMultiple(). This method is also in the Extended MDB2 module, so you need to load it first. The data you specify must be in a multidimensional array where each element at the top level of the array is one record.

```
$sql = 'INSERT INTO people VALUES (?, ?, ?, ?)';
$statement = $mdb2->prepare($sql);
$data = array(
  array($mdb2->nextId('people'), 'James', 'Hetfield',
                                            '1969-06-06'),
  array($mdb2->nextId('people'), 'Lars', 'Ulrich',
                                          '1968-02-02')
             );
$mdb2->loadModule('Extended');
$mdb2->executeMultiple($statement, $data);
$statement->free();
```

Auto Prepare

Instead of writing a generic query and then preparing a statement, you can have the autoPrepare() method do it for you. You supply only the name of the table, an array of field names, and the type of the query—insert, update, or delete. If you do an update or delete, you can also give the WHERE condition as a string or an array containing different conditions, which MDB2 will concatenate with AND for you. An insert example would be:

```
$mdb2->loadModule('Extended');
$table = 'people';
$fields = array('id', 'name', 'family', 'birth_date');
$statement = $mdb2->autoPrepare($table, $fields,
                                         MDB2_AUTOQUERY_INSERT);
```

This way you'll get an `MDB2_Statement` object created from a generic query that looks like this:

```
INSERT INTO people (id, name, family, birth_date) VALUES (?, ?, ?, ?)
```

If you want an update statement, you can do something like this:

```
$mdb2->loadModule('Extended');
$table = 'people';
$fields = array('name', 'family', 'birth_date');
$where = 'id = ?';
$statement = $mdb2->autoPrepare($table, $fields,
                                        MDB2_AUTOQUERY_UPDATE, $where);
```

The code above will prepare this type of generic query:

```
UPDATE people SET name = ?, family = ?, birth_date = ? WHERE  id = ?
```

Internally, `autoPrepare()` uses the `buildManipSQL()` method, which basically does all the work of creating the generic query, but doesn't call `prepare()` once the query is built. You might find this method useful in cases when you just need a query and do not intend to use prepared statements. Here's how you can delete all the records in the table with last names starting with **S** and **s**:

```
$mdb2->loadModule('Extended');
$sql = $mdb2->buildManipSQL(
    'people',
    false,
    MDB2_AUTOQUERY_DELETE,
    'family like "s%"');
echo $mdb2->exec($sql);
```

Auto Execute

The `autoExecute()` method is similar to `autoPrepare()` but it also executes the prepared statement. The difference in the parameters passed is that the array of fields should be an associative array containing bothe the field names and the data to be inserted or updated.

```
$mdb2->loadModule('Extended');
$table = 'people';
$fields = array ( 'id' => $mdb2->nextId('people'),
                  'name' => 'Cliff',
                  'family' => 'Burton',
                  'birth_date' => '1962-02-10'
                );
$result = $mdb2->autoExecute($table, $fields, MDB2_AUTOQUERY_INSERT);
```

Transactions

If transactions are supported by your RDBMS, using them is very good practice to keep your data in a consistent state, should an error occur in the middle of the process of writing several pieces of data to one or more tables.

You begin by checking whether transactions are supported by your RDBMS and then you initiate a new transaction with a call to `beginTransaction()`. Then you start executing the different queries that comprise your transaction. After every query you can check the result and if you find it's a `PEAR_Error`, you can roll back (undo) the transaction and all previously executed queries within it. Otherwise you commit (finalize) the transaction. Before the calls to `rollback()` or `commit()`, you need to check if you really are in transaction, using the `inTransaction()` method.

```
if ($mdb2->supports('transactions'))
{
    $mdb2->beginTransaction();
}
$result = $mdb2->exec('DELETE FROM people WHERE id = 33');
if (PEAR::isError($result))
{
    if ($mdb2->inTransaction())
    {
        $mdb2->rollback();
    }
}
$result = $mdb2->exec('DELETE FROM people WHERE id =
                                        invalid something');
if (PEAR::isError($result))
{
    if ($mdb2->inTransaction())
    {
        $mdb2->rollback();
    }
}
elseif ($mdb2->inTransaction())
{
    $mdb2->commit();
}
```

Note that if transactions are not supported by your RDBMS, MDB2 will not emulate this functionality, so it is your responsibility to keep the data in a consistent state.

MDB2 Modules

When looking at some of the examples earlier in this chapter, you've already seen how the idea of modularity is built into MDB2. The main purpose is to keep the base functionality lightweight and then include more functionality on demand, using the `loadModule()` method.

Earlier in the chapter, the Extended module was loaded like this:

```
$mdb2->loadModule('Extended');
```

After this call you have access to all the methods that the Extended module provides, such as all the `get*()` methods. The methods are accessible through the `extended` property of the `$mdb2` instance:

```
$mdb2->extended->getAssoc($sql);
```

In addition to that, in PHP5, due to the object overloading functionality, you can access the methods directly as methods of the `$mdb2` instance:

```
$mdb2->getAssoc($sql);
```

In this chapter PHP5 was assumed, so all the calls to the module methods benefit from object overloading and are called using this short notation.

Yet another way to access the module's methods is by prefixing them with the short name of the module `ex` (for "Extended"). This is also PHP5-only.

```
$mdb2->exGetAssoc($sql);
```

And finally, you can specify a custom property name to load the module into (works in both PHP 4 and 5):

```
$mdb2->loadModule('Extended', 'mine');
$mdb2->mine->getAssoc($sql);
```

The full list of currently available MDB2 modules is as follows (short access names given in brackets):

- **Extended (ex)**: You already have an idea of some of the methods available in the Extended module. This module is the only one unrelated to the different database drivers and its definition file (`Extended.php`) lies in the root `MDB2` directory, not in the `Drivers` directory. This module is defined in the `MDB2_Extended` class, which inherits the `MDB2_Module_Common` class.
- **Datatype (dt)**: Contains methods for manipulating and converting MDB2 data types and mapping them to types that are native to the underlying database.

- **Manager (mg)**: Contains methods for managing the database structure (schema), like creating, listing, or dropping databases, tables, indices, etc.
- **Reverse (rv)**: Methods for reverse engineering a database structure.
- **Native (na)**: Any methods that are native to the underlying database are placed here.
- **Function (fc)**: Contains wrappers for useful functions that are implemented differently in the different databases.

Let's see a few examples that use some of the modules.

Manager Module

Using the Manager module you have access to methods for managing your database schema. Let's see some of its methods in action.

Create a Database

Here's an example that will create a new blank database:

```
$mdb2->loadModule('Manager');
$mdb2->createDatabase('test_db');
```

Create a Table

You can use the Manager module to recreate the table `people` that was used in the earlier examples in this chapter. This table had four fields:

- `id`: An unsigned integer primary key that cannot be null
- `name`: A text field, like `VARCHAR(255)` in MySQL
- `family`: Same type as `name`
- `birth_date`: A date field

To create this table you use the `createTable()` method, to which you pass the table name and an array containing the table definition.

```
$definition = array ( 'id' => array ( 'type' => 'integer',
                                      'unsigned' => 1,
                                      'notnull' => 1,
                                      'default' => 0,
                                    ),
                      'name' => array ( 'type' => 'text',
                                        'length' => 255
                                      ),
                      'family' => array ( 'type' => 'text',
```

```
                                        'length' => 255
                                    ),
                    'birth_date' => array ( 'type' => 'date'
                                          )
                );
$mdb2->createTable('people', $definition);
```

Alter Table

Let's say that after the table was created, you decide that 255 characters are too much for one name. In this case you'll need to set up a new definition array and call `alterTable()`. The new definition array used for modifications is broken down into the following keys:

- `name`: New name for the table
- `add`: New fields to be added
- `remove`: Fields to be dropped
- `rename`: Fields to rename
- `change`: Fields to modify

Here's how to modify the `name` field to store only a hundred characters:

```
$definition = array(
    'change' => array(
        'name' => array(
            'definition' => array(
                'length' => 100,
                'type' => 'text',
                              )
                          ),
                        )
             );
$mdb2->alterTable('people', $definition, false);
```

If you set the third parameter of `alterTable()` to `true`, MDB2 will not execute the changes, but will only check if they are supported by your DBMS.

Constraints

The `id` field was meant to be the primary key, but so far it isn't. For this purpose you can use the `createConstraint()` method, which accepts the table name, the name we chose for the constraint, and the array containing the constraint definition.

```
$definition = array ( 'primary' => true,
                      'fields' => array ( 'id' => array())
```

```
                    );
$mdb2->createConstraint('people', 'myprimekey', $definition);
```

Note that MySQL will ignore the `myprimekey` name of the constraint, because it requires the primary key to always be named `PRIMARY`.

Now we can specify that the name plus the family name should be unique:

```
$definition = array('unique' => true,
                    'fields' => array('name' => array(),
                                      'family' => array(),
                                     )
                   );
$mdb2->createConstraint('people', 'unique_people',
                                  $definition);
```

On second thoughts, different people sometimes have the same names, so let's drop this constraint:

```
$mdb2->dropConstraint('people', 'unique_people');
```

Indices

If there will be a lot of SELECTs on the `birth_date` field, you can speed them up by creating index on this field.

```
$definition = array('fields' => array('birth_date' => array(),) );
$mdb2->createIndex('people', 'dates', $definition);
```

Note that by default MDB2 will add a `_idx` suffix to all your indices and constraints. If you want to modify this behavior, set the `idxname_format` option:

```
$mdb2->setOption('idxname_format', '%s'); // no suffix
```

Listings

In the Manager module you have also a lot of methods to get information about a database, such as `listDatabases()`, `listUsers()`, `listTables()`, `listTableViews()`, and `listTableFields()`.

Function Module

The Function module contains some methods to access common database functions, such as referring to the current timestamp, and concatenating or getting partial strings. If you want to access the current timestamp in your statements, you can use the `now()` method and it will return you the means to get the timestamp in a way that is native for the currently underlying database system.

```
$mdb2->loadModule('Function');
echo $mdb2->now();
```

This will output `CURRENT_TIMESTAMP` when using MySQL and `datetime('now')` when using SQLite.

`now()` accepts a string parameter (with values `date`, `time`, and `timestamp`) that specifies if you want the current date, time, or both.

If you wish to concatenate strings in your statements in a database-agnostic way, you can use the `concat()` method and pass an unlimited number of string parameters to it. For extracting substrings, you have the `substring()` method. Here's an example that uses both methods:

```
$mdb2->loadModule('Function');
$sql = 'SELECT %s FROM people';
$first_initial = $mdb2->substring('name', 1, 1);
$dot = $mdb2->quote('.');
$all = $mdb2->concat($first_initial, $dot, 'family');
$sql = sprintf($sql, $all);
$data = $mdb2->queryCol($sql);

echo $sql;
print_r($data);
```

The `print_r()` from this code will produce:

```
Array (
    [0] => E.Vedder
    [1] => M.McCready
    [2] => S.Gossard
...
     )
```

The `echo $sql;` line will print a different result, depending on the database driver you use. For MySQL it would be:

```
SELECT CONCAT(SUBSTRING(name FROM 1 FOR 1), '.', family) FROM people
```

Using the Oracle (oci8) driver, you'll get:

```
SELECT (SUBSTR(name, 1, 1) || '.' || family) FROM people
```

In this example only the first character from the value in the `name` field was extracted. Then it was concatenated with the dot symbol and the full value of the `family` field. Note that it was necessary to quote the dot in order for it to be treated as a string and not a field name.

Reverse Module

If you want to get information about the table `people` that was used in the examples in this chapter, you can call the `tableInfo()` method:

```
$mdb2->loadModule('Reverse');
$data = $mdb2->tableInfo('people');
```

If you `print_r()` the result, you'll get something like:

```
Array(  [0] => Array ( [table] => people
                       [name] => id
                       [type] => int
                       [length] => 11
                       [flags] => not_null primary_key
                       [mdb2type] => integer
                     )
        [1] => Array ( [table] => people
                       [name] => name
                       [type] => char
                       [length] => 100
                       [flags] =>
                       [mdb2type] => text
                     )
     ...
     )
```

The real magic about the `tableInfo()` method is that it can return information on the fields based on a query result, not just a table. Let's say you have one more table `phones` in your database that stores phone numbers of the people from the `people` table and it looks like this:

id	person_id	Phone
1	1	555-666-7777
2	1	555-666-7788

You can execute a query that joins the two tables and when you get the result, you can pass it to `tableInfo()`:

```
$mdb2->loadModule('Reverse');

$sql = 'SELECT phones.id, people.name, phones.phone ';
$sql.= ' FROM people ';
$sql.= '  LEFT JOIN phones ';
$sql.= '  ON people.id = phones.person_id ';

$result = $mdb2->query($sql);
$data = $mdb2->tableInfo($result);
```

Now if you `print_r()` what `tableInfo()` returns, you'll get an array that describes the three fields selected in the `JOIN` statement—id, name, and phone:

```
Array (
    [0] => Array ( [table] => phones
                   [name] => id
                   [type] => int
                   [length] => 11
                   [flags] => primary_key
                   [mdb2type] => integer
                 )
    [1] => Array ( [table] => people
                   [name] => name
                   [type] => char
                   [length] => 100
                   [flags] =>
                   [mdb2type] => text
                 )
    [2] => Array ( [table] => phones
                   [name] => phone
                   [type] => char
                   [length] => 20
                   [flags] =>
                   [mdb2type] => text
                 )
     )
```

Extending MDB2

MDB2 is easy to tweak by playing with its numerous setup options, but it's also highly extensible. For example, you can wrap the query results in your custom classes, when you execute a query or fetch data. You can create your own debug handler, provide your own `Iterator` implementation, and finally, you can add new functionality to the package by creating new modules in addition to the existing ones. In this section you'll see the necessary steps for creating custom functionality.

Custom Debug Handler

You already know that you can set the `debug` option to a positive integer like this:

```
$mdb2->setOption('debug', 1);
```

Then at any time you can get a list of executed queries like this:

```
$mdb2->getDebugOutput();
```

You can provide your own custom debug handler to collect the list of queries. The debug handler can be a function or a class method—basically anything that qualifies as a valid PHP callback pseudo-type (`http://php.net/callback`). Let's create a new class that will be responsible for collecting debug information and then printing it. The custom functionality in this example will be that our data collection will keep a running counter of how many times each query has been executed. This can be useful when you do performance testing on a larger application. Often in an application you put small pieces of functionality in different classes and methods and then simply call these methods when you need them, without worrying how exactly they work, which is the beauty of OOP. So it may happen that some methods that do database work are called more often then you thought and perform repeating tasks. Using the custom debugger in the following example, you can identify and optimize such cases.

```
class Custom_Debug_Class
{
    // how many queries were executed
    var $query_count = 0;
    // which queries and their count
    var $queries = array();

    // this method is called on every query
    function collectInfo(&$db, $scope, $message, $is_manip =
                                                            null)
    {
        $this->query_count++;
        @$this->queries[$message]++;
    }

    // print the log
    function dumpInfo()
    {
```

```
            echo 'Total queries in this page: ';
            echo $this->query_count;
            // sort descending
            arsort($this->queries);
            echo '<pre>';
            print_r($this->queries);
            echo '</pre>';
        }
}
```

To see the custom debug handler in action, you need to instantiate the newly created class, set the MBD2 debug handler callback, execute a few queries (one of them is executed twice), and then print the results.

```
$my_debug_handler = new Custom_Debug_Class();
$mdb2->setOption('debug', 1);
$mdb2->setOption('debug_handler', array($my_debug_handler,
                                              'collectInfo'));
$sql = 'SELECT * FROM people';
$result = $mdb2->query($sql);
$sql = 'SELECT * FROM people WHERE id = 1';
$result = $mdb2->query($sql);
$my_debug_handler->dumpInfo();
```

The result of this will be:

Total queries in this page: 3

Array

(

[SELECT * FROM people]=>2

[SELECT * FROM people WHERE id = 1]=>1

)

During the development phase of your application you can even register `dumpInfo()` to be called automatically at the end of each script using:

```
register_shutdown_function(array($my_debug_handler,
                                       'dumpInfo'));
```

Here's an idea for monitoring performance in your application's MySQL queries with MDB2's help. You can create (and register to be executed on a script shutdown) a new method in your custom debug class that will take only the SELECT queries and re-run them by prefixing them with the EXPLAIN statement. Then you can do some automated checks to find suspicious queries that are not using appropriate indices. You can find more on the EXPLAIN statement at `http://dev.mysql.com/doc/refman/5.0/en/explain.html`.

Custom Fetch Classes

As you know already, you can have different fetch modes when you retrieve the data from a query result—associative array, ordered list, or object. When you use the object fetch mode (`MDB2_FETCHMODE_OBJECT`), an instance of PHP's standard class (`stdClass`) is created for every row (by simply casting the array result to an object). This allows you to access the field data as object properties, for example `$row->name` or `$row->id`.

MDB2 gives you the means to customize this functionality by providing your own custom fetch class. Every row in the result set will be passed as an array to the constructor of the custom class. Let's create a simple class that mimics what `stdClass` will give you, only it converts the field with name `id` to an integer.

```
class My_Fetch_Class
{
    function __construct($row)
    {
        foreach ($row as $field => $data)
        {
            if ($field == 'id')
            {
                $data = (int)$data;
            }
            $this->{$field} = $data;
        }
    }
}
```

To test the class, you need to set the fetch mode to `MDB2_FETCHMODE_OBJECT`, and the option `fetch_class` to be the name of the new class.

```
$mdb2->setFetchMode(MDB2_FETCHMODE_OBJECT);
$mdb2->setOption('fetch_class', 'My_Fetch_Class');
```

The same result can be achieved directly with the call to `setFetchMode()`.

```
$mdb2->setFetchMode(MDB2_FETCHMODE_OBJECT, 'My_Fetch_Class');
```

If you execute a query like this:

```
$sql = 'SELECT * FROM people WHERE id=1';
$data = $mdb2->queryRow($sql);
```

and then `var_dump()` the result, you'll get:

```
object(My_Fetch_Class)#3 (2)
{
    ["id"]=>
    int(1)
    ["name"]=>
    string(5) "Eddie"
    ...
}
```

Also note that in the core MDB2 package there exists a class called `MDB2_Row` that does pretty much what the custom class example above does, only it doesn't convert fields named `id` to an integer. If you make your custom fetch classes extend `MDB2_Row`, you can benefit from what it provides and build upon it.

Custom Result Classes

As you know already, once you execute an SQL statement with `query()`, you get an object of the appropriate `MDB2_Result` class. If you're using MySQL, the result class would be `MDB2_Result_mysql` and it will extend the common functionality provided by `MDB2_Result_Common`, which in turn extends `MDB2_Result`. MDB2 provides you the means to extend and customize the result classes, in other words replace or extend `MDB2_Result_*` with your own classes.

What you need to do is:

- Create your custom result class
- Make sure its definition is included
- Pass its name as an MDB2 option

Let's create a class called `MyResult` and make it extend the out-of-the-box `MDB2_Result_mysql` class, so that you can benefit from the existing functionality. To this class, let's add a simple method that demonstrates the feature:

```
class MyResult extends MDB2_Result_mysql
{
    function newResultMethod()
    {
        echo 'I am MyResult::newResultMethod()';
```

```
        // $this->db is your current MDB2 instance
        // in case you need it
    }
}
```

Then, to make this class available when executing queries, let's pass its name as an option:

```
$mdb2->setOption('buffered_result_class', 'MyResult');
```

Now you can execute a query and call the new custom method on its result:

```
$sql = 'SELECT * FROM people';
$result = $mdb2->query($sql);
$result->newResultMethod();
```

As you saw above, the option `buffered_result_class` was set. This is because the default behavior for MDB2 is to use buffered queries. You can change this by setting:

```
$mdb2->setOption('result_buffering', false);
```

In this case, when you're working with unbuffered results, if you want to use the custom result class, you will need to set the `result_class` option, as opposed to the `buffered_result_class` one:

```
$mdb2->setOption('result_class', 'MyResult');
```

If you want to create custom result classes that are database-specific, you can postfix their names with the name of the MDB2 database driver (for example `MyResult_mysql`) and you can use a placeholder for the driver name when setting the custom class option:

```
$mdb2->setOption('result_class', 'MyResult_%s');
```

MDB2 will replace the `%s` placeholder with the name of the database driver used for the current MDB2 instance.

Let's take a look at another, slightly more advanced example. The idea is to create a new method in the custom result class that will calculate the average age of the people matched by any query. Here's the code for the new custom class—`MyResult2`.

```
class MyResult2 extends MDB2_BufferedResult_mysql
{
    function getAverageAge()
    {
        $current_row = $this->rowCount(); // where are we
        $this->seek(); // rewind
        $total_ts = 0; // sum of all birth date timestamps
```

```
        while ($row = $this->fetchRow(MDB2_FETCHMODE_ASSOC))
        {
            $total_ts += strtotime($row['birth_date']);
        }
        $avg_ts = $total_ts / $this->numRows();
                            // average timestamp
        $age = date('Y') - date('Y', $avg_ts);
        if (date('md') < date('md', $avg_ts))
        {
            $age--; // not a birth day yet
        }
        $this->seek($current_row); // back to where we were
        return $age;
    }
}
```

To use a custom result class with a query, apart from the possibility of specifying the class name as an MDB2 option, you can also specify it per query, as the third parameter of the `query()` method. This way you can use the default result class for most of your queries, but overwrite it only for selected ones. So to use the new class you can write:

```
$sql = 'SELECT * FROM people';
// or maybe --> $sql = 'SELECT * FROM people WHERE name
// LIKE "J%"';
$result = $mdb2->query($sql, null, 'MyResult2');
echo $result->getAverageAge();
```

In the implementation of the `getAverageAge()` method you can see that `$this` refers to the result object. First, the method starts with getting the result set pointer position by calling `$this->rowCount()`. Then there is a call to `seek()` to move to the beginning of the result set. Before the method returns, it seeks back to the point in the result set before the method call. This is useful because it lets you navigate back and forth through the result set before calling `getAverageAge()` without affecting the functionality. Otherwise, if you've already fetched a few rows before calling `getAverageAge()`, the pointer to the current row is already advanced and you'll get partial results. Once the record set is reset, we simply fetch all records, sum the timestamps of all birth dates, and perform some date operations to get the average age. Note that `MyResult2` class extends the *buffered* built-in class, otherwise it cannot access the `seek()` and `numRow()` methods.

Custom Iterators

As you know already, MDB2 comes with two implementations of PHP5's SPL `Iterator` interface— `MDB2_Iterator` and `MDB2_BufferedIterator`. It probably won't come as a surprise that you can also use your own `Iterator` implementations. In the next example a simple `My_Iterator` class is created. It builds upon the `MDB2_BufferedIterator` implementation.

```
// load MDB2 iterators
MDB2::loadFile('Iterator');
// custom iterator class
class My_Iterator extends MDB2_BufferedIterator
{
    function foo()
    {
        echo 'bar';
    }
}
// execute query
$sql = 'SELECT * FROM people';
$result = $mdb2->query($sql, null, true, 'My_Iterator');
// iterate over the result set
foreach ($result as $row)
{
    var_dump($row);
}
// call the custom method
$result->foo();
```

Custom Modules

If all the possibilities for customizations are not enough for you and you're looking for some completely missing functionality, you can create a new MDB2 module, on top of the six existing ones (Extended, Manager, Reverse, Function, Datatype, and Native). This would be a custom extension of the core MDB2, but it can still be included using the same `loadModule()` method and behaves as if it is a part of MDB2. Here are the necessary steps to build and use a module.

First, create the class, prefixed with `MDB2_`. In this case let's pick `Mymodule` as the name of the custom extension.

```
class MDB2_Mymodule
{
    function sayHi()
    {
```

```
            echo "OK, hi!";
        }
    }
```

Then place this class in a file named after the module name, `Mymodule.php`, and copy it where `MDB2::loadModule()` will be looking for it—a directory called **MDB2** somewhere in your include path. You can also put this file in the core MDB2 directory of your PEAR installation, but it's probably a good idea to keep the PEAR directory managed only by the PEAR installer. To keep things simple, let's say the MDB2 directory you create is a subdirectory in the same directory as the script that will use the new module.

Then in the test script simply load the module like any built-in MDB2 module and call its method:

```
$mdb2->loadModule('Mymodule');
$mdb2->sayHi();
```

Voilà! You've created and tested the custom module.

Mymodule2

Usually in your custom module you would need more functionality that just `echo`-ing. Most likely you'll need access to the current MDB2 instance. Here is a second example that extends the `MDB2_Module_Common` class and gets a reference to the current MDB2 object (through the call to `getDBInstance()`) in order to perform a database operation—counting the rows in a given table.

```
class MDB2_Mymodule2 extends MDB2_Module_Common
{
    function getNumberOfRecords($table)
    {
        $mdb2 =& $this->getDBInstance();
        $sql = 'SELECT count(*) FROM '
                . $mdb2->quoteIdentifier($table);
        $count = $mdb2->queryOne($sql);
        return $count;
    }
}
```

If you place this code in a file called `Mymodule2.php` in your MDB2 directory, you can then test it:

```
$mdb2->loadModule('Mymodule2');
echo $mdb2->getNumberOfRecords('people');
```

MDB2_Schema

MDB2_Schema is a separate PEAR package that builds upon MDB2 to provide tools to manage your database schema using a platform- and database-independent XML format. The XML format is inherited form the Metabase package and is very simple to read and understand; it actually uses only a subset of what XML offers, known as SML (Simplified Markup Language). You can find a detailed description of the Metabase format in the **docs** folder of your PEAR installation, in a file called `xml_schema_documentation.html`. You can also read it directly from the PEAR CVS repository at `http://cvs.php.net/viewcvs.cgi/pear/MDB2_Schema/docs/`.

MDB2_Schema offers quite a few methods to help you manage your database structure and keep track of the changes you inevitably make during the life of your application. Let's take a look at some examples.

Installation and Instantiation

Since MDB2_Schema is a separate package, it needs to be installed separately. To do so, type:

```
> pear install MDB2_Schema
```

To create an instance of the Schema class, you have `connect()` and `factory()` methods that accept a DSN and an options array, just like MDB2 does. Another option is to create a Schema object using an existing MDB2 object, if you have one at hand.

```
require_once 'MDB2.php';
require_once 'MDB2/Schema.php';

$dsn = 'mysql://root@localhost/test_db';
$options = array('debug' => 0,);
$mdb2 =& MDB2::factory($dsn, $options);
$mdb2->setFetchMode(MDB2_FETCHMODE_ASSOC);

$schema =& MDB2_Schema::factory($mdb2);
```

Dump a Database

If you want to copy your database to a file that uses the Metabase XML format, you can use the `dumpDatabase()` method. It accepts a database definition array that looks similar to the definition arrays you saw earlier in the chapter when looking into the Manager module. If you don't have the definition array, you can have Schema guess the database definition for you, using the `getDefinitionFromDatabase()` method. Here's the code to do so, assuming you already have a Schema object:

```
$definition = $schema->getDefinitionFromDatabase();
$dump_options = array ( 'output_mode' => 'file',
                        'output' => 'test.xml'
                      );
$schema->dumpDatabase($definition, $dump_options,
                      MDB2_SCHEMA_DUMP_STRUCTURE);
```

If you execute this code on the `test_db` database that was created earlier and had one `people` table, and then you `print_r()` the `$definition` array, you'll get something similar to this (partial listing):

```
Array
(
    [name] => test_db
    [create] => 1
    [overwrite] =>
    [tables] => Array
        (
            [people] => Array
                (
                    [fields] => Array
                        (
                            [id] => Array ( [type] => integer
                                            [notnull] => 1
                                            [length] => 4
                                            [unsigned] => 1
                                            [default] => 0
                                          )
                            [name] => Array ( [type] => text
                                              [notnull] =>
                                              [length] => 100
                                              [fixed] =>
                                              [default] =>
                                            )
                            ...
                        )

                    [indexes] => Array (...)
                )
        )
    [sequences] => Array
        (
        )
)
```

The code overleaf will also create a file `test.xml` (in the directory where the script is) with the following content (again, a partial listing with some empty lines removed):

```
<?xml version="1.0" encoding="ISO-8859-1" ?>
<database>
  <name>test_db</name>
  <create>true</create>
  <overwrite>false</overwrite>

  <table>
    <name>people</name>
    <declaration>
    <field>
      <name>id</name>
      <type>integer</type>
      <unsigned>true</unsigned>
      <length>4</length>
      <notnull>true</notnull>
      <default>0</default>
    </field>

    <field>
      <name>name</name>
      <type>text</type>
      <length>100</length>
      <notnull>false</notnull>
      <default></default>
    </field>

      ...

    <index>
    ...
    </index>
    </declaration>
  </table>
</database>
```

The `test.xml` file was created because this was specified in the `$dump_options` array that was passed to the `dumpDatabase()` method. If you don't want to write the XML file to the file system but you need it for other purposes, you can skip the `$dump_options['output_mode']` key and then provide a function name in `$dump_options['output']`. In this case, the XML result will be passed as a string to the function you specify. So if you just want to see the dump in your browser, you can create a simple function like this:

```
function printXml($input)
{
    echo '<pre>';
    print_r(htmlentities($input));
    echo '</pre>';
}
```

Then you can set the `$dump_options` array:

```
$dump_options = array ( 'output' => 'printXml' );
```

The third parameter to `dumpDatabase()` tells the method *what* you want dumped—the structure, the data in the tables, or both. This is defined with a constant where the available options are:

- `MDB2_SCHEMA_DUMP_STRUCTURE`
- `MDB2_SCHEMA_DUMP_CONTENT`
- `MDB2_SCHEMA_DUMP_ALL`

As the API docs say, the `getDefinitionFromDatabase()` method is an *attempt* to figure out the definition directly from the database and sometimes it may require some manual work to make the definition exactly as you want.

Switching your RDBMS

Suppose you decide to move your application from using a MySQL database back end to SQLite (or simply want to test how portable your application is). You can have `MDB2_Schema` do the database structure and data transition for you. Let's say you've created your database dump as shown above and you have your `test.xml` file. All you need now is a new DSN to connect to SQLite, one method call to parse the XML file and extract the database definition from it, and a method call to create the new database.

```
$dsn2 = 'sqlite:///';
$schema2 =& MDB2_Schema::factory($dsn2);
$definition = $schema2->parseDatabaseDefinitionFile('test.xml');
$schema2->createDatabase($definition);
```

For this simple type of transition you don't necessary need the XML file, and can work with only the database definition array. The whole transition can be done in one line, assuming you have your two Schema instances ready:

```
$schema2->createDatabase($schema->getDefinitionFromDatabase());
```

Summary

In this chapter you were presented with an introduction to the MDB2 database abstraction layer. You saw the challenges faced with database abstraction and how they are handled in MDB2. You learned how to install MDB2, instantiate an MDB2 object, and use some of the most common methods. You also learned how MDB2 is built with extensibility in mind and about the existing modules. There were also a few examples of how you can customize the package by using your custom classes for some tasks and how to create your own extensions. Finally, there was a quick example of how to use `MDB2_Schema` for managing your database in an RDBMS-independent way.

2
Displaying Data

One of the primary uses of the Internet is the presentation of data. Whether you are listing your friends' birthdays on your personal website, creating an administration interface for a web portal, or presenting a complex spreadsheet to your boss, what it comes down to is pulling the data out of a source, processing the data, and then formatting it in whichever format you need.

When it comes to creating and formatting data, many programmers have implemented their own scripts or classes to solve the same basic problems. There are many different ways to do this, but unfortunately many of the common implementations are either wrong or inefficient. In an attempt to solve a specific problem, programmers often create a half-baked solution and then move on to other things, leaving what could have been good code incomplete and potentially vulnerable to security or performance issues.

Thankfully PEAR provides several different packages that take care of different aspects of data presentation, and not only take the drudgery of formatting out of the picture, but also allow programmers to expand their scripts to support many formats they would not have been able to use and support before.

In this chapter we'll take a look at data you are familiar with. We will learn how to create simple tables and a monthly calendar, generate a spreadsheet and PDF document, and how to create a flexible DataGrid that uses a combination of these classes to import and export data.

HTML Tables

Of all HTML elements, the humble table is probably the most misunderstood. Initially designed as a way to display tabular data, designers soon discovered that it could also be used as a container for complex layouts. Soon it became common practice to see hideous techniques such as using an obscene number of complex nested tables to display something as simple as a border to a block of text, or using "spacer gifs" to limit the width of table cells.. The backlash by many designers and coders was to pride themselves in the fact that their web pages contained absolutely no tables, and they refused to use a table even for the most legitimate of uses.

We will put all preconceived ideas about tables behind us now and focus on using tables for the simple task for which they were originally designed, which was displaying tabular data.

Table Format

The format of creating tables in HTML is very simple. The top-level tag is `<table>`, to which table-wide attributes can be added. The individual rows of the table are defined by `<tr>` tags. Within the rows of the table reside the cells. The cells can either be data cells (enclosed with `<td>` tags) or header cells (enclosed in `<th>` tags). These elements form the basis of a table as shown in the code example below.

```
<table>
  <tr>
    <th>Header One</th>
    <th>Header Two</th>
   <th>Header Three</th>
  </tr>
  <tr>
    <td>Cell Four</td>
    <td>Cell Five</td>
    <td>Cell Six</td>
  </tr>
</table>
```

As you can see from a quick look at the above code, manually creating HTML tables can be very tedious. Even working with PHP and looping through your data to create the table quickly becomes messy, as we have to deal with the HTML tags directly, calculate when to close tags, etc. In these cases the `HTML_Table` package comes in very handy as an object-oriented wrapper for the creation and manipulation of HTML tables.

Using the `HTML_Table` package we could create this table very simply:

```
include_once 'HTML/Table.php';
$table = new HTML_Table();

$table->addRow(array("one", "two", "three"), null, "th");
$table->addRow(array("one", "two", "three"));

echo $table->toHtml();
```

We start out by creating a new instance of the `HTML_Table` class. To use table-wide attributes we can send them to the class constructor; we will look at this later. Once we have our table object, we can start adding rows to our table. The first parameter of the `addRow()` function is an array that contains the data you want to store, the second parameter allows you to specify any attributes for the row that is created, and the third attribute defines whether or not these cells should use the header cell tag. We want the first row to be a header row using the `<th>` tags, and the rest of the rows to use the regular table cells.

Using HTML_Table to Create a Simple Calendar

Now that we've seen the basics of what `HTML_Table` can do, we'll jump into a real-world example.

We will start off by developing a simple monthly calendar. Our calendar will have a month view and will display weeks and days in a tabular format. We will add more features later in this section, but for now we will use `PEAR::Calendar` and `HTML_Table` to build the calendar for the current month.

```
include_once 'HTML/Table.php';
include_once 'Calendar/Month/Weekdays.php';

$table = new HTML_Table();

$Month = new Calendar_Month_Weekdays(date('Y'), date('n'));
$Month->build();

while ($Day = $Month->fetch())
{
    if ($Day->isFirst())
    {
        if (is_array($week))
        {
          $table->addRow($week);
        }
        $week = array();
    }

    $week[] = $Day->isEmpty() ? "" : $Day->thisDay();
}

$table->addRow($week);
```

```
$table->setColAttributes(0, 'bgcolor="#CCCCCC"');
$table->setColAttributes(6, 'bgcolor="#CCCCff"');
$table->updateAllAttributes('align="center"');

echo $table->toHTML();
```

After including the needed packages we instantiate a new instance of the `HTML_Table` class. If we wanted to give this table a border or apply any other attribute to the table, we could send this attribute to the constructor of `HTML_Table`. This will be described in the next example.

The usage of the Calendar class from PEAR is beyond the scope of this chapter. Put simply, we create a new object that contains the information for the current month and then iterate through the days, handling each day individually. We add each day to an array and then when we reach the first day of the week, we add the previous week to the table and empty the array for the next week. There will be some days of the week that do not belong to the present month; these are *empty* days and we do not include them in the calendar. Once we are finished looping through the weeks, we add the last week to our table.

Now that we have all of our data added to our table, we can add and update the attributes of our rows and columns to add some formatting elements. `HTML_Table` offers functions for setting the attributes of rows, columns, or individual cells. These functions are named `setRowAttributes()`, `setColAttributes()`, and `setCellAttributes()` respectively. When setting the attributes of parts of your table, remember that a cell that is set will have its formatting overwritten if you use the `setRowAttribute()` function on a row of which that cell is a part. To get around this, you can call the "update" functions to update attributes of a cell. In this example, once the colors have been added, we update all the cells in the table to be centered. This does not affect any previous formatting that has been applied.

Setting Individual Cells

As luck would have it, as soon as we complete our sample calendar, someone in upper management suggests that we enhance the calendar to not just highlight the weekends, but any other holiday occurring in the month.

For this we will need more granular access to our table, so instead of adding weeks to the table we will need to add each day on its own. This will require a redesign of how we enter data into the table.

To get the data on the holidays in the month, we will use the `Date_Holidays` package from PEAR. As we loop through the days of the month, we check to see if the current day is a holiday and, if it is, apply the appropriate formatting to the cell. If we were using this calendar in a real application you would probably want to add the name of the holiday, which `Date_Holidays` provides, but for the sake of this example we'll just highlight the cell.

```
require_once 'HTML/Table.php';
require_once 'Calendar/Month/Weekdays.php';
require_once 'Date/Holidays.php';

$tableAttrs = array('border' => "2");
$table = new HTML_Table($tableAttrs);

$Germany =& Date_Holidays::factory('Germany', 2005);
$Month = new Calendar_Month_Weekdays(2005, 12);
$Month->build();

$table->addRow(array('S', 'M', 'T', 'W', 'T', 'F', 'S'),
                                            null, "th");

while ($Day = $Month->fetch())
{
    if ($Day->isFirst())
    {
       $row++;
       $col = 0;
    }

    if (!$Day->isEmpty())
    {

      $table->setCellContents($row, $col, $Day->thisDay());
      $t = sprintf('%4d-%02d-%02d', $Day->thisYear(),
                         $Day- >thisMonth(), $Day->thisDay());

      if ($Germany->isHoliday($t))
      {
        $table->setCellAttributes($row,$col, 'bgcolor="red"');
      }
    }
    $col++;
}

$table->setRowAttributes(0, 'bgcolor="#CC99FF"');

$table->updateAllAttributes('align="center"');
$table->setCaption("Holidays");

echo $table->toHTML();
```

The first change you'll notice is the addition of the border attributes when creating the table. This will add the border attribute to the main table tag.

We have used several new functions in this example. The most important is the `setCellContents()` function. True to its name, this function requires the row and column number of a cell and then fills the cell with the supplied data. We also add a header row to display the days of the week, highlight it, and add a caption for the table.

Our completed calendar now displays the current month with the holidays highlighted in red.

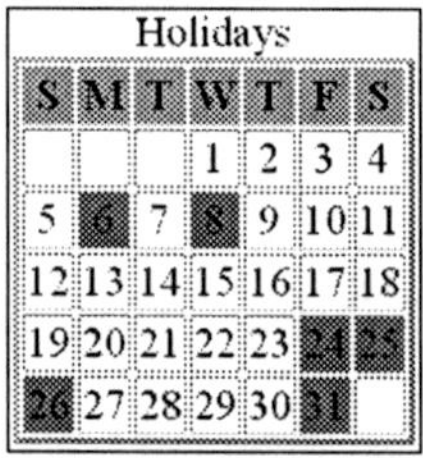

Holidays

S	M	T	W	T	F	S
			1	2	3	4
5	6	7	8	9	10	11
12	13	14	15	16	17	18
19	20	21	22	23	24	25
26	27	28	29	30	31	

Extended HTML_Table with HTML_Table_Matrix

The `HTML_Table_Matrix` (HTM) package is a sub-package of `HTML_Table` and extends it to enable the easy formatting of data in a tabular layout. The main benefit of using HTM is that instead of having to fill each row using the `addRow()` function, you can simply specify how many rows and columns you want in your table and then drop in your array of data and let `HTML_Table_Matrix` sort everything out.

`HTML_Table_Matrix` is designed using **Filler** drivers that handle the order in which your data appears in the table. Fillers currently support filling your table in a natural left-right, top-bottom format, as well as bottom-top or right-left, spiraling outwards in a counter-clockwise fashion, etc.

The Filler simply provides a `next()` method that the rendering class uses to determine where the next piece of data will be placed. While it's unlikely that you will choose to render a table from the center cell out, a flexible mechanism is provided, which should be able to handle any future needs. The data store itself is only queried once.

In this example, we use the `Services_Yahoo` package to fetch the top sixteen images from Yahoo Image Search and display them in a table.

```
include_once 'HTML/Table/Matrix.php';
include_once 'Services/Yahoo/Search.php';
```

```
$table = new HTML_Table_Matrix(array('border' => "2"));


$rows = 4;
$cols = 4;
$term = 'Pears';

$search = Services_Yahoo_Search::factory("image");
$search->setQuery($term);
$search->setResultNumber($rows * $cols);

$results = $search->submit();
foreach($results as $image)
{
    $data[] = "<img src='{$image['Thumbnail']->Url}' />";
}

$table->setTableSize($rows, $cols);
$table->setFillStart(1, 0);
$table->setData($data);


$table->addRow(array("Search for the term '$term'"),
                                        "colspan='$cols'", "th");

$f = HTML_Table_Matrix_Filler::factory("LRTB", $table);

$table->accept($f);
echo $table->toHtml();
```

After including both the packages we are using in this example, we set a couple of variables to hold information about our search. We want a table with four rows and four columns to hold the images found when searching for the term 'Pears'. Once we have received the query data back from Yahoo, we define the size of our table based on the predefined variables. We want to add a header, so we start filling the table one row from the top of the table; this is done using the `setFillStart()` function.

`HTML_Table_Matrix` is a sub-package of `HTML_Table`, so while the `setData` method exists for adding data en masse, we can still manipulate the table or individual rows and cells, which is what we do to add the header row.

When we instantiate the Filler package we supply the table object as well as the driver to be used. To fill in the data left-right and top-bottom, we use the parameter `LRTB`; then we print out the table.

Excel Spreadsheets

Generating Excel spreadsheets is a task that most programmers are regularly called on to do. Whether we like it or not, the fact is that an Excel spreadsheet has become the standard for presenting and sharing tabular data. The easy-to-use format coupled with the general availability of Excel-compatible programs makes it the format of choice for many companies when they need to create reports for their management or exchange data with other offices.

While there are several different techniques for generating Excel-compatible files, which are mentioned briefly at the end of this section, the PEAR class `Spreadsheet_Excel_Writer` stands out as the only pure PHP method of creating native Excel spreadsheets.

`Excel_Spreadsheet_Writer` was ported into PHP from the Perl module `Spreadsheet::WriteExcel`, and supports not only data input, but adding formatting, formulas, multiple worksheets, images, and much more. `Excel_Spreadsheet_Writer` does not utilize any external components like COM, so the package is truly cross-platform and will run on any platform that PHP runs on.

The Excel Format

The format used by Excel Spreadsheet Writer is called BIFF5 (Binary Interchange File Format). This is a binary standard introduced with Excel 5 and all modern versions of Microsoft Excel as well as OpenOffice can parse the BIFF5 format. The BIFF5 format is quite well understood and supported, but lacks some of the features available in later versions of Excel. There is no official documentation of the BIFF5 format from Microsoft, but many projects have done a lot of work in reverse engineering and documenting BIFF5. One of the best sources of documentation is the OpenOffice website. The relevant document is available at `http://sc.openoffice.org/excelfileformat.pdf`.

One of the common complaints about Excel Spreadsheet Writer is the way in which it handles Unicode strings. This is actually not an issue with Excel Spreadsheet writer, since it is simply missing from the BIFF5 format. There have been individual efforts by users to add limited Unicode support into `Excel_Spreadsheet_Writer`. At the time of writing there are no plans to incorporate these features into the official Excel Spreadsheet Writer package.

Older Microsoft formats use a system called OLE to create compound documents and because of this `Spreadsheet_Excel_Writer` depends on the PEAR OLE package to wrap the BIFF5 document it creates into a valid Excel document.

Our First Spreadsheet

Getting started with `Spreadsheet_Excel_Writer` is very simple. In this first basic example we will create a worksheet and add data into two cells. Now that we have a basic understanding of what we are trying to do we'll get to the code.

```
require_once 'Spreadsheet/Excel/Writer.php';
$workbook = new Spreadsheet_Excel_Writer();

$worksheet =& $workbook->addWorksheet('Example 1');
$worksheet->write(0, 0, 'Hello World!');
$worksheet->write(0, 1, 'This is my first Excel Spreadsheet');
$worksheet->send('example1.xls')
$workbook->close();
```

When working with `Spreadsheet_Excel_Writer` we have two different choices for the storing our completed spreadsheet. The first option, used here, is the `send()` method, which will send the Excel headers (`application/vnd.ms-excel`) to your browser followed by the spreadsheet data. This will either open the spreadsheet in your browser for inline viewing, or prompt you to save it on your computer, depending on your browser and its settings.

The second option is to save the generated file on your local file system. To do this you simply give the path to the constructor upon instantiating the `Spreadsheet_Excel_Writer` class. When you close the spreadsheet using `close()` the data will be saved to the file specified. When deciding which method to use, it is important to realize that when you send the spreadsheet directly to the web browser, you will not be able to send any further HTML text. This is useful when the sole task of a script is to dynamically serve spreadsheet documents. However in many cases you'll want to generate the spreadsheet document and then print an HTML page, or alert the user that the spreadsheet generation is complete. In these cases, it is practical to save the spreadsheet to your filesystem and then continue with the generation of your HTML page. For simplicity's sake we will use this method in future examples.

Once we have our worksheet object set up we can go ahead and write some data to a cell.

Finally we close the workbook, which compiles the data and either stores it in a file or sends it to your browser, depending on the options you've chosen.

About Cells

Excel Spreadsheet writer uses two methods to point to cells within the Excel Spreadsheet. When adding data to a spreadsheet we refer to the zero-based X and Y positions of the cell. The first cell in the worksheet is referred to as 0, 0.

To use formulas you need to use a different notation using a letter for the column and the line number. The first cell would be A1 in our example.

The difference between these two styles of referring to cells is most evident when working with formulas. Thankfully, `Spreadsheet_Excel_Writer` provides a useful function for converting from the row/col format to the cell name format.

```
$first = 1;
$last = 10;
for ($i = $first; $i <= $last; $i++) {
    $worksheet1->write($i, 1, $i);
}
$cell1 = Spreadsheet_Excel_Writer::rowcolToCell($first, 1);
$cell2 = Spreadsheet_Excel_Writer::rowcolToCell($last, 1);
$worksheet1->write($last + 1, 0, "Total =");
$worksheet1->writeFormula($last + 1, 1,
                                        "=SUM($cell1:$cell2)");
```

As you can see, we are using the row and column values to write the data to the spreadsheet, then using the static `rowcolToCell()` method to convert the row/column position to the cell address that the formula requires. In this example the string value of `$cell1` will be `A1` and the value of `$cell2` will be `A10`. Thus the formula parsed by Excel will be `=SUM(A1:A10)`.

We will learn more about formulas further on in this chapter.

Setting Up a Page for Printing

There are many options that affect how your spreadsheet is printed. This is particularly useful if you are shipping a spreadsheet to a client and need exact control over how the final spreadsheet is presented.

All page formatting options are applied to the entire spreadsheet.

Function	Usage
`$worksheet->setPaper(1);`	Sets the size of the page using a constant.
`$worksheet->setPortrait();` `$worksheet->setLandscape();`	Sets the orientation of the page.
`$worksheet->setHeader();` `$worksheet->setFooter();`	Adds a header and footer to each page in the spreadsheet
`$worksheet->setMargins(.5);`	Sets each margin to the value in inches; each of the margins can be set individually as well.
`$worksheet->printArea($firstcol, $firstrow, $lastcol, $lastrow);`	Defines what area of the page you want printed.
`$worksheet->hideGridlines();`	Hides the grid when printing
`$worksheet->fitToPages(2, 2);`	Sets the maximum number of pages to use when printing this spreadsheet to 2 pages across and 2 pages down.
`$worksheet->setPrintScale($scale);`	Specifies the percentage by which to scale the spreadsheet. 100% is the default. This option overrides the "fit to page" option.

Adding some Formatting

Now that we have a basic understanding of how we can create Excel files with PHP, we need to work on the formatting of the cells.

Unlike what we saw in `HTML_Table` where we directly edited the attributes of individual cells to change the formatting, `Spreadsheet_Excel_Writer` takes an object-oriented approach when it comes to creating and applying styles to cells.

To create a new style we use the `addFormat()` function from the workbook class. This creates a formatting object, which we can then apply to as many different cells as we like. This is similar to creating CSS classes in HTML, and in a project you are likely to create several standard formatting objects and then use them throughout your project.

```
require_once 'Spreadsheet/Excel/Writer.php';
$workbook = new Spreadsheet_Excel_Writer('example2.xls');

$worksheet =& $workbook->addWorksheet("Example 2");

$header =& $workbook->addFormat(array("bold" => true,
                                      "Color" => "white",
```

```
                                                   "FgColor" => "12",
                                                   "Size"    => "15"));

$worksheet->write(0, 0, 'Hello, World!', $header);
```

Here we create a new worksheet, and then send our formatting parameters to the `addFormat()` function to get our formatting option that we can then apply to the data we send when we add our text.

Each key of the array you send to the `addFormat()` function also has a separate function, which you can use to set that format value independently.

```
$header =& $workbook->addFormat();
$header->setBold();
$header->setColor("white");
$header->setFgColor("12");
```

Because you are able to apply these formatting values independently of each other, using this markup makes your code easier to manage and change in the future.

About Colors

Excel has an interesting way of working with colors. You will have noticed that we set the `FgColor` attribute to `12` and the `Color` of the text to `white`. Excel uses both named colors and its own internal color indexing system.

The following script generates the chart of Excel-compatible colors that you can use in your spreadsheets.

```
require_once 'Spreadsheet/Excel/Writer.php';
$workbook = new Spreadsheet_Excel_Writer('example2a.xls');
$worksheet =& $workbook->addWorksheet("Colors");

$row = 0;
$col = 0;
for ($i = 1; $i <= 128; $i++)
{
    $format =& $workbook->addFormat(array("bold" => true,
                                          "Color" => "white",
                                          "FgColor" => $i));

    $worksheet->write($row, $col, '#'.$i, $format);

    $col++;
    if ($col == 7)
    {
        $col = 0;
```

```
            $row++;
        }
    }
    $workbook->close();
```

This will generate the following chart:

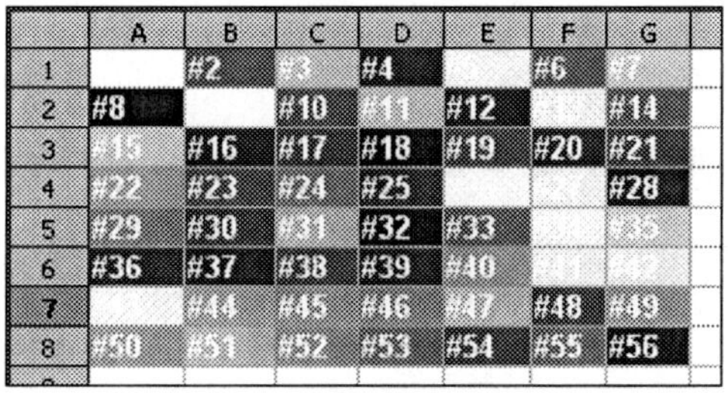

The palette of colors varies slightly between Excel 5 and Excel 97, so if you expect users to be running very old versions of Excel, keep this in mind. The numbers are not hex codes as in HTML; here they simply identify the colors.

You will no doubt notice that we have set the cell background color with the `FgColor` attribute. The reason for the naming of this function is that with Excel you can apply a pattern to the background of a cell. If no pattern is specified it defaults to a solid pattern, and `FgColor` sets the foreground color of the pattern. Yes, it is a bit difficult to understand. Patterns are described in detail in the next section.

If you need to apply a color other than the ones represented on this chart, you can override one of the supplied colors with your own color. We create a new color by first specifying which slot we want to use, in our case place 12, and then specify the RGB values.

```
    $workbook->setCustomColor(12, 10, 200, 10);
```

These substitutions apply to the entire spreadsheet.

Pattern Fill

Along with the unique color system, Excel also supplies background patterns. The default pattern for cells is solid, with only the background color showing. The following image shows the patters that are available as well as their identification numbers. In this image dark grey is the foreground color and light grey as the background color.

	A	B	C	D
1	#1	#2	#3	#4
2	#5	#6	#7	#8
3	#9	#10	#11	#12
4	#13	#14	#15	#16
5	#17	#18		

Number Formatting

Excel also provides a wide array of formatting options for both the format and color of numerical values.

Numbers within formats can be represented either with the `#` or the `0` placeholder. The difference between the two placeholders is that using `0` will pad the results with additional zeros but `#` will just display the number. The format `#####.##` when applied to the number `4201.5` will display just that, while the format `00000.00` will display `04201.50`. The best strategy is to use a combination of both, `#.00`, to give the expected result of `4201.50`.

Another formatting placeholder that can be used is the `?` character. This leaves a space for insignificant 0s, but does not display the character if it is not available. This is useful when you want to align a row of numbers by the decimal point.

When providing the format of a number, Excel allows you to define both the positive and negative formats. The formats are separated by `;` and will be used depending on the value of the text or number in the field. For example, if you want positive numbers to be displayed in blue and negative numbers to be displayed in red surrounded by brackets, use the following formatting string:

```
$format =& $workbook->addFormat();
$format->setNumFormat('[Blue]$0.00;[Red]($0.00)');
$worksheet->write(2, 1, "-4201", $format);
$worksheet->write(2, 2, "4201", $format);
```

You can also specify the format for 0 values or for text values in the field.

```
$format =& $workbook->addFormat();
$format->setNumFormat('[Blue]0;[Red]0;[Green]0;@*-');
$worksheet->write(0, 1, 10, $format);
$worksheet->write(0, 1, -10, $format);
$worksheet->write(0, 1, 0, $format);
$worksheet->write(0, 1, "ten", $format);
```

This format will display positive numbers in blue, negative numbers in red, 0 values in green, and text will be padded with as many dashes as is needed to fill the cell. Being able to manipulate the format allows you to create a format that, for example, doesn't show 0 values, or displays an error if text is added to what should be a numerical field.

If you want the sum of a calculation to return as **6 Dollars and 95 cents** instead of **$6.95**, use the following formatting string.

```
$format =& $workbook->addFormat();
$format->setNumFormat('0 "Dollars and" .00 "cents"');
$worksheet->write(4, 1, 6.95, $format);
```

Taking this example one step further, we can display the cent value as a fraction.

```
$format =& $workbook->addFormat();
$format->setNumFormat('0 ??/?? "Dollars"');
$worksheet->write(0, 1, 42.50, $format);
```

This will display as **42 ½ Dollars**.

Some more commonly used formats are shown in the table below:

Format	Description
`00000`	Shows no less than 5 digits. Pads number with leading 0s
`;;;@`	Suppresses numbers, only displays the text (@)
`#.???`	Lines numbers up with the decimal.
`#,`	Displays numbers in thousands
`0.000,, "Million"`	Displays number in Millions followed by the string "Million"
`0;[Red]"Error!";0;[Red]"Error!"`	Displays a red **Error!** for negative numbers or text values
`0.00_-;0.00-`	Displays the negative sign on the right side of the number and pads the space, so that the decimal points line up
`'0","000'`	Inserts a decimal point into your number: 10000 will display as 10,000
`??/??`	Displays the decimal value as a fraction
`# ??/??`	Displays a fraction with the decimal value
0.00E+#	Displays the number in scientific notation

Adding Formulas

Creating formulas and assigning them to cells is one of the basic functions of Excel. Now that we can add and format data in our spreadsheet we can add a couple of formulas to make Excel do the work for us.

```
require_once 'Spreadsheet/Excel/Writer.php';

$workbook = new Spreadsheet_Excel_Writer('example3.xls');

$worksheet =& $workbook->addWorksheet("Example 3");

$tax =& $workbook->addFormat();
$tax->setNumFormat('.00%');

$price =& $workbook->addFormat();
$price->setNumFormat('$####.00');

$worksheet->write(0, 0, 'Tax Calculation Worksheet');

$worksheet->write(1, 0, 'VAT:');
$worksheet->write(1, 1, ".16", $tax);
$worksheet->write(2, 1, 'Price');
$worksheet->write(2, 2, "With Tax");

$worksheet->freezePanes(array(3));

for ($i = 3; $i < 101; $i++)
{
    $worksheet->write($i, 0, "Item $i");
    $worksheet->write($i, 1, rand(3, 100), $price);
    $cell = Spreadsheet_Excel_Writer::rowcolToCell($i, 1);
    $worksheet->writeFormula($i, 2, "=($cell*B2)+$cell",
                                                $price);
}

$worksheet->writeFormula(102, 1, "=SUM(B4:B102,C4:C102)", $price);
$workbook->close();
```

This example generates 100 random numbers, adds them to the worksheet, and then creates a formula to apply a tax. This formula can be changed by the spreadsheet user. We used the `rowcolToCell()` helper function that enables us to quickly switch from the row/column value to the cell address that Excel expects in its formulas.

The final formula at the end of the worksheet calculates the `SUM` of columns B and C. Excel is picky about the argument separator, and I've added this example to illustrate that when passing arguments to an Excel function, the `writeFormula()`

method requires a comma as the argument separator. In certain localized versions of Excel, the formula `SUM(B4:B102,C4:C102)` would be written as `SUM(B4:B102;C4:C102)` using the ; separator. A small difference, but one that can easily create difficult-to-find bugs.

Since this example scrolls down past the viewable area of our screen we have frozen the top 3 rows using the `freezePanes()` method.

Multiple Worksheets, Borders, and Images

Now that the hard stuff is out of the way, we can return to making our spreadsheet look nice.

To illustrate the use of formats, we will create a simple Invoice generator. For the sake of brevity we have excluded a lot of formats, so further beautification is left as an exercise for the reader.

```
<?php
require_once 'Spreadsheet/Excel/Writer.php';

$workbook = new Spreadsheet_Excel_Writer("example4.xls");
$worksheet =& $workbook->addWorksheet();
$worksheet->writeNote(1, 0, "Invoice For New Customer");

$worksheet->setRow(0, 50);
$worksheet->insertBitmap(0, 0, "logo.bmp", 0, 0);

$left   =& $workbook->addFormat(array("Left" => 2));
$right  =& $workbook->addFormat(array("Right" => 2));
$number  =& $workbook->addFormat(array("NumFormat" =>
                                                     '$####.00'));

$worksheet->write(1, 1, "Client Name:");
$worksheet->write(2, 1, "Tax:");
$worksheet->writeNumber(2, 2, .16);

$cart = array("Monitor" => 12,
              "Printer" => 14.4);

$top = 4;
foreach ($cart as $item => $price)
{
    $worksheet->write($top, 1, $item, $number);
    $worksheet->write($top, 2, $price, $number);
    $cell = "C" . ($top + 1);
```

```
        $worksheet->writeFormula($top, 3, "=($cell*C3)+$cell",
                                                        $number);
        $top++;
    }

    $lastrow = $top + 1;

    for ($i=1; $i <= $lastrow; $i++)
    {
        $worksheet->writeBlank($i, 0, $left);
        $worksheet->writeBlank($i, 7, $right);
    }

    $worksheet->write($lastrow, 2, "Total:");
    $worksheet->writeFormula($lastrow, 3, "=SUM(D5:D$lastrow)",
                                                        $number);

    $workbook->close();
```

The important points to note are the adding of the image and the borders that have been created. Bitmap images can be included into your spreadsheet using the `insertBitmap()` method.

This is fairly straightforward, but because it works in a way that many people don't expect, many people have reported a bug when trying to change the height of the row in which the Bitmap sits.

The reason for this behavior is that the height of the row must be set before the image is included into the spreadsheet. If you add the image and then change the row height the image will be stretched or shrunken, which is most likely not what you want. In this example, we first call the `setRow()` method, and once we have set the row to the correct height we use `insertBitmap()` to embed the image.

Borders work exactly the same as a text format. Simply add the style of border to your format and apply it to the cell. In this case we don't need to put any data into the cells formatted with the border formats, so we use the `writeBlank()` method to add a format to a cell without inserting data. You will also notice that we use the `writeNumber()` and `writeNote()` methods in this example; these are just a few of the different ways to write specific data to a spreadsheet with `Spreadsheet_Excel_Writer`.

In this example we only generated one invoice. However if you are pulling data from an external source and need to create multiple invoices, you can easily add as many worksheets as you need, by adding each of them with the `addWorksheet()` method of the workbook class.

example4.xls

	A	B	C	D	E	F	G	H
1	Our Company Header							
2		Client Name:						
3		Tax:	0.16					
4								
5		Monitor	$12.00	$13.92				
6		Printer	$14.40	$16.70				
7								
8			Total:	$30.62				

Other ways to create Spreadsheets

`Spreadsheet_Excel_Writer` is the best way to create high quality pure Excel spreadsheets. However, in instances where you do not need all the features that `Excel_Spreadsheet_Writer` supports, and would prefer to use something simpler for displaying your data, there are simpler options.

CSV

The humble CSV (comma separated value) is the simplest of data exchange formats and many programs enable the import and the export of CSV data. PEAR offers easy read and write access to CSV files through the File module.

The Content-Type Trick

One commonly used technique that works quite well in modern Excel versions is to simply create an HTML table containing your data, and then send a content-type HTTP header with the value of `application/vnd.ms-excel` followed by your table. The web browser will accept the header and treat the HTML table as if it were an Excel spreadsheet. Excel will accept the HTML table and will display it, but you will have less functionality than with native Excel documents.

The reason why this works is that the most recent Excel file formats are XML-based and Excel is fairly lenient when it comes to the formatting.

Generating Excel 2003 Files

Unlike the difficult-to-use BIFF format, the new Microsoft document formats are based on XML, standards compliant, and well documented. One technique in use is to create your document using a recent version of Excel, then edit the generated XML document and add PHP tags within the XML document. You would need to change your web server configuration to parse the Excel Documents as PHP files, but once this is done you can have fun using PHP inside Excel Documents.

Creating Spreadsheets using PEAR_OpenDocument

Thanks to a Google Summer of Code project, work is being done to create an OpenDocument reader/writer for PEAR. When this is complete, it will be possible to create full-featured OpenDocument spreadsheets. In the most recent versions of Microsoft Office, steps have been taken for interoperability with OpenDocument formats. While at the time of writing there is no way to open an OpenDocument spreadsheet with Office, it is on the roadmap for future releases.

DataGrids

Windows programmers are familiar with the concept of using a DataGrid component to display data in a flexible and sortable grid. In simple scenarios, all a programmer needs is to pull data out of a DataSource (database, text file, array) and display it in an easily configurable HTML web page. In more complex scenarios a programmer will want to make the grid sortable, enable data filtering, and render it to multiple formats.

On the web front, ASP.NET programmers have a DataGrid component available to them. PHP has no standard implementation of the DataGrid, and most PHP programmers have had to write their own component or settle for a third-party component or commercial implementation.

As mentioned above, a DataGrid component requires several elements.

- You need to get the data from somewhere; this is referred to as your DataSource.
- You need to create your DataGrid and select an output format, which is referred to as the Renderer.
- You need to bind the DataSource to the DataGrid and display the latter. These requirements are generally standardized between DataGrid implementations.

`Structures_DataGrid` from PEAR fills this space nicely. Not only does `Structures_DataGrid` give you the standard options of fetching data from a database and binding it to an HTML table, it also offers a driver-based approach for both fetching and rendering data. This allows `Structures_DataGrid` to, for example, use its XML DataSource driver to import data from an XML file, choose which fields you want to display, and then render the tabular data in any format for which a rendering driver exists. If project requirements change and you need to render your DataGrid into additional formats, this is as simple as creating a new `Structures_DataGrid` renderer.

As you may have already guessed, this flexibility not only enables you to create extremely powerful DataGrids, but has the side benefit of being a powerful data conversion engine, as you are now able to convert data from any format for which a DataSource driver exists into any format for which a renderer exists. In the following table the currently available DataSources and renders are listed. The third column in the tables represents the constant that represents the DataSource or renderer and is sent as a parameter to the `Structures_Datagrid` constructor.

DataSources

Name	Function	Constant
`CSV`	Parses data from the Comma Separated Value format	`DATAGRID_SOURCE_CSV`
`DataObject`	Uses the PEAR Object Interface to database tables `DB_DataObject` to query data from a database	`DATAGRID_SOURCE_DATAOBJECT`
`RSS`	Fetches and parses data from an external RSS feed	`DATAGRID_SOURCE_RSS`
`DB`	Fetches data using `PEAR::DB`	`DATAGRID_SOURCE_DB`
`XML`	Parses an XML file	`DATAGRID_SOURCE_XML`

Renderers

Name	Function	Constant
`Excel`	Generates native MS Excel files using `PEAR::Spreadsheet_Excel_Writer`	`DATAGRID_RENDER_XLS`
`HTML_Table`	The default Renderer; shows the data as a configurable, sortable, and pageable HTML table	`DATAGRID_RENDER_TABLE`
`XML`	Formats the data into an XML file	`DATAGRID_RENDER_XML`
`XUL`	Renders the DataGrid into an XUL grid for Mozilla, Firefox, and other Gecko-based web browsers	`DATAGRID_RENDER_XUL`
`CSV`	Renders the DataGrid to the Comma Separated Value format	`DATAGRID_RENDER_CSV`
`Console`	Renders the DataGrid into a table that can be displayed on a console	`DATAGRID_RENDER_CONSOLE`

First we will start off with some simple examples of `Structures_DataGrid` usage, and then jump into rendering, formatting, and extending the `Structures_DataGrid` package.

A Simple DataGrid

Now that we've understood what `Structures_DataGrid` does, let's dig into some code to see how it works.

```
require_once 'Structures/DataGrid.php';

$data = array(array('First Name' => 'Aaron',
                    'Last Name'  => 'Wormus',
                    'Email'      => 'aaron@wormus.com'),
              array('First Name' => 'Clark',
                    'Last Name'  => 'Kent',
                    'Email'      => 'clark@kent.com'),
              array('First Name' => 'Peter',
                    'Last Name'  => 'Parker',
                    'Email'      => 'peter@parker.com'),
              array('First Name' => 'Bruce',
                    'Last Name'  => 'Wayne',
                    'Email'      => 'bruce@wayne.com')
              );

$dg =& new Structures_DataGrid;
$dg->bind($data);
$dg->render();
```

This example clearly shows the three steps involved in creating a DataGrid. First we create an instance of the `Structures_DataGrid` package. Next we use the `bind()` method to bind the data array to the DataGrid. The default DataSource driver that `Structures_DataGrid` uses is `ARRAY`, so we can simply pass an array to our DataGrid without setting any other options. Once the DataSource is bound to our DataGrid, we render it using the `render()` method, which gives us a fully functional DataGrid.

An important part of this code snippet is the fact that the instance of the `DataGrid` class must be instantiated as a reference using the `=&` syntax. This design change had to do with how `Structures_DataGrid` dealt with its drivers. Since this broke backwards compatibility, keep this in mind when creating or upgrading your DataGrid instances.

First Name	Last Name	Email
Aaron	Wormus	aaron@wormus.com
Bruce	Wayne	bruce@wayne.com
Clark	Kent	clark@kent.com
Peter	Parker	peter@parker.com

As you can see, the default usage of the DataGrid includes sorting of the records presented. Simply click on the header links to sort the DataGrid using that column. We will give more examples of this later on in the chapter.

Paging the Results

`Structures_DataGrid` uses the PEAR class `PAGER` to offer the ability to add Google-like paging to your DataGrid. To limit the results displayed on each page, simply send the number of records you want to display per page to the constructor.

```
$dg =& new Structures_DataGrid('2');
```

After displaying your DataGrid, you will need to display the paging control to give your users access to the records on pages that are not displayed on the front page.

```
echo $dg->renderer->getPaging();
```

This calls the HTML renderer and prints out the paging control. Paging is specific to the renderer used; at this point only the HTML renderer supports paging.

Using a DataSource

In a real-life scenario, we wouldn't be adding data through an array, but will most likely be pulling data from an external source. To do this we use DataGrid's DataSource drivers.

To create a new DataSource we use the `create()` method of the `Structures_DataGrid_DataSource` class. This method takes three parameters. The first parameter points to the location of the data, the second holds an array with the driver-specific options, and the third parameter is a constant that defines the DataSource driver.

In this example, we use the CSV DataSource driver to read data from a customer list database that has been exported from our address book.

```
require_once 'Structures/DataGrid.php';
require_once 'Structures/DataGrid/DataSource.php';
$opt = array('delimiter' => ',',
```

```
            'fields' => array(0, 1, 2),
            'labels' => array("First Name", "Last Name", "Email"),
            'generate_columns' => true);
$data = Structures_DataGrid_DataSource::create('data.csv',
        $opt, DATAGRID_SOURCE_CSV);
$dg =& new Structures_DataGrid();
$dg->bindDataSource($data);
$dg->render();
```

The options specify what we are using as the field delimiter, the fields we want to include in our DataGrid, the labels of the fields, and finally whether we want to generate the columns with the headers. We will talk more about manually generating columns later, but for now setting this option will do what we need.

We bind our data to the DataGrid using the `bindDataSource()` method and then render the output.

Using a Renderer

Now we have our DataGrid and it is pulling the data out of our CSV file and displaying it as an HTML DataGrid, but we want to use the power of `Structures_DataGrid`'s renderers to export our data into an Excel document. We do this by changing the following lines in the above example.

```
// Instruct the Structures_Datagrid to use the XLS renderer
$dg =& new Structures_DataGrid(null, null, DATAGRID_RENDER_XLS);

// Set the filename which we will be using
$dg->renderer->setFilename('datagrid.xls');

// Bind the data, and render the output
$dg->bindDataSource($data);
$dg->render();
```

Now we have a fully functional CSV to XLS converter. Unfortunately the XLS renderer does not use the full functionality of `Spreadsheet_Excel_Writer` to add formatting to the rows and headers, but for now this is good enough. We can use the other renderers by simply changing the constant in the constructor of `Structures_DataGrid`.

Structures_Datagrid Constructor Options

The `Structures_DataGrid` constructor takes three parameters. The first parameter specifies the limit of how many results are displayed on the current page, the second parameter specifies which page is displayed, and the third option defines which renderer is used.

Making it Pretty

Now that we have `Structures_DataGrid` doing what we want, we need to make the result look pretty enough for us to impress the management. Each renderer provides a variety of different formatting options. We will use the default `HTML_Table` renderer and insert some options into the last script.

```
$dg =& new Structures_DataGrid(2, null, DATAGRID_RENDER_TABLE);
$dg->renderer->setTableHeaderAttributes(array('bgcolor' =>
                                              '#3399FF'));
$dg->renderer->setTableOddRowAttributes(array('bgcolor' =>
                                              '#CCCCCC'));
$dg->renderer->setTableEvenRowAttributes(array('bgcolor' =>
                                              '#EEEEEE'));

// Define DataGrid Table Attributes
$dg->renderer->setTableAttribute('width', '100%');
$dg->renderer->setTableAttribute('cellspacing', '1');

// Set sorting icons
$dg->renderer->sortIconASC = '&uarr;';
$dg->renderer->sortIconDESC = '&darr;';
$dg->bind($data);
```

You will notice that we are sending additional parameters to `Structures_DataGrid` when instantiating the class. The second attribute specifies which page we want to display, and the third specifies the driver we will use for rendering the DataGrid. While it is not necessary to explicitly set the `DATAGRID_RENDER_TABLE` renderer since it is the default renderer, we have set it for the sake of this example.

After initiating an instance of the DataGrid object, we can start playing with the renderer. As you can see from the example, you can set the individual attributes of the table, the headers, or the even and odd rows. The `HTML_Table` renderer is one of the most complete renderers and offers several more formatting options than the others. We have only used a small subset of the options here.

Before we are done, we add the sort icons, which will show in the header when a specific column is being sorted. We use the HTML entities for "Up Arrow" and "Down Arrow". Note that any HTML code can be entered here, so using an image is also possible.

Extending DataGrid

In the previous section, the code for setting the table attributes was fairly long, and you wouldn't want to have to repeat this code each time you want to display a DataGrid. To solve this problem, we can create a class that extends the `Structures_DataGrid` package so that each time you call your new class, all the renderer attributes will be automatically added.

```
require 'Structures/DataGrid.php';
class myDataGrid extends Structures_DataGrid
{
    function myDataGrid($limit = null, $page = 0)
    {
        parent::Structures_DataGrid($limit, $page);
        $this->renderer->setTableAttribute('width', '100%');
        // ... Enter the rest of your formatting code here ...
        $this->renderer->sortIconDESC = '&darr;';
    }
}


$dg =& myDataGrid();
```

Now whenever we instantiate a new `myDataGrid` object, all the table attributes will already be set, and we will have a central place to change the look of the DataGrids used in our project.

A more flexible approach if you have a site in which you use several different DataGrids is to create several classes that extend `Structures_DataGrid` in the specific ways that you need, and then instantiate the class you are creating using a simplified factory pattern.

```
function getDGInstance($type)
{
    if (class_exists($type))
    {
        $datagrid =& new $type;
        return $datagrid;
    } else
      {
```

```
            return false;
        }
    }

    $dg = getDGInstance('myDataGrid');

    // We can create another instance of DataGrid using a
    // seperate extended class like this

    $dg = getDGInstance('myDataGrid2');
```

This example is fairly limited, but it gives a good idea of how to easily deal with multiple instances of extended `Structures_DataGrid` classes.

Adding Columns

The columns of your DataGrid are actually instances of the `Structures_DataGrid_Column` class. Until now, DataGrid has taken care of this behind the scenes, so it was not necessary for us to create the columns ourselves. However, if you want to add a column to your DataGrid, you will need to do this manually.

In this example, we will use the `RSS` DataSource driver to pull data from an external RSS file and then display it with several additional columns.

```
require_once 'Structures/DataGrid/DataSource.php';

// Specify the Columns from the RSS we want to use
$options = array('fields' => array('title', 'link'));
$rss   = "http://rss.slashdot.org/Slashdot/slashdot";
$ds = Structures_DataGrid_DataSource::create($rss, $options,
                                             DATAGRID_SOURCE_RSS);
// Instantiate our extended DataGrid class
$dg =& new myDataGrid;
// Create 2 columns
$titleCol = new Structures_DataGrid_Column('Title', 'title');
$funcCol  = new Structures_DataGrid_Column('Function', null);
// Attach Formatters
$titleCol->setFormatter('printLink()');
$funcCol->setFormatter('sendLink()');
// Add Columns to DataGrid
$dg->addColumn($titleCol);
$dg->addColumn($funcCol);
// Bind DataSet to DataGrid and render
$dg->bindDataSource($ds);
$dg->render();
```

You have seen most of this code in previous examples. We create a DataSource using the RSS driver and set the options to display the title and link fields.

The interesting part comes when we create our columns by creating instances of the Structures_DataGrid_Column class. The parameters we use are the title of the column and name of the field it is associated with. Structures_DataGrid_Column accepts several other values, such as formatting options, table attributes, auto-fill values, and sort-by values, but we will keep this example simple.

We want to add some special features to the column that contains the URL and our function column, so we use the setFormatter() method to point to functions that will format the columns; the functions follow:

```
function printLink($params)
{
    $data = $params['record'];
    return "<a href=\"{$data[link]}\">$data[title]</a>";
}
function sendLink($params)
{
    $data  = $params['record'];
    $link = urlencode($data["link"]);
    return "<a href=\"send2friend.php?url=$link\">Send Link to
                                                         Friend</a>";
}
```

The $params variable is an array that contains all the data from the current record of the dataset. We put the record data into the $data variable and then return the data as we need it formatted in the column of our DataGrid. In this case we only have two columns; the first is a link to the article, and the second formats the URL and connects it to our script so we can send this link to a friend.

Generating PDF Files

When discussing file formats, something must be said about the PDF format. PDF (Portable Document Format) is the 600-Pound gorilla of file documents. Originally a proprietary document format created by Adobe, PDFs have gained popularity as solving a specific problem, that is to create a document and be assured that it will look exactly the same on any system that the document is viewed on.

Unfortunately, there is a cost to the portability of PDF documents. It is an extremely complex format and is notoriously difficult to decipher, even for those who read the 1,000+ pages of the specification.

Thankfully, as PEAR users, we don't have to worry about reading the lengthy technical specification and can simply use the `File_PDF` library to handle our PDF creation needs. With a simple API we are able to do the majority of the tasks that present themselves, including displaying text, drawing lines and other objects, displaying images, writing to
tables, etc.

The following is a simple business letter created with `File_PDF`. For the sake of a simple, yet fully functional example, we use the `setXY()` function. This function sets the starting point to the X and Y position specified. When creating a larger document, or a document that contains dynamic content, you will probably want to stick to the more flexible methods of inserting content detailed in the section about Cells.

```
require_once "File/PDF.php";

$company_name = "Wormus Consulting";
$my_address = "123 Aaron Way, Gotham City, 12421 RQ, USA";

// Set some initial margins
$lm = 22;
$rm = 22;
$tm = 22;
$bm = 22;

$padding = 10;

$pdf = File_PDF::factory();
$pdf->open();

// Can also be done with setMargins
$pdf->setLeftMargin($lm + $padding);
$pdf->setRightMargin($rm + $padding);
$pdf->addPage();

// Set the typeface for the title
$pdf->setFont('Arial', 'B', '12');
$pos = $tm + $padding;
$pdf->setXY(10, $pos);

// Draw the Company Name
$pdf->cell(0, $padding, $company_name, null, 0, 'R');
$pdf->setFont('Arial', 'B', '8');

$pos += 10;
$pdf->setXY(10, $pos);

$pdf->cell(0, 0, $my_address, null, 1, 'R');
```

```
$pos += 3;
$pdf->setXY($lm, $pos);
$pdf->line($lm + $padding, $pos, 210 - $rm - $lm, $pos);

$pos += 10;
$pdf->setXY($lm, $pos);
$pdf->newLine();
$pdf->write('4', "John Smith");
$pdf->newLine();
$pdf->write('4', "122 Peters Lane");
$pdf->newLine();
$pdf->write('4', "32235 City, State");
$pdf->newLine();
$pdf->write('4', "Country");
$pdf->newLine();
$pos += 20;
$pdf->setXY($lm, $pos);
$pdf->newLine();

$pdf->write('4', "To whom it may Concern:");
$pos += 6;
$pdf->setXY($lm, $pos);
$pdf->newLine();

// shortened for the sake of brevity
$text = "Lorem ipsum dolor ... porta eleifend. ";
$pdf->MultiCell(210 -$lm -$rm - $padding *2, 3, $text, null, "J");
$pdf->newLine(10);
$pdf->write("10", "Best Regards,");
$pdf->output();
```

This simple example demonstrates some of the functionality of `File_PDF` and creates a good-looking example of a business letter.

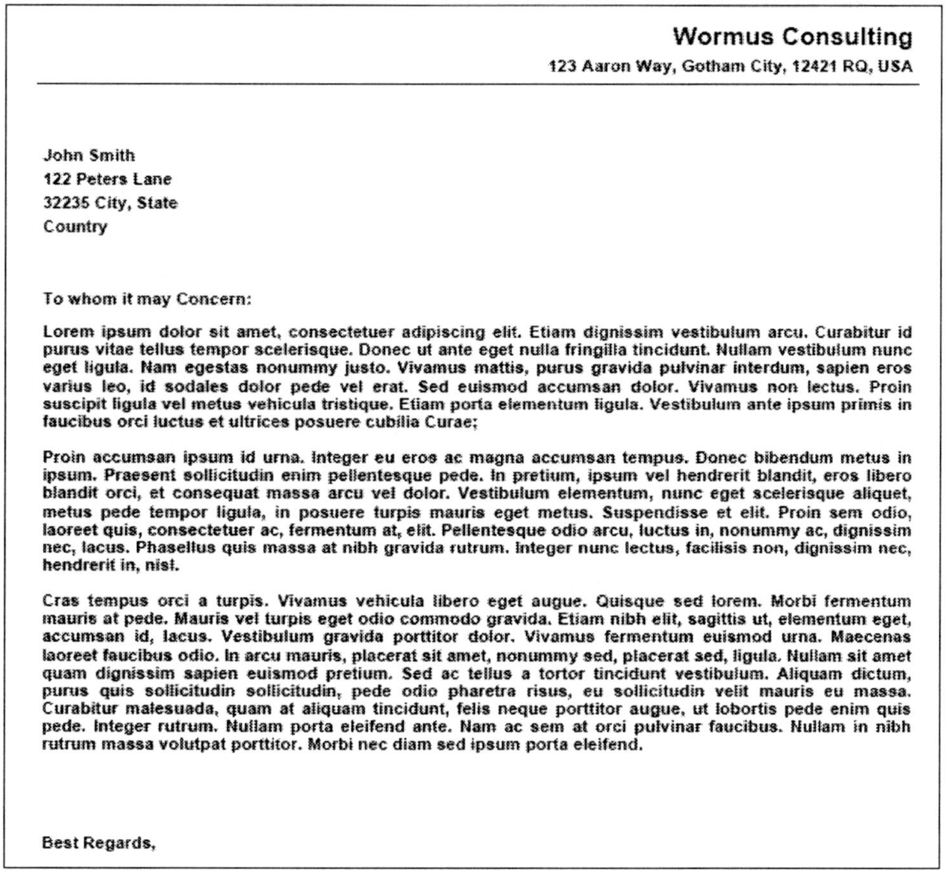

Wormus Consulting

123 Aaron Way, Gotham City, 12421 RQ, USA

John Smith
122 Peters Lane
32235 City, State
Country

To whom it may Concern:

Lorem ipsum dolor sit amet, consectetuer adipiscing elit. Etiam dignissim vestibulum arcu. Curabitur id purus vitae tellus tempor scelerisque. Donec ut ante eget nulla fringilla tincidunt. Nullam vestibulum nunc eget ligula. Nam egestas nonummy justo. Vivamus mattis, purus gravida pulvinar interdum, sapien eros varius leo, id sodales dolor pede vel erat. Sed euismod accumsan dolor. Vivamus non lectus. Proin suscipit ligula vel metus vehicula tristique. Etiam porta elementum ligula. Vestibulum ante ipsum primis in faucibus orci luctus et ultrices posuere cubilia Curae;

Proin accumsan ipsum id urna. Integer eu eros ac magna accumsan tempus. Donec bibendum metus in ipsum. Praesent sollicitudin enim pellentesque pede. In pretium, ipsum vel hendrerit blandit, eros libero blandit orci, et consequat massa arcu vel dolor. Vestibulum elementum, nunc eget scelerisque aliquet, metus pede tempor ligula, in posuere turpis mauris eget metus. Suspendisse et elit. Proin sem odio, laoreet quis, consectetuer ac, fermentum at, elit. Pellentesque odio arcu, luctus in, nonummy ac, dignissim nec, lacus. Phasellus quis massa at nibh gravida rutrum. Integer nunc lectus, facilisis non, dignissim nec, hendrerit in, nisl.

Cras tempus orci a turpis. Vivamus vehicula libero eget augue. Quisque sed lorem. Morbi fermentum mauris at pede. Mauris vel turpis eget odio commodo gravida. Etiam nibh elit, sagittis ut, elementum eget, accumsan id, lacus. Vestibulum gravida porttitor dolor. Vivamus fermentum euismod urna. Maecenas laoreet faucibus odio. In arcu mauris, placerat sit amet, nonummy sed, placerat sed, ligula. Nullam sit amet quam dignissim sapien euismod pretium. Sed ac tellus a tortor tincidunt vestibulum. Aliquam dictum, purus quis sollicitudin sollicitudin, pede odio pharetra risus, eu sollicitudin velit mauris eu massa. Curabitur malesuada, quam at aliquam tincidunt, felis neque porttitor augue, ut lobortis pede enim quis pede. Integer rutrum. Nullam porta eleifend ante. Nam ac sem at orci pulvinar faucibus. Nullam in nibh rutrum massa volutpat porttitor. Morbi nec diam sed ipsum porta eleifend.

Best Regards,

After including the main package, the process for creating a new page is very simple. The factory method creates a new instance of the `File_PDF` class and also accepts several parameters:

```
$pdf = File_PDF::factory(array('orientation' => 'P',
                               'unit' => 'mm',
                               'format' => 'A4'));
```

This sets the orientation to portrait, the unit size to millimeters, and the paper format to A4. These are the default parameters, so if you want to use these parameters there is no reason to explicitly set these values.

Once we have a new instance of the class we can call the `open()` method to start the document, and then add a page to the document. When adding a new page, the first thing that happens is that the `header()` and `footer()` methods are called; more about this later on in this chapter.

We now have a page and can begin to add data to the page.

Colors

We didn't change any colors in our simple example, but adding colors is very easy to do. `File_PDF` offers two functions for adding colors to your document. When specifying a color in your document, you are specifying that you want this color to be used from the point you initiated the color until the end of the page. When `File_PDF` creates a new page, it will re-instate the color options that are set, so unless you change the color or reset it to the previous value the color will remain until the end of the document.

The two functions you will use for this are `setDrawColor()` and `setFillColor()`. Each of these functions uses the first parameter to specify which color space is being used (`rgb`, `cymk`, or `gray`), and the proceeding parameters to set the values for each of the colors being used.

The `setDrawColor()` applies the specified color to lines that are drawn, and `setFillColor()` applies the color to text, areas, and cells that do not have a transparent background.

```
$pdf->setDrawColor("rgb", 0, 0, 255);
$pdf->setFillColor("rgb", 255, 0, 0);
```

Adding these lines to the top of your file will make your document use red text and blue lines.

Fonts

Like setting colors, a font setting also applies to the entire document from the point where the font is set. The following example will set the font to a bold 8-point Arial typeface.

```
$pdf->setFont("Arial", "B", 8);
```

A standard set of fonts that are readily available on most systems are predefined in `File_PDF`. If you want to use any other fonts you will need to make sure that they are available on the system, else you will need to convert them to a Type1 or TrueType font and then add it to the system. The description of how this is done is beyond the scope of this chapter, but it involves creating a font definition file using the included `makefont.php` utility, and then loading that data using the `addFont()` function. Once these steps have been taken you will be able to use the font in the `setFont()` function.

Cells

An easy way to write structured data to a PDF is to write to cells. A cell is simply a rectangular area to which you can add text and optionally borders and a background color.

```
$pdf->cell(0, $padding, $company_name, null, 0, 'R');
```

The first parameter is the width of the cell. If it is set to 0 then the cell will stretch to the right margin. The second parameter specifies the height of the cell, and the third parameter specifies the text to be displayed within the cell. The fourth parameter specifies whether or not a border should be drawn. A `null` setting implies no border. You can also specify which sides of the cell you want the border drawn on using the fifth parameter. In the example below, we are drawing borders on the left and right sides of the cell.

```
$pdf->cell(0, $padding, $company_name, null, 0, "LR", 'R', 0,
                                        "http://example.com");
```

The next parameter specifies that the text will be right-aligned, the seventh (optional) parameter specifies whether a cell background is transparent or painted using the assigned background color. Finally, we can optionally add a link that we want this cell to point to when clicked and also create a link identifier using the `addLink()` function and add the identifier here instead of the URL.

Creating Headers and Footers

`File_PDF` is designed to let programmers extend the base package to enable the addition of headers and footers called when each page is created. To use these methods, you will need to create a new class that you will use when creating your PDF document.

```
class My_File_PDF extends File_PDF
{
    function header()
    {
        // Select Arial bold 15
        $this->setFont('Arial', 'B', 15);
```

```
            // Move to the right
            $this->cell(80);
            // Framed title
            $this->cell(30, 10, 'Title', 1, 0, 'C');
            // Line break
            $this->newLine(20);
        }
    }
```

This is just one example of how you can extend `File_PDF` to override the default functionality. When using `File_PDF` in your projects, you'll want to extend the base class to utilize this functionality. The manual and code samples distributed with the package give more insight into what you can do with this.

Summary

While this chapter covers the highlights of how you can utilize PEAR packages to display your data, the examples given only cover a small part of the functionality available within these very fully featured packages.

There are other packages available for reading and writing to other formats, such as vcards and BibTeX. There are powerful parsers for reading and writing data into Wiki syntax, and much more that we did not touch in this chapter.

3

Working with XML

XML has been drawing more and more attention during recent years. In fact, in the new PHP version, PHP 5, XML support has been completely revamped and is now based on the libraries `libxml2` and `libxsl`, which implement the W3C standards and recommendations in nearly every aspect.

But XML is not only hype; there are several applications where XML is definitely the best choice. If you need to store hierarchical data structures, such as the structure and contents of a page in a content management system, XML is perfectly suited for the job. But a content management system is not the only application where XML comes in handy. Even if you develop a smaller application, you can use XML for your configuration files. This way they are more flexible and can more easily be extended if new features are added. An XML document does not only contain key/value pairs like a standard INI configuration; the values are always related to a context through their position in the XML tree structure. Another common use of XML is data exchange between different companies, applications, or servers. One particular data exchange will be covered in Chapter 4, as nearly all modern web services use XML as their data format.

The multiple use cases of XML are not the only advantage of this simple, but powerful format. Through its resemblance to HTML, it can be easily read and interpreted by humans. In contrast to HTML, XML has to follow stricter rules, which makes it easer to process by machines and applications. Furthermore XML brings a lot more flexibility to the developer than HTML. While HTML defines which tags may be used in a document, XML only defines some basic rules that a document needs to follow but lets the developer choose which tags may be used in a document and how the application processing the document should interpret them. Creating a new XML application is simply creating a new set of tags that are used together in a document. Currently there are already several of these XML applications, like XHTML (the XML-compatible version of HTML), SVG (Scalable Vector Graphics), XML Schema (an XML language to define rules for other XML applications), or XUL, the language used by Mozilla to build its user interface. You do not need to be part of any organization or committee in order to create your own XML application; this can be done by anyone who needs it.

PEAR Packages for Working with XML

As XML got more attention from developers and even from PHP, it got more important for the PEAR project and the XML category has become one of the fastest-growing categories of PEAR. At the time of writing, PEAR offers 28 packages (web services not included) that aid you in creating and processing XML documents. This chapter will introduce you to the most important packages that this category provides. The chapter is split into two parts. While the first half shows you how to leverage PEAR to create new XML documents from scratch, the second part introduces parsing and analyzing existing documents. On the following pages, you will learn how to use XML_Util or XML_FastCreate to turn any object tree into a valid XML document by iterating over the data. After that, we will use the powerful XML_Serializer package to create an XML document from any data you pass in. As you will see, this makes the creation of XML documents with PEAR easy as cake, irrespective of whether you have your data organized in arrays, objects, or any arbitrary data source.

In the second part of this chapter we will use XML_Parser to create a configuration reader that is able to extract information from an XML document and provides an object-oriented API to the configuration. Later, we will use the XML_Unserializer class, which comes packaged with XML_Serializer, to convert various XML documents into nested arrays and object structures. We will also use this class to read the same XML configuration we processed with XML_Parser but without having to worry about the actual XML parsing. Finally we will use the XML_RSS package to include news feeds from any website that provides RSS feeds into your PHP application.

Before we start with PEAR, let us take a look at the rules that apply for XML documents.

Creating XML Documents

At first glance, creating XML documents seems to be extremely easy. After all, a document only consists of tags in plain text, so it is nothing more than an HTML document and you should be able to use concatenation or PHP's string functions for this task. However, there are some points that are often overlooked when creating XML and which can haunt you as a developer if your application is used in production. These points are closely related to the rules that any XML document must follow:

- XML is (in contrast to HTML) case sensitive; <foo/> is not equivalent to <Foo/>.
- Every XML tag must be closed. If the tag contains no data, the closing tag may be omitted and the tag can be written as an empty element tag. That means you have to use <br/> instead of just <br>.
- Tags must be nested correctly and the last opened tag must be closed first. So the XML snippet <i>Clark Ken t<b>is</i> Superman</b> is not valid but <i>Clark Kent</i> <b><i>is</i> Superman</b> is.
- Every XML document needs *exactly* one root element, which is opened at the top of the document and closed as the last tag in the document.
- The characters &, <, >, ", and ' need to be replaced with their matching XML entities &, <, >, ", and ' when used as data or attribute values. These are the only entities that can be used in an XML document without declaring them beforehand.
- All attributes must be quoted either using double or single quotes.
- The document must comply with its character-set definition. This character set can be defined in the XML declaration that precedes the actual XML. If the document is delivered via HTTP, it can also be supplied by a header. If no encoding is given, the default encoding UTF-8 is assumed.

An XML document that meets all these requirements is called a well-formed document. Here is an example of a well-formed XML document.

```
<?xml version="1.0" encoding="ISO-8859-1"?>
<labels>
  <label name="Sun Records">
    <artists>
      <artist id="1">
        <name>Elvis Presley</name>
        <records>
          <record id="SUN 209" released="July 19, 1954">
            <name>
              That&apos;s All Right (Mama) &amp; Blue Moon Of Kentucky
            </name>
          </record>
          <record id="SUN 210" released="September, 1954">
            <name>
              Good Rockin&apos; Tonight
            </name>
          </record>
        </records>
      </artist>
```

```
        <artist id="2">
          <name>Carl Perkins</name>
          <records>
            <record id="SUN 224" released="October 22, 1955">
              <name>
                Gone, Gone, Gone
              </name>
            </record>
          </records>
        </artist>
      </artists>
    </label>
  <labels>
```

Now it looks difficult to create this XML document using only PHP's basic string capabilities and string functions. On the following pages, you will learn how to use several PEAR packages to generate this XML document.

Creating a Record Label from Objects

Before we use PEAR to create the XML document, let us build the PHP data structure that will be used to hold the actual data used for the XML generation. If you take a close look at the document, you will see that it contains information about three different entities: a record label (Sun Records), artists that the record label signed (Elvis Presley and Carl Perkins), and the records these artists recorded. So first we need to implement classes that can be used to store the properties of these three entities. As the root element is the record label, we start with the `Label` class:

```
/**
 * Store information about a record label
 * and the signed artists
 */
class Label {
    public $name    = null;
    public $artists = array();

    public function __construct($name) {
        $this->name = $name;
    }
    public function signArtist(Artist $artist) {
        // get the next higher id
        $artist->setId(count($this->artists)+1);
        $this->artists[] = $artist;
    }
}
```

Besides the `$name` property this class also has an `$artists` property, which will later store objects of the signed artists. The name of the label is passed to the constructor, and the `signArtist()` method is used to add a new artist to the list. This method accepts an instance of the `Artist` class, which is implemented next:

```
/**
 * Store information about an artist
 * and the records he released
 */
class Artist {
    public $id      = null;
    public $name    = null;
    public $records = array();

    public function __construct($name) {
        $this->name = $name;
    }
    public function setId($id) {
        $this->id = $id;
    }
    public function recordAlbum(Record $album) {
        $this->records[] = $album;
    }
}
```

Again the constructor of the class is used to set the name of the artist, and with the `recordAlbum()` method it is possible to add an instance of the `Album` class to the list of recorded albums. This class also provides a `setId()` method, which is called by the `Label` object when the artist is added to the list of signed artists. Last we need to implement the `Record` class, which stores all information about a recorded album:

```
/**
 * Store information about a record.
 */
class Record {
    public $id       = null;
    public $name     = null;
    public $released = null;

    public function __construct($id, $name, $released) {
        $this->id       = $id;
        $this->name     = $name;
        $this->released = $released;
    }
}
```

Now that all container classes have been implemented, creating the data structure is extremely easy:

```
// create the new label
$sun    = new Label('Sun Records');
// create a new artist
$elvis  = new Artist('Elvis Presley');

// add the artist to the list of signed artists
$sun->signArtist($elvis);

// record two albums
$elvis->recordAlbum(
                new Record('SUN 209',
                    'That\'s All Right (Mama) & Blue Moon Of Kentucky',
                           'July 19, 1954'
                          )
                );
$elvis->recordAlbum(
                new Record('SUN 210',
                           'Good Rockin\' Tonight',
                           'September, 1954'
                          )
                );

// Create a second artist and record an album
$carl = new Artist('Carl Perkins');
$carl->recordAlbum(
                new Record('SUN 224',
                           'Gone, Gone, Gone',
                           'July 19, 1954'
                          )
                );
// Add the artist to the label
$sun->signArtist($carl);

// create a list of labels (if we have more
// than one label at a later point)
$labels = array($sun);
```

After creating a new `Label` object, we can easily add as many `Artist` objects as we like and for each of these artists we just add any number of `Record` objects. So if the data of the record label is stored in the database you can easily write a script that fetches the data and builds the needed structure using these three classes.

Now if the resulting structure is printed to the screen using `print_r()` the following output is generated:

```
Array (
    [0] => Label Object (
            [name] => Sun Records
            [artists] => Array (
                    [0] => Artist Object (
                            [id] => 1
                            [name] => Elvis Presley
                            [records] => Array (
                                    [0] => Record Object (
                                            [id] => SUN 209
                                            [name] => That's All
                                                      Right...
                                            [released] => July 19,
                                                      1954
                                    )
                            )

                    )
                    [1] => Artist Object (
                            [id] => 2
                            [name] => Carl Perkins
                            [records] => Array (
                                    [0] => Record Object (
                                            [id] => SUN 224
                                            [name] => Gone, Gone, Gone
                                            [released] => July 19,
                                                        1954
                                    )
                            )
                    )
            )
    )
)
```

Note that the `print_r()` output has been slightly modified to save some space.

Why not generate XML directly from the database?

You may wonder why these three helper classes have been implemented as value objects when the XML could as well be generated directly from the database. The new classes act as a kind of data-storage abstraction and they are especially handy once you decide to pick a different storage layer instead of a database.

As we have finished building our data structure, let us take a look at how several PEAR packages can be used to generate XML documents based on the data.

Creating XML Documents with XML_Util

XML_Util is a utility class for working with XML documents. It provides several methods that execute common XML-related tasks. All of these methods can be invoked statically, so you never need to create a new instance of XML_Util in your scripts in order to use its features; all that is needed is requiring the class in your code:

```
require_once 'XML/Util.php';
```

Once you have included the XML_Util class, it provides the methods to:

- Create the XML and document type declaration
- Create opening and closing tags
- Create complete tags (with the tag content) or other XML elements like comments
- Replace XML entities in any string
- Create XML attributes from associative arrays
- Help you with other XML related tasks

As the task at hand is to create an XML document from PHP objects, this package seems perfect. The API of all the methods XML_Util offers is quite simple, so to generate an opening tag, all you need to do is call the `createStartElement()` method and pass the name of the XML tag:

```
$label = XML_Util::createStartElement('label');
```

As this will only produce the string `<label>`, you might wonder what the benefits of using XML_Util are. The benefits come into play when you need to create a tag that also contains attributes. Those can be passed to `createStartElement()` as an associative array:

```
$attributes = array(
                  'name'     => 'Sun Records',
                  'location' => 'Nashville'
                );
$label = XML_Util::createStartElement('label', $attributes);
```

This code snippet will create an opening tag with the attributes specified in the array. XML_Util will automatically sort the attributes alphabetically.

```
<label location="Nashville" name="Sun Records">
```

The `createStartElement()` method also provides support for XML namespaces; you just need to pass the namespace URI as the third parameter. Furthermore we can also influence how the tag is rendered: if a tag has a lot of attributes the readability often suffers as the line gets extremely long. As whitespace in XML is ignored, XML_Util is able to split the tag into multiple lines, and place each attribute in its own line. Here is an example that uses the namespace support as well as multi-line attributes:

```
$attributes = array(
                  'name'     => 'Sun Records',
                  'location' => 'Nashville'
                );
$label = XML_Util::createStartElement('records:label', $attributes,
                                      'http://www.example.com', true);
```

And this is what the tag looks like:

```
<records:label location="Nashville"
               name="Sun Records"
               xmlns:records="http://www.example.com">
```

XML_Util also provides means to create the closing tags using the `createEndElement()` method:

```
$label = XML_Util::createEndElement('label');
```

Of course, this method does not support any additional parameters as a closing tag does not contain anything except the tag name. If you want to create the opening and closing tag at once and even pass in the content of the tag to be generated, then `createTag()` is the method of your choice. Like the `createStartElement()` method, `createTag()` accepts the name of the tag and an array with attributes as the first two arguments. However starting with the third argument, the method signatures differ. When using `createTag()` you may pass the content of the tag as the third parameter:

```
$attributes = array(
                  'name'     => 'Sun Records',
```

```
                    'location' => 'Nashville'
                   );
$tag = XML_Util::createTag('label', $attributes, 'Tag content');
```

The method accepts more arguments, which influence how the tag is created; you may pass the following arguments in this order; use `null` if you do not want to pass in a value.

- URI of the namespace, if any.
- Whether to replace XML entities in the tag content (`true`) or not (`false`). This is useful if the tag will contain more tags and you do not want the entities escaped.
- Whether to split the attributes among several lines (`true`), or not (`false`).

If the last parameter is set to `true`, you may pass two additional arguments to control the indenting and the line breaks used to split the attribute list among several lines. In 99% of all cases the default values for these parameters will be sufficient.

As you have learned how to create XML tags using XML_Util, the only thing left to learn is how to create an XML declaration and you will know enough to create the complete XML document from the object tree. XML_Util offers a method that creates the XML declaration for you:

```
$decl = XML_Util::getXMLDeclaration('1.0', 'ISO-8859-1');
```

This method accepts three parameters: the XML version, the desired encoding, and a Boolean flag to indicate whether the generated document will be a standalone document or not.

These four methods are the only ones you will need to create the XML document. All that is left is to iterate over the objects using several `foreach` loops and pass the object properties to the methods of XML_Util. If you want to send the document to the browser, you can use `echo` to directly output the result.

So the complete script to create the XML document from the object tree is:

```
require_once 'XML/Util.php';
echo XML_Util::getXMLDeclaration('1.0', 'ISO-8859-1');
echo XML_Util::createStartElement('labels') . "\n";

foreach ($labels as $label) {
    echo XML_Util::createStartElement('label',
                              array('name' => $label->name)) . "\n";
    echo XML_Util::createStartElement('artists') . "\n";
    foreach ($label->artists as $artist) {
        echo XML_Util::createStartElement('artist',
```

```
                                    array('id' => $artist->id)) . "\n";
        echo XML_Util::createTag('name', array(), $artist->name) . "\n";
          echo XML_Util::createStartElement('records') . "\n";
          foreach ($artist->records as $record) {
              echo XML_Util::createStartElement('record', array(
                                           'id'       => $record->id,
                                           'released' => $record->released
                                                )
                                                  ) . "\n";
              echo XML_Util::createTag('name', array(), $record->name) .
                                         "\n";
              echo XML_Util::createEndElement('record') . "\n";
          }
          echo XML_Util::createEndElement('records') . "\n";

          echo XML_Util::createEndElement('artist') . "\n";
      }
      echo XML_Util::createEndElement('artists') . "\n";
      echo XML_Util::createEndElement('label') . "\n";
  }
  echo XML_Util::createEndElement('labels') . "\n";
```

After including the file that contains the XML_Util class, we create the XML declaration that precedes the document and supply the encoding we want to use. Then, the opening tag of the root element is created using the `createStartElement()` method. After that, we iterate over all `Label` objects that are stored in the `$labels` array; actually there is only one element, the `Sun Records` label, but you do not need to change the code after adding additional objects. For each record label we create a `<label>` element and pass the `$name` property of the `Label` object to the list of attributes:

```
echo XML_Util::createStartElement('label',
                                  array('name' => $label->name)) . "\n";
```

Inside this loop, we iterate over all `Artist` objects that are stored in the `$artists` property of the `Label` object after an opening `<artists>` tag has been created. For each of the `Artist` objects we create a matching `<artist>` tag and pass the value of the `$id` property to the attributes. Finally inside the second loop we only need to iterate over all `Record` objects that have been added to the `$records` property of the `Artist` object and create the matching `<record/>` tag. Of course these tags are surrounded by a `<records/>` tag. At the end of each loop, closing tags are created to match the opening tags that have been created before the loop so the document will be well-formed.

If you run this script, it will output the exact same XML document that we started this chapter with, except that the tags will not be indented. XML_Util provides methods to create single tags or any other XML elements, but it will not create a complete document for you. You will learn about other PEAR packages that provide this feature later in this chapter. You will later use packages that allow passing virtually any data structure, instead of just strings or associative arrays, and transform your data to an XML document.

Additional Features

XML_Util provides some more methods that come in handy when working with XML. If you are generating XML dynamically and do not know how the tags will be named, you can use XML_Util to check whether a string can be used as a tag name.

```
$result = XML_Util::isValidName('My tag name');
if (PEAR::isError($result)) {
    echo 'No valid tag name: ' . $result->getMessage();
} else {
    echo 'Tag name is valid';
}
```

If the string you passed to the method can be used as a tag name in XML, the method will return `true`. If the string cannot be used as a tag name as it violates XML rules, `isValidName()` returns a `PEAR_Error` object that contains information on the rule that is violated. So if you run this script, it will output:

No valid tag name: XML names may only contain alphanumeric chars, period, hyphen, colon and underscores

Another useful feature is to replace disallowed characters with their respective entities in any string by using the `replaceEntities()` method:

```
echo XML_Util::replaceEntities('This text contains " & \'.');
```

After applying this method to a string, you can safely use it in any XML document. To reverse the result of this method, you can use the `reverseEntities()` method of XML_Util.

To learn about new features of XML_Util or take a close look at the API, you can browse the end-user documentation online on the PEAR website: `http://pear.php.net/manual/en/package.xml.xml-util.php`.

Creating XML Documents with XML_FastCreate

XML_FastCreate is a package that creates XML in a very fast and efficient manner (but you've probably already guessed this from the name, haven't you). To do this, it takes a totally different approach than XML_Util. XML_FastCreate does not create fragments of an XML document, but always creates a complete well-formed document. So XML_FastCreate ensures that you always get a valid XML document, whereas with XML_Util you get valid tags but still are able to omit closing tags or make mistakes when it comes to tag nesting.

XML_FastCreate can be used to:

- Create a string that contains an XML document
- Create a tree structure in memory that contains the XML document

You can use either approach with the same API to create an XML document, as XML_FastCreate provides different drivers for these two different ways. So instead of creating a new XML_FastCreate instance by using the `new` operator you must always use the factory method of the XML_FastCreate class.

```
require_once 'XML/FastCreate.php';
$xml = XML_FastCreate::factory('Text');
```

In this case the factory method returns a driver that will directly create a string containing the XML document. We will be using this driver for most of the following examples as it's easier to use and more stable than the alternative driver based on the XML_Tree package. If you still would like to use the driver based on XML_Tree, be advised that the following examples might not work as expected, as some features are not supported by this driver. Furthermore you will need to use version 2.0.0 of XML_Tree, which is still in the beta state. The difference between the text driver and the XML_Tree-based driver is that the latter allows you to modify the XML document as an object before it is written to a string. The text driver will directly generate a string containing the XML document, which cannot be easily modified (unless you resort to regular expressions).

Now that you have obtained a new instance of XML_FastCreate you will probably want to create the tags of the document. This is very easy! All you need to do is call a method with the name of the tag you want to create and pass the text that should be enclosed between the opening and closing tag:

```
$xml->artist('Elvis Presley');
```

This way you have added a new `<artist/>` tag to your XML document. You can print the resulting document to `STDOUT` using the `toXML()` method:

```
$xml->toXML();
```

If you run this code it will display:

```
<?xml version="1.0" encoding="UTF-8" standalone="no" ?>
<artist>Elvis Presley</artist>
```

Now you are probably wondering how XML_FastCreate knew that you need to create an `<artist/>` tag and offered the `artist()` method. As an XML document might contain virtually any tag, XML_FastCreate would have to offer an unlimited number of methods to be able to create all tags. You probably already guessed that XML_FastCreate does not implement all these methods; instead it uses a technique called **overloading**.

Overloading is supported natively by PHP5 but XML_FastCreate also supports PHP4 if you enable the overload extension (which is enabled by default in all versions of PHP4.3.x). If you want to use XML_FastCreate with PHP4, you can learn more about the overloading extension in the PHP manual at `http://www.php.net/overload`. In the following examples we will focus on the overloading support provided by PHP5.

Interlude: Overloading in PHP5

In order to understand how XML_FastCreate works, you need to understand the basic principles behind object overloading. Overloading allows you to intercept calls to undefined methods of an object. Consider the following code snippet:

```
class Bird {
    public function fly() {
        print "I'm flying.\n";
    }
}

$bird = new Bird();
$bird->fly();
$bird->swim();
```

If you run this script, you will see the following output:

I'm flying.

Fatal error: Call to undefined method Bird::swim() in c:\wamp\www\books\packt\pear\xml\overloading.php on line 10

This script terminates with a fatal error as you tried to call the `swim()` method on the `Bird` object and the method has not been implemented. This is where object overloading comes into play: overloading allows you to intercept method calls (and property access) to undefined methods (and properties). In order to intercept the call to the undefined method `swim()` you need to implement a *magic* `__call()` method that has to accept two arguments:

1. The name of the original method that has been called
2. An array containing all arguments that have originally been passed to the method call

After adding this method to the `Bird` class it might look like this:

```
class Bird {
    public function fly() {
        print "I'm flying.\n";
    }
    public function __call($method, $args) {
        print "I can't $method.\n";
    }
}
```

Now if you run the script again, you will get a different output:

I'm flying.

I can't swim.

Whenever you call a method that has not been implemented in the class, the `__call()` method will be invoked instead:

```
$bird->playPoker();
$bird->raiseTaxes();
```

Of course the output is as expected:

I can't playPoker.

I can't raiseTaxes.

Back to XML

This is exactly how XML_FastCreate works; whenever you call any method that matches the name of the tag that you want to create, PHP will invoke the `__call()` method instead and pass the name of the tag you want to create as well as the tag content.

XML_FastCreate also allows you to nest tags by nesting method calls:

```
require_once 'XML/FastCreate.php';

$xml = XML_FastCreate::factory('Text');
$xml->artist(
    $xml->name('Elvis Presley'),
    $xml->hometown('Memphis')
        );

$xml->toXML();
```

The output of this code is an XML document with the following structure (indentations have been added for improved readability):

```
<?xml version="1.0" encoding="UTF-8" standalone="no" ?>
<artist>
    <name>Elvis Presley</name>
    <hometown>Memphis</hometown>
</artist>
```

Until now, all tags contained only text content and did not include any attributes. But adding attributes to the tags of your XML content is also extremely easy. As with XML_Util, you have to supply the list of attributes for an XML tag as an associative array. This array has to be passed in as the first parameter to any method call that creates an XML tag. To add two attributes to the root tag of the previously generated XML document, make a small change:

```
require_once 'XML/FastCreate.php';

$xml = XML_FastCreate::factory('Text');
$xml->artist(
    array(
        'id'    => 56,
        'label' => 'Sun Records'
    ),
    $xml->name('Elvis Presley'),
    $xml->hometown('Memphis')
        );

$xml->toXML();
```

The resulting document now has the two attributes `id` and `label` set in the root tag:

```
<?xml version="1.0" encoding="UTF-8" standalone="no" ?>
<artist id="56" label="Sun Records">
    <name>Elvis Presley</name>
```

```
    <hometown>Memphis</hometown>
</artist>
```

The next thing that may strike you is that XML_FastCreate automatically creates an XML declaration for the document using UTF-8 encoding, while we have been using ISO-8859-1 in the previous examples. Do not worry! XML_FastCreate enables you to set a different encoding. When creating an instance of an XML_FastCreate driver using the factory method, you may pass a list of options as a second argument; one of these options can be used to set the encoding of the resulting document:

```
$options = array(
                 'encoding' => 'ISO-8859-1'
               );
$xml = XML_FastCreate::factory('Text', $options);
```

The encoding is only one of the possible options that can be set via the factory method; the following table shows a list of the most important options. These options are supported by both drivers included in the current version of XML_FastCreate. Take a look at the source code and inline documentation of the drivers and the base class to learn more about additional options that are not supported by both drivers.

Option name	Description	Default value
`version`	The XML version to use.	1.0
`encoding`	The XML encoding to use.	UTF-8
`standalone`	Whether the document is standalone or not.	No
`indent`	Whether to apply indentations to the XML document (requires the `XML_Beautifier` package).	False
`quote`	Whether to automatically replace special characters with their entities.	True
`doctype`	Which document type declaration should be added.	No value
`exec`	External program that should be used to validate the XML document according to the specified DTD.	No value
`file`	File to write the validation output to. If no file is specified, the validation output will be printed to the screen.	No value

The XML_Beautifier package

XML_Beautifier is a package that helps you make an XML document more readable by humans. XML documents do not require line breaks or indentation to be well-formed. Any application that is processing an XML document simply relies on the opening and closing tags that structure the contained information.

However, line breaks and indentation help humans easily grasp the structure of the XML document. So if you need to display an XML document that is not structured using whitespace to a user, XML_Beautifier comes in handy. It is able to read any XML document and apply formatting rules to it (like your editor is able to format PHP code). It will add line breaks, indentation, automatically wrap long lines, etc.

With the new DOM extension in PHP5, XML_Beautifier has become less important, as this extension is able to format an XML document to a certain degree (although it is not able to mimic all features of XML_Beautifier).

Now you know nearly everything you need to create the XML containing the record labels from the objects we built previously. There's only one thing left that we haven't covered, yet. When creating an XML tag by calling any method, we always ignored the return value of the method. However these methods will return an XML snippet, depending on the driver you are using. When using the Text driver, the method will return a string, while the XML_Tree will return an instance of the `XML_Tree_Node` class.

Creating the XML Document

If you are using the Text driver, the different tags created by XML_FastCreate can be joined to one XML document using the standard string functions provided by PHP. All that's left for you to do is iterate over the object structures in three nested loops: one for the record labels, one for the artists of each record label, and one for the records of each artist. While this approach is quite similar to the solution using XML_Util, there is one important difference: XML_FastCreate always creates the complete XML element (that means the opening and the closing tag) at once. As a consequence you always have to compile the content of the tag before creating the tag; this leads to the document being generated from the inside-out. The first tags created are the `<record/>` tags, followed by the `<artist/>` tags, again followed by the `<label/>` tags. Finally, in the last lines of the script, we create the `<labels/>` tag, which surrounds all other created tags. When using XML_Util we created the tags in the same order as we wanted them to appear in the document. When using XML_FastCreate, you will have to think about the correct nesting order, which makes creating XML documents a bit more complicated if you are not familiar with this type of recursion.

The complete script that creates the desired XML document from the object tree using XML_FastCreate is:

```
require_once 'XML/FastCreate.php';

// set the basic options for the XML document
$options = array(
                 'encoding'   => 'ISO-8859-1',
                 'standalone' => 'yes'
               );
// Get a new instance with the 'Text' driver
$xml = XML_FastCreate::factory('Text', $options);

// This variable will store all labels as XML
$labelsXML = '';

// Traverse the record labels in the array
foreach ($labels as $label) {

    // This variable will store all artists of the label as XML
    $artistsXML = '';

    // traverse all artists
    foreach ($label->artists as $artist) {

        // This variable will store all records of the artist as XML
        $records = '';

        // traverse all records
        foreach ($artist->records as $record) {
            $recordAtts = array(
                                'id'       => $record->id,
                                'released' => $record->released
                              );
            // Create and append one <record/>
            $records .= $xml->record($recordAtts, $xml->name(
                                                  $record->name));
        }
        $artistAtts = array('id' => $artist->id);
```

```
        // Create and append one <artist/>
        $artistsXML .= $xml->artist($artistAtts,
                                       $xml->records($records));
    }
    $labelAtts = array('name' => $label->name);

    // Create and append one <label/>
    $labelsXML .= $xml->label($labelAtts, $xml->artists($artistsXML));
}
$xml->labels($labelsXML);

// Send the resulting XML to STDOUT
$xml->toXML();
```

For each loop we create a new variable and initialize it with an empty string (`$labelsXML`, `$artistsXML`, and `$recordsXML`). The inner loops will then store their results in these variables and after all inner loops are completed, the variables will be used as content for the surrounding `<labels>`, `<artists>`, or `<records>` tags. If you run this script you will get the same output as in the XML_Util example. If you have the package XML_Beautifier installed, you can also enable the `indent` option of XML_FastCreate, which will then return nicely indented XML.

Pitfalls in XML_FastCreate

While XML_FastCreate may seem more powerful than XML_Util (and in a lot of cases certainly is), do not overlook the following pitfalls:

- As overloading only intercepts calls to non-existent methods, there are some reserved words (the names of all methods provided by XML_FastCreate), that cannot be used as tag names. One of these methods is the `xml()` method, which is used by the `__call()` interceptor to create the actual tags. So if you are invoking `$fastcreate->xml('foo')`, the method call will not be intercepted as the method you are calling exists. So this will not produce the desired result and you will have to use `$fastcreate->xml('xml', 'foo');` instead, as you will have to use the correct method signature for the `xml()` method.
- XML_FastCreate heavily relies on alpha or beta packages (XML_DTD, XML_Tree), which might lead to backward compatibility breaks when upgrading one of these packages. This could even mean that XML_FastCreate suddenly stops working.
- Creating XML documents with a dynamic structure is extremely complicated using the XML_Tree driver of XML_FastCreate. This driver returns objects instead of strings when creating tags, so you cannot just use the built-in string functions of PHP to create a larger document that uses dynamic tag

names and data. This driver should not be used for documents that contain complex structures determined at run time.

Creating XML Documents with XML_Serializer

While XML_Serializer is a package for creating XML documents, it takes a totally different approach from the last two packages, XML_Util and XML_FastCreate. When working with one of these packages, you are creating the document tag by tag with each method call. When using XML_Serializer, you are calling one method to create the complete document at once. It will extract the raw information from an array or an object and convert it to an XML document. While this may sound inflexible, when compared to the previous approaches, XML_Serializer still is one of the most powerful packages when creating XML documents. It can serialize any data that you pass in as an XML document. So it can create an XML-based string representation of any data. Think of it as the XML equivalent of the built-in `serialize()` function, which lets you create a string representation of any data, be it a deeply nested array or a complex tree of objects. This string representation may then be saved in a file, the user session, or even a database. PHP also provides an `unserialize()` function to restore the original data from the string representation. In the second part of this chapter, you will also learn about the matching XML_Unserializer class, which does this for the XML documents created by XML_Serializer.

The typical way to work with XML_Serializer follows these steps:

- Include XML_Serializer and create a new instance
- Configure the instance using options
- Create the XML document
- Fetch the document and do whatever you want with it

If you are using XML_Serializer in real-life applications, it will never get any harder than this. As you only call one method to actually create the XML document, you will need to pass all information that should be contained in the XML document to this method. To make life as easy as possible, XML_Serializer accepts virtually *any input* to this method as data for the generated XML document. But now enough theory, the best way to describe XML_Serializer is to show what it can do through an example:

```
// include the class
require_once('XML/Serializer.php');

// create a new object
$serializer = new XML_Serializer();
```

```
// create the XML document
$serializer->serialize('This is a string');

// fetch the document
echo $serializer->getSerializedData();
```

In this example, we followed exactly the steps described above and if you execute it you will get:

```
<string>This is a string</string>
```

This is not a complex XML document, and would have been easier to create using XML_Util, XML_FastCreate, or even PHP's string concatenation. But if you take a look at the next example, you will probably change your opinion:

```
$data = array(
          'artist' => 'Elvis Presley',
          'label'  => 'Sun Records',
          'record' => 'Viva Las Vegas'
        );
// include the class
require_once('XML/Serializer.php');

// create a new object
$serializer = new XML_Serializer();

// create the XML document
$serializer->serialize($data);

// fetch the document
echo $serializer->getSerializedData();
```

In this example, only two things have changed:

- A variable `$data` has been created and contains an array.
- The `$data` variable is passed to the `serialize()` method instead of a string.

The rest of the script remained unchanged and still follows the same steps mentioned above. Now let us take a look at the output of this script:

```
<array>
<artist>Elvis Presley</artist>
<label>Sun Records</label>
<record>Viva Las Vegas</record>
</array>
```

Creating this XML document would have been a lot harder using a different approach. If we added more data and nested the XML tags deeper it would be harder to create the document using XML_Util or XML_FastCreate. With XML_Serializer, the needed code always stays the same and you could as well pass the following data to `serialize()` and not change anything else:

```
$data = array(
            'artist' => array(
                            'name'  => 'Elvis Presley',
                            'email' => 'elvis@graceland.com'
                        ),
            'label'  => 'Sun Records',
            'record' => 'Viva Las Vegas'
        );
```

As expected, the script will generate the following XML document:

```
<array>
<artist>
<name>Elvis Presley</name>
<email>elvis@graceland.com</email>
</artist>
<label>Sun Records</label>
<record>Viva Las Vegas</record>
</array>
```

Now you know how XML_Serializer basically works: You pass any PHP data structure to the `serialize()` method and it will create XML for you based on the data you passed. While generating the XML document, XML_Serializer tries to guess how the document should be created, i.e. it uses the type of the data as root tag name, array keys as tag names, and nests the tags in the same manner the arrays have been nested. The previously mentioned options allow you to influence how the *guessing* will work; we will now explain how to use the most important options of XML_Serializer.

XML_Serializer Options

As of version 0.17.0, XML_Serializer offers 27 different options. For each of these options, XML_Serializer provides a constant that starts with XML_SERIALIZER_OPTION_, followed by the name of the option. To set the values of these options, use one of the following techniques:

- Pass an associative array containing the selected options and their values to the constructor of XML_Serializer.
- Use the `setOption()` and `setOptions()` methods of XML_Serializer.
- Pass an associative array containing the selected options and their values as a second argument to the `serialize()` method.

While the first two techniques are equivalent and can be used to set the options for all following XML documents, the last one will only override the options for the document that is created by the current call to `serialize()`. For most cases, the multiple usage of `setOption()` is recommended to ensure better readability of your scripts.

Now, that you know how to set options for XML_Serializer, let's get back to the XML document that has been created and try using some options to influence the result. The first thing that may strike you is that the XML declaration has been missing from the created XML document. Of course it would be easy to add it after XML_Serializer has created the document, but it is even easier to let XML_Serializer do the work for you. All you need to add are two lines of code:

```
// include the class
require_once('XML/Serializer.php');

// create a new object
$serializer = new XML_Serializer();

// set options
$serializer->setOption(XML_SERIALIZER_OPTION_XML_DECL_ENABLED, true);
$serializer->setOption(XML_SERIALIZER_OPTION_XML_ENCODING,
                                                          'ISO-8859-1');

// create the XML document
$serializer->serialize($data);

// fetch the document
echo $serializer->getSerializedData();
```

Now your document will have a valid XML declaration that defines the encoding you are using in your document. Next, we want to make some beauty corrections to the document by indenting the tags nicely and choose a different tag name for the root, as `array` is not very self-explanatory. Again, we only add two new lines:

```
$serializer->setOption(XML_SERIALIZER_OPTION_INDENT, '    ');
$serializer->setOption(XML_SERIALIZER_OPTION_ROOT_NAME,
                                                'artist-info');
```

If you take a look at the result, you will see that the XML document looks a lot better:

```
<?xml version="1.0" encoding="ISO-8859-1"?>
<artist-info>
    <artist>
        <name>Elvis Presley</name>
        <email>elvis@graceland.com</email>
    </artist>
```

```
    <label>Sun Records</label>
    <record>Viva Las Vegas</record>
</artist-info>
```

Adding Attributes

XML documents seldom consist only of tags without attributes. So you might want to use XML_Serializer to create tags that contain attributes as well as nested tags and character data. And of course, achieving this is as easy as everything else we have done using XML_Serializer before.

XML_Serializer is able to automatically convert scalar variables (strings, Boolean values, integers, etc.) to attributes of the parent tag. All that is required is setting one option:

```
$serializer->setOption(XML_SERIALIZER_OPTION_SCALAR_AS_ATTRIBUTES,
                                                              true);
```

If you add this to your script and run it again, the resulting XML document will look totally different:

```
<?xml version="1.0" encoding="ISO-8859-1"?>
<artist-info label="Sun Records" record="Viva Las Vegas">
    <artist email="elvis@graceland.com" name="Elvis Presley"/>
</artist-info>
```

If you only want to convert the string values stored in the `artist` array to attributes of the `<artist/>` tag, but keep the `<label/>` and `<record/>` tags, this is possible as well:

```
$serializer->setOption(XML_SERIALIZER_OPTION_SCALAR_AS_ATTRIBUTES,
                       array(
                          'artist' => true
                            )
                       );
```

You can even selectively choose which value you want to add as an attribute on a per-tag basis. If you want the email address stored in an attribute, but still wish to add a nested tag for the name of an artist, all you need to change is one line in your script:

```
$serializer->setOption(XML_SERIALIZER_OPTION_SCALAR_AS_ATTRIBUTES,
                       array(
                         'artist' => array('email')
                           )
                       );
```

If you execute the script now, it will output:

```
<?xml version="1.0" encoding="ISO-8859-1"?>
<artist-info>
    <artist email="elvis@graceland.com">
        <name>Elvis Presley</name>
    </artist>
    <label>Sun Records</label>
    <record>Viva Las Vegas</record>
</artist-info>
```

Another option that allows you to add attributes to the XML document is `ROOT_ATTRIBS`; you may pass an associative array with this option to build the attributes of the root element.

Treating Indexed Arrays

Most musical artists release more than one record and they often sign contracts with more than one label during their career. If you apply this to our simple example, you will probably end up with a data structure similar to the following array:

```
$data = array(
          'artist'  => array(
                         'name'   => 'Elvis Presley',
                         'email'  => 'elvis@graceland.com'
                       ),
          'labels'  => array(
                         'Sun Records',
                         'Sony Music'
                       ),
          'records' => array(
                         'Viva Las Vegas',
                         'Hound Dog',
                         'In the Ghetto'
                       )
        );
```

Since XML_Serializer will transform any data to XML, you will probably pass this data to XML_Serializer as well and hope that it creates useful XML. So if you try and run the script, it will output an XML document looking like this:

```
<?xml version="1.0" encoding="ISO-8859-1"?>
<artist-info>
    <artist email="elvis@graceland.com">
        <name>Elvis Presley</name>
    </artist>
```

```
        <labels>
            <XML_Serializer_Tag>Sun Records</XML_Serializer_Tag>
            <XML_Serializer_Tag>Sony Music</XML_Serializer_Tag>
        </labels>
        <records>
            <XML_Serializer_Tag>Viva Las Vegas</XML_Serializer_Tag>
            <XML_Serializer_Tag>Hound Dog</XML_Serializer_Tag>
            <XML_Serializer_Tag>In the Ghetto</XML_Serializer_Tag>
        </records>
    </artist-info>
```

What probably strikes you as soon as the document is outputted to your screen is the frequent use of the `<XML_Serializer_Tag/>` in the document. If you are familiar with XML, you probably already guessed why it is there. When serializing an array, XML_Serializer uses the array key as the name for the tag and the value as the content of the tag. In this example, the data contains two indexed arrays and they contain keys like "0", "1" and "2". But `<0/>`, `<1/>`, and `<2/>` are not valid XML tags. Since XML_Serializer can create a well-formed XML document, it will use a default tag name instead of creating an invalid tag. Of course, it is possible to change the name of the default tag:

```
$serializer->setOption(XML_SERIALIZER_OPTION_DEFAULT_TAG, 'item');
```

Once you have added this line to the script, you will get a slightly different XML document, as all `<XML_Serializer_Tag/>` occurrences have been replaced by `<item/>` tags. But still XML_Serializer allows you to be more flexible when it comes to choosing default tags. The nicest solution would be if the `<records/>` tag contained `<record/>` tags for each record and the `<labels/>` tag contained a `<label/>` tag for each label the artist signed a contract with. This is easily possible, as XML_Serializer allows you to specify a default tag name depending on the context. Instead of a string containing the default tag, you have to pass an associative array to the `DEFAULT_TAG` option. The array keys define the names of the parent tag and the array values define the name of the default tag for the specified parent:

```
$serializer->setOption(XML_SERIALIZER_OPTION_DEFAULT_TAG,
                       array(
                         'labels'  => 'label',
                         'records' => 'record'
                           )
                      );
```

So the resulting document is:

```
<?xml version="1.0" encoding="ISO-8859-1"?>
<artist-info>
    <artist email="elvis@graceland.com">
        <name>Elvis Presley</name>
```

```
        </artist>
        <labels>
            <label>Sun Records</label>
            <label>Sony Music</label>
        </labels>
        <records>
            <record>Viva Las Vegas</record>
            <record>Hound Dog</record>
            <record>In the Ghetto</record>
        </records>
    </artist-info>
```

Now you have learned how to use the most important options of XML_Serializer. Before implementing a script that creates the desired XML from the pre-built object tree, you might want to take a look at all other options of XML_Serializer listed in the following table.

Option name	Description	Default value
INDENT	String used for indenting tags.	Empty
LINEBREAKS	String used for line breaks.	\n
XML_DECL_ENABLED	Whether to add an XML declaration to the resulting document.	false
XML_ENCODING	Encoding to be used for the document if XML_DECL_ENABLED is set to true.	UTF-8
DOCTYPE_ENABLED	Whether to add a document type declaration to the document.	false
DOCTYPE	Filename of the document declaration file; only used if DOCTYPE_ENABLED is set to true.	No value
ROOT_NAME	Name of the root tag.	Depends on the serialized data
ROOT_ATTRIBS	Attributes of the root tag.	Empty array
NAMESPACE	Namespace to use for the document.	No value
ENTITIES	Whether to encode XML entities in character data and attributes.	true
RETURN_RESULT	Whether serialize() should return the result or only return true if the serialization was successful.	false
CLASSNAME_AS_TAGNAME	Whether to use the name of the class as tag name, when serializing objects.	false

Option name	Description	Default value
DEFAULT_TAG	Name of the default tag. Used when serializing indexed arrays. Can either use a string or an associative array to set this option depending on the parent tag.	XML_ Serializer_ Tag
TYPEHINTS	Whether to add type information to the tags.	false
ATTRIBUTE_TYPE	Name of the attribute that stores the type information, if TYPEHINTS is enabled.	_type
ATTRIBUTE_CLASS	Name of the attribute that stores the class name, if TYPEHINTS is enabled.	_class
ATTRIBUTE_KEY	Name of the attribute that stores the name of the array key, if TYPEHINTS is enabled.	_originalKey
SCALAR_AS_ ATTRIBUTES	Whether scalar values (strings, integers, etc.) should be added as attributes.	false
PREPEND_ ATTRIBUTES	String to prefix attributes' names with.	No value
INDENT_ATTRIBUTES	String to use for attribute indentation, when using one line per attribute. Can be set to _auto.	No value
IGNORE_NULL	Whether to ignore null values when serializing objects or arrays.	false
TAGMAP	Associative array to map keys and property names to different tag names.	No value
MODE	Which mode to use for serializing indexed arrays, either XML_SERIALIZER_MODE_ DEFAULT or XML_SERIALIZER_MODE_ SIMPLEXML.	DEFAULT
ATTRIBUTES_KEY	All values stored with this key will be serialized as attributes.	No value
CONTENT_KEY	All values stored with this key will be directly used as character data instead of creating another tag. Must be used in conjunction with ATTRIBUTES_KEY.	No value
COMMENT_KEY	All values stored with this key will be converted to XML comments.	No value
ENCODE_FUNC	Name of a PHP function or method that will be applied to all values before serializing.	No value

Creating the XML Document from the Object Tree

As you are now familiar with XML_Serializer, let us go back to the initial task we need to accomplish and create an XML document from the objects we instantiated that contained information about record labels, artists, and their recorded albums. As XML_Serializer accepts any PHP variable as input for the XML document, the easiest way to start this task is just passing the `$labels` variable, which contains one or more `Label` objects. Additionally we set some options that we are already sure of:

```
// include the class
require_once('XML/Serializer.php');

// create a new object
$serializer = new XML_Serializer();

// configure the XML declaration
$serializer->setOption(XML_SERIALIZER_OPTION_XML_DECL_ENABLED, true);
$serializer->setOption(XML_SERIALIZER_OPTION_XML_ENCODING,
                                                    'ISO-8859-1');

// configure the layout
$serializer->setOption(XML_SERIALIZER_OPTION_INDENT, '    ');
$serializer->setOption(XML_SERIALIZER_OPTION_LINEBREAKS, "\n");

// create the XML document
$serializer->serialize($labels);

// fetch the document
echo $serializer->getSerializedData();
```

This code will create the following XML document, which already looks a lot like the XML document we need to create:

```
<?xml version="1.0" encoding="ISO-8859-1"?>
<array>
    <XML_Serializer_Tag>
        <name>Sun Records</name>
        <artists>
            <XML_Serializer_Tag>
                <id>1</id>
                <name>Elvis Presley</name>
                <records>
                    <XML_Serializer_Tag>
                        <id>SUN 209</id>
                        <name>That&apos;s All Right (Mama) &amp;
                                    Blue Moon Of Kentucky</name>
                        <released>July 19, 1954</released>
```

```
                </XML_Serializer_Tag>
                <XML_Serializer_Tag>
                    <id>SUN 210</id>
                    <name>Good Rockin&apos; Tonight</name>
                    <released>September, 1954</released>
                </XML_Serializer_Tag>
            </records>
        </XML_Serializer_Tag>
        <XML_Serializer_Tag>
            <id>2</id>
            <name>Carl Perkins</name>
            <records>
                <XML_Serializer_Tag>
                    <id>SUN 224</id>
                    <name>Gone, Gone, Gone</name>
                    <released>July 19, 1954</released>
                </XML_Serializer_Tag>
            </records>
        </XML_Serializer_Tag>
    </artists>
  </XML_Serializer_Tag>
</array>
```

The main issues with this document are:

- The root element should be <labels/>.
- <XML_Serializer_Tag/> instances should be replaced with <label/>, <artist/>, and <record/> tags.
- Some tags (like <id/>, <name/>, and <released/>) should be replaced by matching elements.

You have already learned how to fix these issues in the previous examples, by setting the appropriate options:

- The root element can be changed using the ROOT_NAME option.
- The <XML_Serializer_Tag/> instances can be replaced using the DEFAULT_TAG option and passing an array to this option.
- The SCALAR_AS_ATTRIBUTES option can be used to influence which information will be serialized as attributes instead of tags.

Here is the complete script with all options set correctly. The changes have been highlighted:

```
// include the class
require_once('XML/Serializer.php');

// create a new object
$serializer = new XML_Serializer();

// configure the XML declaration
$serializer->setOption(XML_SERIALIZER_OPTION_XML_DECL_ENABLED, true);
$serializer->setOption(XML_SERIALIZER_OPTION_XML_ENCODING,
                                                      'ISO-8859-1');

// configure the layout
$serializer->setOption(XML_SERIALIZER_OPTION_INDENT, '    ');
$serializer->setOption(XML_SERIALIZER_OPTION_LINEBREAKS, "\n");

// configure tag names
$serializer->setOption(XML_SERIALIZER_OPTION_ROOT_NAME, 'labels');
$tagNames = array(
                  'labels'  => 'label',
                  'artists' => 'artist',
                  'records' => 'record'
                );
$serializer->setOption(XML_SERIALIZER_OPTION_DEFAULT_TAG, $tagNames);

$attributes = array(
                  'label'  => array('name'),
                  'artist' => array('id'),
                  'record' => array('id', 'released')
                );
$serializer->setOption(XML_SERIALIZER_OPTION_SCALAR_AS_ATTRIBUTES,
                       $attributes);

$result = $serializer->serialize($labels);
echo $serializer->getSerializedData();
```

Putting Objects to Sleep

The last example showed that XML_Serializer can work with objects in the same way it works with arrays. It will fetch all public properties and serialize them to the XML document as if they were values stored in an array. However, in some cases this might not be the desired result. Take the following code for example:

```
class UrlFetcher {
    public $url  = null;
```

```
    public $html = null;

    public function __construct($url) {
        $this->url  = $url;
        $this->html = file_get_contents($this->url);
    }
}
$pear = new UrlFetcher('http://pear.php.net');

$serializer = new XML_Serializer();
$serializer->setOption(XML_SERIALIZER_OPTION_XML_DECL_ENABLED, true);
$serializer->setOption(XML_SERIALIZER_OPTION_XML_ENCODING,
                                                        'ISO-8859-1');
$serializer->setOption(XML_SERIALIZER_OPTION_INDENT, '    ');
$serializer->serialize($pear);
echo $serializer->getSerializedData();
```

If you instantiate a new object of the class `UrlFetcher`, this object will fetch the HTML content from the URL content specified in the constructor. If you pass the object to XML_Serializer, it will extract all public properties and add them to the resulting XML document, which will look like this:

```
<?xml version="1.0" encoding="ISO-8859-1"?>
<UrlFetcher>
    <url>http://pear.php.net</url>
    <html>&lt;?xml version=&quot;1.0&quot; encoding=&quot;iso-8859-
1&quot; ?&gt;&lt;!DOCTYPE html PUBLIC &quot;-//W3C//DTD XHTML 1.0
Transitional//EN&quot; &quot;http://www.w3.org/TR/xhtml1/DTD/xhtml1-
transitional.dtd&quot;&gt;
...a lot of HTML code has been removed...
    </html>
</UrlFetcher>
```

In this case you probably do not want XML_Serializer to put all the HTML code from `pear.php.net` into the XML document. This can be easily avoided using a technique that you might know from serializing objects using PHP's `serialize()` function. If the object that will be serialized by XML_Serializer implements a `__sleep()` method, this method will be invoked and the return value used for the serialization. The `__sleep()` method should return an array with the names of the object properties that should be included in the result document. To prohibit serialization of the `$html` property, only a small change to the `UrlFetcher` class is necessary:

```
class UrlFetcher {
    public $url  = null;
    public $html = null;
```

```
    public function __construct($url) {
        $this->url  = $url;
        $this->html = file_get_contents($this->url);
    }

    public function __sleep() {
        return array('url');
    }
}
```

With this change applied to the code, the resulting document will be:

```
<?xml version="1.0" encoding="ISO-8859-1"?>
<UrlFetcher>
    <url>http://pear.php.net</url>
</UrlFetcher>
```

What's your Type?

The last feature of XML_Serializer to be highlighted in this book is its ability to add type information to the XML tags. This feature is enabled using one option:

```
$serializer = new XML_Serializer();

// configure the XML declaration
$serializer->setOption(XML_SERIALIZER_OPTION_XML_DECL_ENABLED, true);
$serializer->setOption(XML_SERIALIZER_OPTION_XML_ENCODING,
                                                       'ISO-8859-1');

$serializer->setOption(XML_SERIALIZER_OPTION_TYPEHINTS, true);

// configure the layout
$serializer->setOption(XML_SERIALIZER_OPTION_INDENT, '    ');
$serializer->setOption(XML_SERIALIZER_OPTION_LINEBREAKS, "\n");

$serializer->setOption(XML_SERIALIZER_OPTION_DEFAULT_TAG, $tagNames);

$result = $serializer->serialize($labels);

echo $serializer->getSerializedData();
```

By setting the `TYPEHINTS` option to `true` you tell XML_Serializer to include information about the type of the data enclosed in a tag as an attribute as well as the original array key or property name, if it could not be used as a tag name.

The resulting document (when the array of `Label` objects is passed to `serialize()`) is:

```
<?xml version="1.0" encoding="ISO-8859-1"?>
<array _type="array">
    <XML_Serializer_Tag _class="Label" _originalKey="0"
                                _type="object">
        <name _type="string">Sun Records</name>
        <artists _type="array">
            <XML_Serializer_Tag _class="Artist" _originalKey="0"
                                _type="object">
                <id _type="integer">1</id>
                <name _type="string">Elvis Presley</name>
                <records _type="array">
                    <XML_Serializer_Tag _class="Record"
                                _originalKey="0"
                                _type="object">
                        <id _type="string">SUN 209</id>
                        <name _type="string">That&apos;s ...
                                                Kentucky</name>
                        <released _type="string">July 19, 1954
                                                  </released>
                    </XML_Serializer_Tag>
                    <XML_Serializer_Tag _class="Record"
                                 _originalKey="1"
                                 _type="object">
                        <id _type="string">SUN 210</id>
                        <name _type="string">Good Rockin&apos;
                                                 Tonight</name>
                        <released _type="string">September, 1954
                                                  </released>
                    </XML_Serializer_Tag>
                </records>
            </XML_Serializer_Tag>
            <XML_Serializer_Tag _class="Artist" _originalKey="1"
                                _type="object">
                <id _type="integer">2</id>
                <name _type="string">Carl Perkins</name>
                <records _type="array">
                    <XML_Serializer_Tag _class="Record"
                                    _originalKey="0"
                                    _type="object">
                        <id _type="string">SUN 224</id>
                        <name _type="string">Gone, Gone, Gone</name>
                        <released _type="string">July 19, 1954
                                                  </released>
```

```
                    </XML_Serializer_Tag>
                </records>
            </XML_Serializer_Tag>
        </artists>
    </XML_Serializer_Tag>
</array>
```

This feature is helpful when you need to restore the converted XML data to the exact same data structure it was before. This way, you can use XML_Serializer (and the matching XML_Unserializer, which will be dealt with later in this chapter) as a drop-in replacement for `serialize()` and `unserialize()`.

In this part of the chapter you have used three different packages to create XML documents. But how should you decide which package you should use to solve the task at hand?

- With the power of all of its options, XML_Serializer is the right tool to use, if you already have all the data collected in one huge data structure.
- If you are creating a structure from data that is computed while you are creating the document, XML_FastCreate is probably the right choice. It can also be used to create HTML documents programmatically. This was the original intent behind the package.
- XML_Util should be used if you either need to create a very small XML document or if you only create a fragment of a document.

Creating Mozilla Applications with XML_XUL

Up to now, you have only created XML in a format that we defined ourselves. But of course, there are already XML applications that have created some kind of standard and are acknowledged by the W3C. PEAR has several packages that help you create XML for these applications, and one of these is the XML_XUL package.

XUL Documents

XUL stands for XML User Interface Language and is part of the Mozilla Project. The specification of XUL v1.0 can be found on the Mozilla website at `http://www.mozilla.org/projects/xul/xul.html`.

XUL is used by Mozilla applications (like Firefox and Thunderbird) to define how the user interface should be structured. XUL can be combined with JavaScript, CSS, and RDF to create interactive applications that can access various data sources. Actually any plug-in for either Firefox or Thunderbird is built with XUL and JavaScript. XUL makes it a lot easier than HTML to build rich user interfaces, because that is exactly what it has been designed for, whereas HTML has originally been designed to publish structured content to the Web. So while HTML ships with tags to structure text in paragraphs, lists, and static HTML tables, XUL provides tags for sortable data grids, color pickers, or explorer-like tree elements.

Enough talk; let us take a look at an XUL document:

```
<?xml version="1.0" encoding="ISO-8859-1" standalone="yes"?>
<?xml-stylesheet href="chrome://global/skin/" type="text/css"?>
<window title="Simple XUL"
        xmlns="http://www.mozilla.org/keymaster/gatekeeper/there.
is.only.xul">
  <tabbox height="500">
    <tabs>
      <tab label="Labels" />
      <tab label="Misc" />
    </tabs>
    <tabpanels>
      <tabpanel label="Labels">
        <tree flex="1" height="200">
          <treecols>
            <treecol flex="1" id="id" label="Id" primary="true" />
            <treecol flex="1" id="name" label="Name" />
            <treecol flex="1" id="email" label="E-Mail" />
          </treecols>
          <treechildren>
            <treeitem container="true">
              <treerow>
                <treecell label="SUN" />
                <treecell label="Sun Records" />
                <treecell label="info@sun-records.com" />
              </treerow>
              <treechildren>
                <treeitem>
                  <treerow>
                    <treecell label="elvis" />
                    <treecell label="Elvis Presley" />
                    <treecell label="elvis@graceland.com" />
                  </treerow>
                </treeitem>
                <treeitem>
                  <treerow>
                    <treecell label="carl" />
                    <treecell label="Carl Perkins" />
                    <treecell label="carl@sun-records.com" />
```

```
                    </treerow>
                  </treeitem>
                </treechildren>
              </treeitem>
              <treeitem>
                <treerow>
                  <treecell label="SONY" />
                  <treecell label="Sony Records" />
                  <treecell label="info@sony.com" />
                </treerow>
              </treeitem>
            </treechildren>
          </tree>
        </tabpanel>
        <tabpanel label="Misc">
          <description>Place any content here.</description>
        </tabpanel>
      </tabpanels>
    </tabbox>
  </window>
```

As XUL is XML, the document starts with an XML declaration. This is followed by another declaration, which is used to include a stylesheet from the URL `chrome://global/skin/`. `chrome` is a special protocol used whenever you need to access internal data from Mozilla. In this case, it is used to include the stylesheet that has been selected by the user for his/her Mozilla installation, so that the XUL application fits perfectly with the look of the browser.

After this declaration comes the root element of the document; this is the `<window/>` element in most cases. Inside the `<window/>` element we nested several other elements like `<tabbox/>` and `<tree/>`. If you open this document in Firefox or Mozilla, you should see a result resembling the following image:

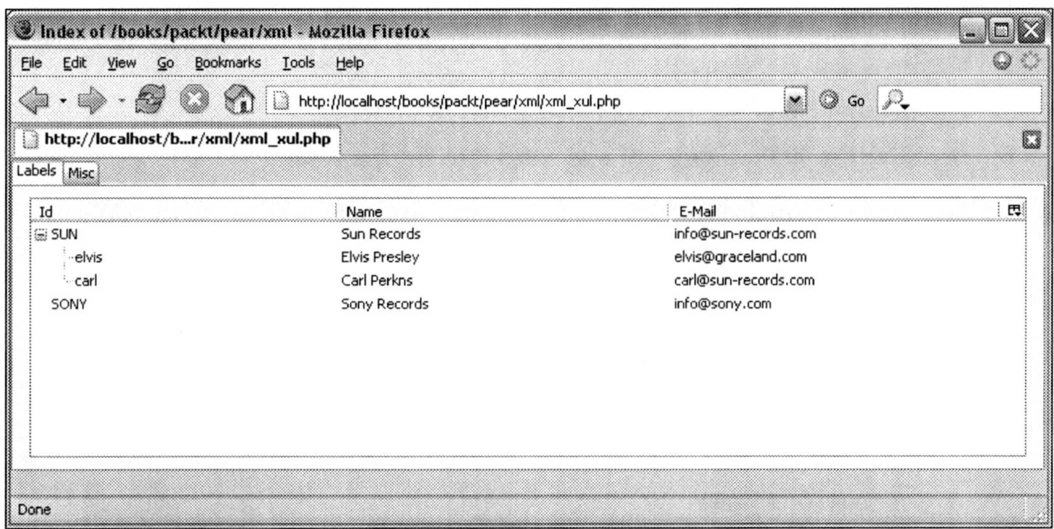

Of course the exact layout depends on the theme you are using in your Mozilla or Firefox installation. If you start to click around in this window, you will realize that the tabs and the tree element are already functional and that you can easily hide columns from the tree element. Imagine implementing this functionality with plain HTML, CSS, and JavaScript and how many hours you would have to work to make this possible! This example already shows a big advantage that XUL has compared to XML—it is great for building intuitive user interfaces for web applications. However, XUL has also its dark side:

- XUL only works in applications of the Mozilla project; users of Microsoft Internet Explorer or Opera will never be able to use your application.
- XUL is (as most XML applications) quite verbose and contains a lot of deeply nested XML documents.

Creating XUL Documents with XML_XUL

PEAR provides a package to help you solve the second problem: the package XML_XUL can be used to create an XUL document with an easy-to-use PHP API. The API of XML_XUL resembles a standard DOM-API—you use the package to build an object tree in memory, which you can move around and modify until you reach the desired result. Once you are satisfied with the tree, you can serialize it to XML, which will then be sent to the browser. The difference to DOM is that there is not only one class that represents an element, but several different classes for the different types of widgets provided by XUL. These classes provide helper methods so you can add a new tab to a tab box with one method call instead of building a complex object tree on your own. The basic steps to creating a script using XML_XUL are always the same:

1. Include the main XML_XUL class
2. Create a new document
3. Create new elements and compose a tree in memory
3. Serialize the XUL document and send it to the browser

Does that sound too hard? Well, it isn't; here is our first script using XML_XUL:

```
require_once 'XML/XUL.php';

// create a new document
$doc = XML_XUL::createDocument();

// link to the stylesheet selected by the user
$doc->addStylesheet('chrome://global/skin/');

// create a new window
$win = $doc->createElement('window',array(
                                          'title'=> 'Simple XUL'
                                         )
                          );
// add it to the document
$doc->addRoot($win);

// create another element
$desc = $doc->createElement('description', array(),
                            'This is XUL, believe it or not.');
$win->appendChild($desc);

header('Content-type: application/vnd.mozilla.xul+xml');
$doc->send();
```

The steps are exactly as described before. The main class is included and a new document object created using `XML_XUL::createDocument()`. After that we add the internal stylesheet to the document instead of providing our own CSS using the `addStylesheet()` method. After that, we start creating elements and composing a tree with them (actually, this is a very small tree, but a tree nevertheless). All elements that will be added to a document always have to be created using the `createElement()` method, which accepts the following parameters:

- Name of the element, which is also the name of the tag that will be created
- Associative array containing the attributes of the element
- The content of the element
- Whether to replace XML entities in the content (default is `true`).

This method will return an instance of a subclass of XML_XUL_Element. If you want to know which elements are supported by XML_XUL, you can take a look at the XML/XUL/Element folder of your PEAR installation.

To build a tree of elements, you may add a child element to any element using its appendChild() method. After we finish building the tree, we send the correct header, so Firefox knows how to treat the data, and then send it to the browser using the send() method. If you open the script in your browser you should see your first dynamically created XUL document. If you take a look at the source code of the document you will see the XUL code that was necessary:

```
<?xml version="1.0"?>
<?xml-stylesheet href="chrome://global/skin/" type="text/css"?>
<window title="Simple XUL"
        xmlns="http://www.mozilla.org/keymaster/gatekeeper/there.
                                                         is.only.xul">
  <description>This is XUL, believe it or not.</description>
</window>
```

You will easily recognize the elements <window/> and <description/> you created using the createElement() method. We mentioned before that XML_XUL will make it easier to create XUL documents from within PHP than it would be using DOM, so here is the first improvement:

```
require_once 'XML/XUL.php';

// create a new document
$doc = XML_XUL::createDocument();

// link to the stylesheet selected by the user
$doc->addStylesheet('chrome://global/skin/');

// create a new window
$win = $doc->createElement('window',array(
                                    'title'=> 'Simple XUL'
                                   )
                          );
// add it to the document
$doc->addRoot($win);

$win->addDescription('This is XUL, believe it or not.');

header( 'Content-type: application/vnd.mozilla.xul+xml' );
$doc->send();
```

The difference in this example is the use of $win->addDescription() to add a <description/> element to the window, instead of creating and appending the element manually. This method is supported by all classes representing elements, as adding text content is needed quite often.

Next we want to create a tree like the one displayed in the example before. The main element needed for this is the `XML_XUL_Element_Tree` class, which is created like every other element:

```
$tree = $doc->createElement('Tree',
                                    array(
                                      'flex' => 1,
                                      'height' => 200
                                    )
                                );
```

To complete the tree, you would have to create nested `<treecols/>` and `<treecol/>` elements, to specify the columns of the tree. Using XML_XUL, this is a lot easier. The `XML_XUL_Element_Tree` class provides a method that does this for you:

```
$tree->setColumns(3,
                      array(
                        'id'      => 'id',
                        'label'   => 'Id',
                        'flex'    => 1,
                        'primary' => 'true'
                      ),
                      array(
                        'id'      => 'name',
                        'label'   => 'Name',
                        'flex'    => 1
                      ),
                      array(
                        'id'      => 'email',
                        'label'   => 'E-Mail',
                        'flex'    => 1
                      )
                  );
```

In the first argument you specify the number of columns you want and in all following arguments you pass the array of attributes for each column. Now that we have built the basic structure, we can start adding data to the tree using the `addItem()` method of the `Tree` element:

```
$sun = $tree->addItem(array('SUN', 'Sun Records',
                                               'info@sun-records.com'));
```

When calling this method, you need to pass an array containing the values for each column. You can either pass a string value, which will be used as a label, or pass an associative array containing all attributes for this column. This method will return an instance of the `XML_XUL_Element_Treeitem` class, which can be stored in a variable for later use. For example, you can directly add child elements to this item, as we are not building a simple table, but a recursive tree structure:

```
$sun->addItem(array('elvis', 'Elvis Presley', 'elvis@graceland.com'));
$sun->addItem(array('carl', 'Carl Perkins', 'carl@sun-records.com'));
```

Of course you can still add new root items to the tree or even nest the tree to a deeper level by calling the `addItem()` method on the return values of the previous `addItem()` calls. After we have built the tree we finally add it to the window:

```
$win->appendChild($tree);
```

If you open the resulting script in your Mozilla-compatible browser, you will see an interactive tree widget. The main difference to the first example is that the tree has been built dynamically using PHP and so you could use any resource PHP can access to fill the tree with data.

Creating a Tab Box

We will now learn how to add tabs to our example. The approach is quite similar; there is an element `XML_XUL_Element_Tabbox`, which can be created like any other element:

```
$tabbox = &$doc->createElement('Tabbox', array('height' => 500));
$win->appendChild($tabbox);
```

After creating the `tabbox` element, it is added to the main window. This newly created object provides the `addTab()` method, which is used to create a new tab:

```
$tab1 = $tabbox->addTab('Labels');
```

You may add any child elements to the object returned by the `addTab()` method. The children of this element will be used as content of the created tab. The `addTab()` method accepts several parameters:

- Label for the tab
- `XML_XUL_Element`, which will be used for the tab content
- Array containing attributes of the tab
- Array containing attributes of the tab panel

As we have learned how to build tab boxes and trees using XML_XUL, we can now implement a script that creates the XUL code shown at the start of this section.

```
require_once 'XML/XUL.php';

// create a new document
$doc = XML_XUL::createDocument();

// link to the stylesheet selected by the user
$doc->addStylesheet('chrome://global/skin/');

// create a new window
$win = $doc->createElement('window',array(
                                          'title'=> 'Simple XUL'
                                         )
                          );
// add it to the document
$doc->addRoot($win);

// Create a tabbox and add it to the window
$tabbox = &$doc->createElement('Tabbox', array('height' => 500));
$win->appendChild($tabbox);

// Create a new tree
$tree = &$doc->createElement('Tree',
                             array(
                               'flex' => 1,
                               'height' => 200
                             )
                           );

// Set the column labels
$tree->setColumns(3,
                  array(
                    'id'      => 'id',
                    'label'   => 'Id',
                    'flex'    => 1,
                    'primary' => 'true'
                  ),
                  array(
                    'id'      => 'name',
                    'label'   => 'Name',
                    'flex'    => 1
                  ),
                  array(
                    'id'      => 'email',
                    'label'   => 'E-Mail',
                    'flex'    => 1
                  )
```

```
                    );

    // add a new entry to the tree
    $sun = $tree->addItem(array('SUN', 'Sun Records', 'info@sun-records.
                                                                    com'));

    // Add two new subentries to the created entry
    $sun->addItem(array('elvis', 'Elvis Presley', 'elvis@graceland.com'));
    $sun->addItem(array('carl', 'Carl Perkins', 'carl@sun-records.com'));

    // add another entry to the tree
    $tree->addItem(array('SONY', 'Sony Records', 'info@sony.com'));

    // Add a new tab to the label and use the tree as content
    $tabbox->addTab('Labels', $tree, array(), array('height' => 200));

    // Add another tab without content
    $tab2 = $tabbox->addTab('Misc');

    // Add simple text content to the second tab
    $tab2->addDescription('Place any content here.');

    header( 'Content-type: application/vnd.mozilla.xul+xml' );
    $doc->send();
```

In most cases creating XUL with PHP and XML_XUL is easier than writing the XUL code by hand—all XUL example code in this book has been created using PHP. XML_XUL allows you to read existing XUL documents, modify them, and write them back to a file or the web browser. Furthermore XML_XUL provides debug output to help you analyze the tree you built in memory. Last, XML_XUL provides classes for over 70 XUL elements.

Processing XML Documents

In the first part of this chapter, you learned how to create XML documents from any data source using various PEAR packages. But creating XML would make no sense unless someone on the other side processes the XML you have created. So in the second part of this chapter you will learn which PEAR packages to use for processing XML documents.

The need to process might arise in several situations, as the use of XML in software development is getting more popular every day. Common usage scenarios where you might need to read XML documents and extract information could be:

- Read configuration files in XML format
- Import data to your application that has been exported by any other application in an XML format
- Display content on your website that has been syndicated by any application or website
- Accept web service requests
- Parse web service responses

While the last two scenarios will be the topic of the next chapter, there still are a lot of usages of XML documents beyond the huge field of web services. PEAR has a lot to offer to help you accomplish these tasks. Before we take a look at the PEAR packages responsible for XML parsing, let us talk about the XML support in PHP in general.

In PHP4 there has been only one stable way to work the XML, the expat-based `xml` extension. This extension allowed you to parse XML documents using a SAX API. SAX, which is short for Simple API to XML, is event based. When using a SAX API, you define several functions or methods to handle the different events that occur while analyzing the document. These events include opening tags and closing tags, as well as character data, processing instructions, or XML comments. After registering the callbacks you pass the document to the parser, which will analyze it character by character and steadily move its internal cursor through the document. You will later learn more about SAX-based parsing, when we deal with the XML_Parser package.

PHP5 provides four extensions that help you process XML data:

- `ext/xml`, which is compatible to the PHP4 version
- `ext/dom`, an extension that follows the W3C DOM standard
- `ext/simplexml`, a new approach, which is unique to PHP
- `ext/xmlreader`, an XML-pull parser, which is some kind of mixture between SAX and DOM

Looking at these APIs you might think that using PEAR for XML processing does not earn you anything. But do not let these APIs blind you, all of them are low-level APIs, while PEAR has to offer some packages that work on a higher level and thus make it easier for you to work with XML documents.

On the following pages we will be using three different packages, XML_Parser, XML_Unserializer, and XML_RSS. All of these packages are built on top of the SAX API and all of them work fine with PHP4 or PHP5. While XML_Parser can be used to read any XML document and XML_Unserializer allows you to process nearly every XML document, XML_RSS is built specifically to parse RSS feeds.

Parsing XML with XML_Parser

XML_Parser is an object-oriented wrapper built around the XML parsing functions available in PHP. The documentation on these functions can be found on the PHP website at `http://www.php.net/xml`; these functions can be used to process any XML document using a SAX API. When using a SAX API, the parser moves an internal cursor forwards through the document and at the same time tokenizes the document. These tokens can be:

- Opening or closing tags (empty tags are the same as an opening and closing tag without any data in between them)
- Character data
- Processing instructions like `<?php ...?>` or `<?xml ...?>`
- External entities that reference other XML documents
- Notation declarations
- Unparsed entity declarations
- Other parts of XML documents like the document type declaration or XML comments

While the parser moves its cursor through the document it will trigger an event for each token it finds. Your application should be able to handle these events using any PHP callback (function, method, or static method) and extract the information you need from the document. You need to register these callbacks for all tokens you want to handle prior to parsing the document. So your typical PHP code using the `xml` functions will look a lot like this:

```
// acquire a new parser resource
$xml_parser = xml_parser_create();

// register callbacks for opening and closing tags.
// The implementations of startElement() and endElement() have been
// left out
xml_set_element_handler($xml_parser, "startElement", "endElement");

// open the file you want to parser
if (!($fp = fopen($file, "r"))) {
   die("could not open XML input");
}

// read the file and pass the read data to the parser for tokenizing
// If an error occurs (e.g. document is not well-formed, exit the
// script)
while ($data = fread($fp, 4096)) {
```

```
        if (!xml_parse($xml_parser, $data, feof($fp))) {
            die(sprintf("XML error: %s at line %d",
                        xml_error_string(xml_get_error_code($xml_parser)),
                        xml_get_current_line_number($xml_parser)));
        }
    }

    // free the parser resource
    xml_parser_free($xml_parser);
```

When using these functions you will be using the same code in different places of your application as you will always have to acquire a parser resource, register the callback, open files or other streams, pass the data from the file to the parser, handle any errors that occur while parsing, and free the parser you have set up.

Enter XML_Parser

XML_Parser has been developed to allow you to reuse as much code as possible when using the SAX API of PHP. Furthermore it provides some convenience functions and enables you to use the SAX functions in an object-oriented way, which should be the preferred approach of large scale applications.

To learn how to work with XML_Parser, we will be using the following example document:

```
<?xml version="1.0" encoding="ISO-8859-1"?>
<configuration>
    <section name="paths">
        <includes>/usr/share/php/myapp</includes>
        <cache>/tmp/myapp</cache>
        <templates>/var/www/skins/myapp</templates>
    </section>
    <section name="db" environment="online">
        <dsn>mysql://user:pass@localhost/myapp</dsn>
        <prefix>myapp_</prefix>
    </section>
    <section name="db" environment="stage">
        <dsn>mysql://root:@localhost/myapp</dsn>
        <prefix>myapp_testing_</prefix>
    </section>
</configuration>
```

This document could have been copied from any application that uses XML-based configuration files. The configuration is split into different sections to configure different parts of the application; in this case there are sections to configure the folders that will be used to include PHP and templates files, and for temporary files, as well as to configure the database access. The section for database access is available twice in the configuration file and an `environment` attribute has been added to these sections. This could be used to store different configurations for the testing, staging, and online environments of the configurations in the same file. On the following pages, we will be using XML_Parser to implement a configuration reader that is able to parse the above file and return the values stored in the configuration while respecting the environment in which it is used.

Using XML_Parser is quite different from using any other PEAR packages you have used before. Instead of instantiating a new instance of XML_Parser you create a new class that extends XML_Parser, and instantiate a new object of this class instead. In this new class, you will only need to implement the different handlers for all tokens you want to process. All other work needed to parse the document (acquiring a parser, opening files, handling errors, etc.) is done automatically by the base class. In order for XML_Parser to be able to invoke the callbacks for the different tokens in your XML document, you have to comply with its naming scheme when implementing the callbacks in your derived class. The following table lists all possible callbacks and their names. The signatures of the methods are exactly the same as described in the PHP manual.

Token	Callback name
opening tag	`startElement`
closing tag	`endElement`
character data	`cdataHandler`
external entities	`entityrefHandler`
processing instructions	`piHandler`
unparsed entity declarations	`unparsedHandler`
notation declarations	`notationHandler`
any other token	`defaultHandler`

Implementing the Callbacks

As we now know the names of the callbacks, implementing a first class that parses the document is extremely easy; just take a look at the following code:

```
// include the base class
require_once 'XML/Parser.php';

// create a class that extends XML_Parser
class ConfigReader extends XML_Parser
{
```

```
    /**
     * handle opening tags
     *
     * @param    resource    parser resource
     * @param    string      tag name
     * @param    array       attributes
     */
     public function startHandler($parser, $name, $attribs)
     {
         echo "Start element $name found\n";
     }

    /**
     * handle character data
     *
     * @param    resource    parser resource
     * @param    string      character data
     */
     public function cdataHandler($parser, $cData)
     {
         $cData = trim($cData);
         if ($cData === '') {
             return;
         }
         echo "...data '$cData' found\n";
     }

    /**
     * handle closing tags
     *
     * @param    resource    parser resource
     * @param    string      tag name
     */
     public function endHandler($parser, $name)
     {
         echo "End element $name found\n";
     }
}

// Create a new instance of the class
$config = new ConfigReader();

// set the name of the file to parse
$config->setInputFile('config.xml');
```

```
// parse the file and catch errors
$result = $config->parse();
if (PEAR::isError($result)) {
    echo 'Parsing failed: ' . $result->getMessage();
}
$config->free();
```

For our example, we only need to handle three types of different tokens: opening tags, closing tags, and the character data enclosed within them. So we only need to implement the methods `startElement()`, `endElement()`, and `cDataHandler()` in our class, after including and extending XML_Parser. For the first example, some debugging output in these methods is enough to get acquainted with the XML_Parser package. Right after implementing the new `ConfigReader` class, we create a new instance of it. As the class extends the XML_Parser class, it already provides useful methods for XML parsing; one of these is the `setInputFile()` method, which enables you to pass the name of a file (or any other stream) that needs to be parsed. To start the actual parsing, you will need to call the `parse()` method. This method will either return `true`, if the document could be parsed, or an instance of `PEAR_Error` if any errors occur during the parsing process. If you pass the filename of our example XML document, you will see the following output on your screen:

```
Start element CONFIGURATION found
Start element SECTION found
Start element INCLUDES found
...data '/usr/share/php/myapp' found
End element INCLUDES found
Start element CACHE found
...data '/tmp/myapp' found
End element CACHE found
Start element TEMPLATES found
...data '/var/www/skins/myapp' found
End element TEMPLATES found
End element SECTION found
Start element SECTION found
Start element DSN found
...data 'mysql://user:pass@localhost/myapp' found
End element DSN found
Start element PREFIX found
...data 'myapp_' found
End element PREFIX found
End element SECTION found
Start element SECTION found
Start element DSN found
...data 'mysql://root:@localhost/myapp' found
End element DSN found
```

```
Start element PREFIX found
...data 'myapp_testing_' found
End element PREFIX found
End element SECTION found
End element CONFIGURATION found
```

A quick glance reveals that this is not exactly the result we expected. While the callbacks for opening and closing tags as well as the data are called in the same order as they occur in the source document, all tag names have been converted to uppercase. This is the default behavior of XML_Parser and can be easily switched off by adding another property to the implemented `ConfigReader` class:

```
// create a class that extends XML_Parser
class ConfigReader extends XML_Parser
{
   /**
    * disable case folding to uppercase
    */
    public $folding = false;

    /* ... rest of the code remains unchanged ...*/
}
```

After setting this property to `false`, XML_Parser will not change the case of the tag names prior to passing them to the callbacks.

Adding Logic to the Callbacks

As we now know how XML_Parser works, we can finally use it to implement the planned configuration reader. As we will need to store state information while parsing, we start by adding some properties to the new class.

```
/**
 * Class to read XML configuration files
 */
class ConfigReader extends XML_Parser
{
   /**
    * disable case folding to uppercase
    */
    public $folding = false;

   /**
    * sections that already have been parsed
    */
    private $sections = array();
```

```
    /**
     * selected environment
     */
     private $environment;

    /**
     * temporarily store data during parsing
     */
     private $currentSection = null;
     private $currentData = null;
}
```

The `$sections` property will later store the configuration options, the `$environment` property will store the environment in which we will be using the configuration reader, and the last two properties will be used to temporarily store the current section while the cursor and current character data is inside a `<section/>` tag.

Next, we implement a constructor to pass the selected environment on instantiation of the parser object:

```
/**
 * Create a new ConfigReader
 *
 * @param    string  environment to use
 */
 public function __construct($environment = 'online')
 {
     parent::__construct();
     $this->environment = $environment;
 }
```

The constructor takes a string parameter whose value will be stored in the `$environment` property. Now that we have set up all properties and the constructor we will implement the actual logic in the callbacks. First is the callback for opening tags:

```
/**
 * handle opening tags
 *
 * @param    resource    parser resource
 * @param    string      tag name
 * @param    array       attributes
 */
 public function startHandler($parser, $name, $attribs)
 {
     switch ($name) {
       case 'configuration':
```

```
            break;
          case 'section':
            // check, whether the correct environment is set
              if (!isset($attribs['environment'])
                    || $attribs['environment'] == $this->environment) {

                // store the name of the section
                    $this->currentSection = $attribs['name'];
                // create an empty array for this section
                    $this->sections[$this->currentSection] = array();
              }
                break;
          default:
            $this->currentData = '';
             break;
      }
  }
```

The technique used here is quite common when implementing SAX-based XML parsers. A `switch` statement is used to execute different actions depending on the tag name. If the opening `<configuration>` tag is found, the parser will ignore it. If an opening `<section>` tag is found, we check whether an environment attribute has been specified and if the value of this attribute is identical to the environment specified in the constructor. If yes, the name of this section is stored in an object property and a new array for this section is created in the `$sections` property. If the environments do not match, we assign `null` value to the `$currentSection` property and ignore all tags inside this section.

If any other tag is found, we set the current character data to an empty string. After the start element handler has been implemented, we continue with the character data handler.

```
/**
 * handle character data
 *
 * @param    resource    parser resource
 * @param    string      character data
 */
public function cDataHandler($parser, $cData)
{
    if (trim($cData) === '') {
        return;
    }
    $this->currentData .= $cData;
}
```

This handler is quite simple: If the data consists only of whitespace, it is ignored, otherwise we append it to the `$currentData` property. The last handler left to implement is the method handling closing tags:

```
/**
 * handle closing tags
 *
 * @param    resource    parser resource
 * @param    string      tag name
 */
public function endHandler($parser, $name)
{
    switch ($name) {
        case 'configuration':
             break;
        // end of </section>, clear the current section
           case 'section':
             $this->currentSection = null;
             break;
        default:
             if ($this->currentSection == null) {
                 return;
             }
             // store the current data in the configuration
             $this->sections[$this->currentSection][$name] = trim(
                                                     $this->currentData);
             break;
    }
}
```

Again, the closing `</configuration>` tag is ignored as it is only used as a container for the document. If we find a closing `</section>` tag, we just reset the `$currentSection` property, as we are not inside a section anymore. Any other tag will be treated as a configuration directive and the text that has been found inside this tag (and which we stored in the `$currentData` property) will be used as the value for this directive. So we store this value in the `$sections` array using the name of the current section and the name of the closing tag, except when the current section is `null`.

Accessing the Configuration Options

Last we need to add a method to access the data collected while parsing the XML document:

```
/**
 * Fetch a configuration option
 *
 * @param    string      name of the section
 * @param    string      name of the option
 * @return   mixed       configuration option or false if not set
 */
public function getConfigurationOption($section, $value)
{
    if (!isset($this->sections[$section])) {
        return false;
    }
    if (!isset($this->sections[$section][$value])) {
        return false;
    }
    return $this->sections[$section][$value];
}
}
```

This method accepts the name of a section as well as the name of a configuration option. It will check whether the section and the option have been defined in the XML document and return its value. Otherwise it will return `null`. Finally our configuration reader is ready to use:

```
$config = new ConfigReader('online');
$result = $config->setInputFile('config.xml');
$result = $config->parse();

printf("Cache folder  : %s\n",
        $config->getConfigurationOption('paths', 'cache'));
printf("DB connection : %s\n",$config->getConfigurationOption('db',
                                                               'dsn'));
```

Running this script will output the configuration values stored in the XML file for the `online` environment:

```
Cache folder  : /tmp/myapp
DB connection : mysql://user:pass@localhost/myapp
```

Our first XML parser that actually does something useful has now been implemented and using XML_Parser helped a lot. However, XML_Parser has much more to offer!

Avoiding Inheritance

In the previous example we had to extend XML_Parser. In a simple example this does not pose a problem, but if you are developing a large framework or application you might want all your classes to extend a base class to provide some common functionality. As you cannot change XML_Parser to extend your base class, you might think that this is a severe limitation of XML_Parser. Luckily, extending XML_Parser is not required for using XML_Parser since version 1.2.0. The following code shows the `ConfigReader` class without the dependency on XML_Parser. Besides the `extends` statement, we also removed the `$folding` property and the call to `parent::__construct()` in the constructor.

```
/**
 * Class to read XML configuration files
 */
class ConfigReader
{
   /**
    * selected environment
    */
    private $environment;

   /**
    * sections that already have been parsed
    */
    private $sections = array();

   /**
    * temporarily store data during parsing
    */
    private $currentSection = null;
    private $currentData = null;

   /**
    * Create a new ConfigReader
    *
    * @param    string  environment to use
    */
    public function __construct($environment = 'online')
    {
        $this->environment = $environment;
    }

    // The handler functions should go in here
    // They have been left out to save some paper
}
```

As our class does not extend XML_Parser anymore, it does not inherit any of the parsing functionality we need. Still, it can be used with XML_Parser. The following code shows how the same XML document can now be parsed with the ConfigReader class without the need to extend the XML_Parser class:

```
$config = new ConfigReader('online');
$parser = new XML_Parser();
$parser->setHandlerObj($config);
$parser->folding = false;
$parser->setInputFile('XML_Parser-001.xml');
$parser->parse();

printf("Cache folder  : %s\n",
       $config->getConfigurationOption('paths', 'cache'));
printf("DB connection : %s\n", $config->getConfigurationOption('db',
                                                               'dsn'));
```

Instead of creating one object, we are creating two objects: the ConfigReader and an instance of the XML_Parser class. As the XML_Parser class does not provide the callbacks for handling the XML data, we pass the ConfigReader instance to the parser and it uses this object to call the handlers. This is the only new method we will be using in this example. We only need to set the $folding property so XML_Parser will not convert the tags to uppercase and then pass in the filename and start the parsing process. The output of the script will be exactly the same as in the previous example, but we did it without extending XML_Parser.

Additional XML_Parser Features

Although you have learned about the most important features of XML_Parser, it can still do more for you. Here you will find a short summary of the features that have not been explained in detail:

- XML_Parser is able to convert the data from one encoding to the other. This means you could read a document encoded in UTF-8 and automatically convert the character data to ISO-8859-1 while parsing the document.
- XML_Parser can help you to get rid of the switch statements. By passing func as the second argument to the constructor, you switch the parsing mode to the so-called function mode. In this mode, XML_Parser will not call startElement() and endElement(), but search for methods xmltag_$tagname() and _xmltag_$tagname() for opening tags, where $tagname is the name of the tag it currently handles.
- XML_Parser even provides an XML_Parser_Simple class that already implements the startElement() and cDataHandler() methods for you. In these methods, it will just store the data and pass the collected information to the endElement() method. In this way you will be able to handle all data associated with one tag at once.

Processing XML with XML_Unserializer

While XML_Parser helps you process XML documents, there is still a lot work left for the developer. In most cases you only want to extract the raw information contained in the XML document and convert it to a PHP data structure (like an array or a collection of objects). This is where XML_Unserializer comes into play. XML_Unserializer is the counterpart to XML_Serializer, and while XML_Serializer creates XML from any PHP data structure, XML_Unserializer creates PHP data structures from any XML. If you have XML_Serializer installed, you will not need to install another package, as XML_Unserializer is part of the same package.

The usage of XML_Unserializer resembles that of XML_Serializer, as you use exactly the same steps (of course with one difference):

- Include XML_Unserializer and create a new instance
- Configure the instance using options
- Read the XML document
- Fetch the data and do whatever you want with it

Now let us take a look at a very simple example:

```
// include the class
require_once 'XML/Unserializer.php';

// create a new object
$unserializer = new XML_Unserializer();

// construct some XML
$xml = <<<XML
<artists>
    <artist>Elvis Presley</artist>
    <artist>Carl Perkins</artist>
</artists>
XML;

$unserializer->unserialize($xml);
$artists = $unserializer->getUnserializedData();

print_r($artists);
```

If you run this script, it will output:

```
Array
(
    [artist] => Array
        (
```

```
                [0] => Elvis Presley
                [1] => Carl Perkins
            )
    )
```

As you can easily see, XML_Unserializer converted the XML document into a set of nested arrays. The root array contains only one value, which is stored under the key `artist`. This key has been used because the XML document contains two `<artist/>` tags in the first nesting level. The `artist` value is again an array, but this time it is not an associative array, but a numbered one. It contains the names of the two artists that have been stored in the XML document. So nearly all the data stored in the document is available in the resulting array. The only information missing is the root tag of the document, `<artists/>`. We used this information as the name of the PHP variable that stores the array, but we could only do this as we knew what kind of information was stored in the XML document. However, if we did not know this, XML_Unserializer still gives access to this information:

```
echo $unserializer->getRootName();
```

As expected, this will display the name of the root tag of the previously processed XML document:

```
artists
```

So instead of having to implement a new class, you can use XML_Unserializer to extract all the information from the XML document while preserving the actual structure of the information. And all that was needed was four lines of code!

So let us try XML_Unserializer with the XML configuration file that we parsed using XML_Parser and see what we get in return. As the XML document is stored in a separate file, you might want to use `file_get_contents()` to read the XML into a variable. This is not needed, as XML_Unserializer can process any inputs supported by XML_Parser. To tell XML_Unserializer to treat the data we passed to `unserialize()` as a filename instead of the actual XML document, you only need to pass an additional parameter:

```
require_once 'XML/Unserializer.php';
$unserializer = new XML_Unserializer();

$unserializer->unserialize('config.xml', true);
$config = $unserializer->getUnserializedData();
print_r($config);
```

Running this script will output the following array:

```
Array
(
```

```
        [section] => Array
            (
                [0] => Array
                    (
                        [includes] => /usr/share/php/myapp
                        [cache] => /tmp/myapp
                        [templates] => /var/www/skins/myapp
                    )
                [1] => Array
                    (
                        [dsn] => mysql://user:pass@localhost/myapp
                        [prefix] => myapp_
                    )
                [2] => Array
                    (
                        [dsn] => mysql://root:@localhost/myapp
                        [prefix] => myapp_testing_
                    )
            )
    )
```

If you take a look at the XML document from the XML_Parser examples, you will recognize that XML_Unserializer extracted all information that has been stored between the XML tags. We had several sections defined in the configuration file and all the configuration directives that have been included in the XML document are available in the resulting array. However, the names and the environments of the sections are missing. This information was stored in attributes of the `<section/>` tags, which have been ignored by XML_Unserializer.

Parsing Attributes

Of course, this behavior can be changed. Like XML_Serializer, XML_Unserializer provides the means to influence parsing behavior by accepting different values for several options. Options can be set in exactly the same way as with XML_Serializer:

- Passing an array of options to the constructor or the `setOptions()` method
- Passing an array of options to the `unserialize()` call
- Setting a single option via the `setOption()` method

If we want to parse the attributes as well, a very small change is necessary:

```
require_once 'XML/Unserializer.php';
$unserializer = new XML_Unserializer();
```

```
// parse attributes as well
$unserializer->setOption(XML_UNSERIALIZER_OPTION_ATTRIBUTES_PARSE,
                                                                  true);

$unserializer->unserialize('XML_Parser-001.xml', true);
$config = $unserializer->getUnserializedData();
print_r($config);
```

We only added one line of code to the script to set the `ATTRIBUTES_PARSE` option of XML_Unserializer to `true` and here is how it influences the output of the script:

```
Array
(
    [section] => Array
        (
            [0] => Array
                (
                    [name] => paths
                    [includes] => /usr/share/php/myapp
                    [cache] => /tmp/myapp
                    [templates] => /var/www/skins/myapp
                )
            [1] => Array
                (
                    [name] => db
                    [environment] => online
                    [dsn] => mysql://user:pass@localhost/myapp
                    [prefix] => myapp_
                )
            [2] => Array
                (
                    [name] => db
                    [environment] => stage
                    [dsn] => mysql://root:@localhost/myapp
                    [prefix] => myapp_testing_
                )
        )
)
```

Now the resulting array contains the configuration directives as well as meta-information for each section, which was stored in attributes. However, configuration directives and meta-information got mixed up, which will cause problems when you are using `<name/>` or `<environment/>` directives, as they will overwrite the values stored in the attributes. Again, only a small modification to the script is necessary to solve this problem:

```
require_once 'XML/Unserializer.php';
$unserializer = new XML_Unserializer();

// parse attributes as well
$unserializer->setOption(XML_UNSERIALIZER_OPTION_ATTRIBUTES_PARSE,
                                                                   true);
// store attributes in a separate array
$unserializer->setOption(XML_UNSERIALIZER_OPTION_ATTRIBUTES_ARRAYKEY,
                                '_meta');

$unserializer->unserialize('config.xml', true);
$config = $unserializer->getUnserializedData();
print_r($config);
```

By setting the `ATTRIBUTES_ARRAYKEY` option, we tell XML_Unserializer to store the attributes in a separate array instead of mixing them with the tags. And here is the result:

```
Array
(
    [section] => Array
        (
            [0] => Array
                (
                    [_meta] => Array
                        (
                            [name] => paths
                        )
                    [includes] => /usr/share/php/myapp
                    [cache] => /tmp/myapp
                    [templates] => /var/www/skins/myapp
                )
            [1] => Array
                (
                    [_meta] => Array
                        (
                            [name] => db
                            [environment] => online
                        )
                    [dsn] => mysql://user:pass@localhost/myapp
                    [prefix] => myapp_
                )
            [2] => Array
                (
                    [_meta] => Array
                        (
                            [name] => db
```

```
                                [environment] => stage
                            )
                        [dsn] => mysql://root:@localhost/myapp
                        [prefix] => myapp_testing_
                    )
            )
    )
```

Now you can easily extract all configuration options without having to implement your own parser for every XML format. But if you are obsessed with object-oriented development, you might complain that the OO interface the XML_Parser approach provided for the configuration options was a lot more convenient than working with simple PHP arrays. If this is what you were thinking, then please read on.

Mapping XML to Objects

By default, XML_Unserializer will convert complex XML structures (i.e. every tag that contains nested tags or attributes) to an associative array. This behavior can be changed by setting the following option:

```
$unserializer->setOption(XML_UNSERIALIZER_OPTION_COMPLEXTYPE,
'object');
```

If you add this line of code to the script, the output will be changed:

```
stdClass Object
(
    [section] => Array
        (
            [0] => stdClass Object
                (
                    [_meta] => Array
                        (
                            [name] => paths
                        )
                    [includes] => /usr/share/php/myapp
                    [cache] => /tmp/myapp
                    [templates] => /var/www/skins/myapp
                )
             ...the other sections have been left out...
)
```

Instead of associative arrays, XML_Unserializer will create an instance of the `stdClass` class, which is always defined in PHP and does not provide any methods. While this will now provide object-oriented access to the configuration directives, it is not better than using arrays, as you still have to write code like this:

```
echo $config->section[0]->templates;
```

Well at least this looks a lot like simpleXML, which a lot of people think is a cool way of dealing with XML. But it is not cool enough for us, and XML_Unserializer is able to do a lot more, as the following example will show you.

XML_Unserializer is able to use different classes for different tags. For each tag, it will check whether a class of the same name has been defined and create an instance of this class instead of just `stdClass`. When setting the properties of the classes, it will check whether a setter method for each property has been defined. Setter methods always start with `set` followed by the name of the property. So you can implement classes that provide functionality and let XML_Unserializer automatically create them for you and set all properties according to the data in the XML document. In our configuration example, we would need two classes: one for the configuration and one for each section in the configuration. Here is an example implementation of these classes:

```
/**
 * Class to provide access to the configuration
 */
class configuration
{
    /**
     * Will store the section
     */
     private $sections = null;

    /**
     * selected environment
     */
     private $environment = 'online';

    /**
     * Setter method for the section tag
     */
     public function setSection($section)
     {
         $this->sections = $section;
     }

    /**
     * Set the environment for the configuration
     *
     * Will not be called by XML_Unserialiazer, but
     * the user.
```

```
    */
    public function setEnvironment($environment)
    {
        $this->environment = $environment;
    }

   /**
    * Fetch a configuration option
    *
    * @param    string      name of the section
    * @param    string      name of the option
    * @return   mixed       configuration option or false if not set
    */
    public function getConfigurationOption($section, $value)
    {
        foreach ($this->sections as $currentSection) {
            if ($currentSection->getName() !== $section) {
                continue;
            }
            if (!$currentSection->isEnvironment($this->environment)) {
                continue;
            }
            return $currentSection->getValue($value);
        }
        return null;
    }
}
```

The implementation of the `configuration` class is quite simple: we have got a property to store all sections of the configuration as well as a property that stores the selected environment, the matching setter methods, and one method to retrieve configuration values. The only thing that might strike you in the implementation of the configuration class is that the method to set the sections is called `setSection()` instead of `setSections()`. This is because the tag is also called `<section/>`. Next is the implementation of the `section` class:

```
/**
 * Class to store information about one section
 */
class section
{
   /**
    * stores meta information
    */
    private $meta = null;
```

```
    /**
     * setter for the meta information
     */
    public function setMeta($meta)
    {
        if (!isset($meta['name'])) {
            throw new Exception('Sections require a name.');
        }
        $this->meta = $meta;
    }

    /**
     * Get the name of the section
     */
    public function getName()
    {
        return $this->meta['name'];
    }

    /**
     * check for the specified environment
     */
    public function isEnvironment($environment)
    {
        if (!isset($this->meta['environment'])) {
            return true;
        }
        return ($environment === $this->meta['environment']);
    }

    /**
     * Get a value from the section
     */
    public function getValue($name)
    {
        if (isset($this->$name)) {
            return $this->$name;
        }
        return null;
    }
}
```

Again, this is mainly a container for information stored in the session with some setters and getters. Now, that both classes have been implemented, you can easily make XML_Unserializer use them:

```
require_once 'XML/Unserializer.php';
$unserializer = new XML_Unserializer();

// parse attributes as well
$unserializer->setOption(XML_UNSERIALIZER_OPTION_ATTRIBUTES_PARSE,
                                                              true);
// store attributes in a separate array
$unserializer->setOption(XML_UNSERIALIZER_OPTION_ATTRIBUTES_ARRAYKEY,
                                                            'meta');
// use objects instead of arrays
$unserializer->setOption(XML_UNSERIALIZER_OPTION_COMPLEXTYPE,
                                                          'object');
$unserializer->setOption(XML_UNSERIALIZER_OPTION_TAG_AS_CLASSNAME,
                                                             true);

$unserializer->unserialize('config.xml', true);
$config = $unserializer->getUnserializedData();

printf("Cache folder  : %s\n", $config->getConfigurationOption(
                                                          'paths',
                                                          'cache'));
printf("DB connection : %s\n", $config->getConfigurationOption('db',
                                                           'dsn'));

$config->setEnvironment('stage');
print "\nChanged the environment:\n";
printf("Cache folder  : %s\n", $config->getConfigurationOption(
                                                          'paths',
                                                          'cache'));
printf("DB connection : %s\n", $config->getConfigurationOption('db',
                                                           'dsn'));
```

Again, setting one option is enough to completely change the parsing behavior of XML_Unserializer. When you run the script, you will see the following output:

```
Cache folder  : /tmp/myapp
DB connection : mysql://user:pass@localhost/myapp

Changed the environment:
Cache folder  : /tmp/myapp
DB connection : mysql://root:@localhost/myapp
```

There is only one thing that might break your new configuration reader. If a configuration contains only one section, the `configuration::setSection()` method will be invoked by passing an instance of `section` instead of a numbered array of several `section` objects. This will lead to an error when iterating over this non-existent array. You could either automatically create an array in this case while implementing `setSection()` or let XML_Unserializer do the work:

```
$unserializer->setOption(XML_UNSERIALIZER_OPTION_FORCE_ENUM,
                         array('section'));
```

Now XML_Unserializer will create a numbered array even if there is only one occurrence of the `<section/>` tag. As you now know how to set options for XML_Unserializer, you may want to take a look at the following table, which is a complete list of all options XML_Unserializer provides.

Option name	Description	Default value
`COMPLEXTYPE`	Defines how tags that do not only contain character data should be unserialized. May either be `array` or `object`.	`array`
`ATTRIBUTE_KEY`	Defines the name of the attribute from which the original key or property name is taken.	`_originalKey`
`ATTRIBUTE_TYPE`	Defines the name of the attribute from which the type of the value is taken.	`_type`
`ATTRIBUTE_CLASS`	Defines the name of the attribute from which the class name is taken when creating an object from the tag.	`_class`
`TAG_AS_CLASSNAME`	Whether the tag name should be used as class name.	`false`
`DEFAULT_CLASS`	Name of the default class to use when creating objects.	`stdClass`
`ATTRIBUTES_PARSE`	Whether to parse attributes (`true`) or ignore them (`false`).	`false`
`ATTRIBUTES_PREPEND`	String to prepend attribute names with.	empty
`ATTRIBUTES_ARRAYKEY`	Key or property name under which all attributes will be stored in a separate array. Use `false` to disable this.	`false`
`CONTENT_KEY`	Key or property name for the character data contained in a tag that does not only contain character data.	`_content`
`TAG_MAP`	Associative array of tag names that should be converted to different names.	empty array
`FORCE_ENUM`	Array of tag names that will be automatically treated as if there was more than one occurrence of the tag. So there will always be numeric arrays that contain the actual data.	empty array

Option name	Description	Default value
ENCODING_SOURCE	The source encoding of the document; will be passed to XML_Parser.	null
ENCODING_TARGET	The desired target encoding; will be passed to XML_Parser.	null
DECODE_FUNC	PHP callback that will be applied to all character data and attribute values.	null
RETURN_RESULT	Whether unserialize() should return the result or only true, if the unserialization was successful.	false
WHITESPACE	Defines how whitespace in the document will be treated. Possible values are: XML_..._WHITESPACE_KEEP, XML_..._WHITESPACE_TRIM and XML_..._WHITESPACE_NORMALIZE.	XML_..._WHITESPACE_TRIM
IGNORE_KEYS	List of tags whose contents will automatically be passed to the parent tag instead of creating a new tag.	empty array
GUESS_TYPES	Whether to enable automatic type guessing for character data and attributes.	false

Unserializing the Record Labels

In the XML_Serializer examples we created an XML document based on a PHP data structure composed of objects. In this last XML_Unserializer example we will close the circle by creating the same data structure from the XML document. Here is the code that we will use to achieve this:

```
require_once 'XML/Unserializer.php';
$unserializer = new XML_Unserializer();

// Do not ignore attributes
$unserializer->setOption(XML_UNSERIALIZER_OPTION_ATTRIBUTES_PARSE,
                                                               true);

// Some complex tags should be objects, but enumerations should be
// arrays
$types = array(
            '#default' => 'object',
            'artists'  => 'array',
            'labels'   => 'array',
            'records'  => 'array'
```

```
        );
$unserializer->setOption(XML_UNSERIALIZER_OPTION_COMPLEXTYPE, $types);

// Always create numbered arrays of labels, artists and records
$unserializer->setOption(XML_UNSERIALIZER_OPTION_FORCE_ENUM,
array('label', 'artist', 'record'));

// do not add nested keys for label, artist and record
$unserializer->setOption(XML_UNSERIALIZER_OPTION_IGNORE_KEYS,
array('label', 'artist', 'record'));

// parse the file
$unserializer->unserialize('first-xml-document.xml', true);
print_r($unserializer->getUnserializedData());
```

When running this script you will see several warnings like this one on your screen:

```
Warning: Missing argument 1 for Record::__construct() in c:\wamp\www\
books\packt\pear\xml\example-classes.php on line 48
```

This is because we implemented constructors in the `Label`, `Artist`, and `Record` classes that require some parameters to be passed when creating new instances. XML_Unserializer will not pass these parameters to the constructor, so we need to make some small adjustments to our class definitions:

```
class Label {
    ...
    public function __construct($name = null) {
        $this->name = $name;
    }
    ...
}

class Artist {
    ...
    public function __construct($name = null) {
        $this->name = $name;
    }
    ...
}

class Record {
    ...
    public function __construct($id = null, $name = null, $released =
                                                                null) {
        $this->id       = $id;
        $this->name     = $name;
```

```
            $this->released = $released;
        }
    }
```

By making the arguments in the constructor optional, we can easily get rid of the warnings. XML_Unserializer will nevertheless set all properties of the objects after instantiating them. So if you run the script now, you will get the result we expected—the complete object tree has been restored and there was no need to write a custom XML parser for this task.

Additional Features

Even though we have used XML_Unserializer to create some really cool scripts with a few lines of code, we have not used all of the features XML_Unserializer provides. XML_Unserializer also allows you to:

- Map tag names to any class name by specifying an associative array
- Use type guessing, so it will automatically convert the data to Booleans, integers, or floats
- Use XML_Serializer/XML_Unserializer as a drop-in replacement for `serialize()`/`unserialize()`
- Apply any PHP callback to all character data and attribute values
- Remove or keep all whitespace in the document

XML_Parser vs. XML_Unserializer

Whenever you need to extract information from an XML document, you should check whether XML_Unserializer can accomplish the task at hand before implementing your custom parser. In more than 90% of all cases XML_Unserializer will be the right tool for you. If your first attempt does not succeed, a little tweaking of the options is usually enough to get the job done.

XML_Parser should be used in any of the following scenarios:

- If your document is extremely complex and does not follow any rules, XML_Unserializer might not be able to extract the needed information. XML_Parser still can do that, although it requires more work.
- If you only need to extract a portion of an XML document, XML_Parser might be faster than XML_Unserializer, as you can tell it to ignore the rest of the document.
- When parsing large XML documents, XML_Parser might be better suited for the task, as its memory footprint is lower than XML_Unserializer's.

XML_Unserializer will keep all the data contained in the document in memory. XML_Parser stores the information collected from the XML document in a database while parsing the document, not after you have finished parsing it.

Parsing RSS with XML_RSS

RSS is an acronym that refers to the following three terms:

- Rich Site Summary
- RDF Site Summary
- Really Simple Syndication

As the last term implies, RSS is used for syndication of the content, so you can offer other websites and clients access to your content or include third-party content in your website. RSS is commonly used by web logs and news aggregators.

As RSS is an XML application, you may use any of the previously covered packages, but PEAR provides a package that is aimed only at extracting information from any RSS document and which makes working with RSS extremely easy. Using XML_RSS you can display the headline from your favorite blogs on your website with less than ten lines of code. Or you could even list the latest releases of your favorite PEAR packages, developer, or category on your website and offer links to the download pages. The PEAR website offers various feeds (this is how URLs providing RSS documents are commonly called), that include either all package releases or only the latest releases of a package, a category, or a developer. You will find a list of all available feeds and the matching URLs on the PEAR website at `http://pear.php.net/feeds/`. In the following examples we will be working with the feed that provides information about the latest releases in the XML category; this feed is available at `http://pear.php.net/feeds/cat_xml.rss`. If you open this URL in your browser or download it, you will see an XML document with the following structure.

```
<?xml version="1.0" encoding="iso-8859-1"?>
<rdf:RDF xmlns:rdf="http://www.w3.org/1999/02/22-rdf-syntax-ns#"
         xmlns="http://purl.org/rss/1.0/"
         xmlns:dc="http://purl.org/dc/elements/1.1/">
  <channel rdf:about="http://pear.php.net/">
    <link>http://pear.php.net/</link>
    <dc:creator>pear-webmaster@lists.php.net</dc:creator>
    <dc:publisher>pear-webmaster@lists.php.net</dc:publisher>
    <dc:language>en-us</dc:language>
    <items>
      <rdf:Seq>
```

```
        <rdf:li rdf:resource="http://.../XML_Serializer/
                                            download/0.16.0/" />
        <rdf:li rdf:resource="http://.../XML_SVG/download/1.0.0/" />
        <rdf:li rdf:resource="http://.../XML_FastCreate/
                                            download/1.0.0/" />
      </rdf:Seq>
    </items>
    <title>PEAR: Latest releases in category xml</title>
    <description>The latest releases in the category xml</description>
  </channel>
  <item rdf:about="http://.../XML_Serializer/download/0.16.0/">
    <title>XML_Serializer 0.16.0</title>
    <link>http://pear.php.net/package/XML_Serializer/
                                          download/0.16.0/</link>
    <description>
XML_Serializer:
- introduced constants for all options (this helps avoiding typos in
                                                  the option names)
- deprecated option &apos;tagName&apos; is no longer supported, use
                XML_SERIALIZER_OPTION_ROOT_NAME (or rootName) instead
- implement Request #3762: added new ignoreNull option to ignore
properties that are set to null when serializing objects or arrays
- fixed bug with encoding function
- use new header comment blocks
XML_Unserializer:
- fix bug #4075 (allow tagMap option to influence any kind of
                                                value)</description>
    <dc:date>2005-06-05T09:26:53-05:00</dc:date>
  </item>
  <item rdf:about="http://.../XML_SVG/download/1.0.0/">
    <title>XML_SVG 1.0.0</title>
    <link>http://pear.php.net/package/XML_SVG/download/1.0.0/</link>
    <description>PHP5 compatible copy() method.</description>
    <dc:date>2005-04-13T19:33:56-05:00</dc:date>
  </item>
  <item rdf:about="http://.../XML_FastCreate/download/1.0.0/">
    <title>XML_FastCreate 1.0.0</title>
    <link>http://pear.php.net/package/XML_FastCreate/download/1.0.0/
                                                            </link>
    <description>BugFix PHP5 ; scripts/example added ; stable
                                            release.</description>
    <dc:date>2005-03-31T10:41:23-05:00</dc:date>
  </item>
  <!--
    ...More item elements have been removed to save space...
```

```
    -->
</rdf:RDF>
```

This document contains information about two things. First is the global information about the **channel** that provides the feed and the feed itself. This information includes the title and the description of the feed, the URL of the website that provides the feed, the language of the feed, and information about the publisher and creator of the feed. Next, the feed contains several entities that describe the news entries in the feed; in this case the news entries refer to package releases. Each of these entries is enclosed in an `<item>` tag and stores the following information:

- Title
- Description
- URL of a page that provides further information about the entry
- Date this information was published

Accessing all the information is extremely easy using XML_RSS; just execute these three steps:

1. Include XML_RSS in your code and create a new instance of XML_RSS.
2. Parse the RSS feed.
3. Fetch the information from the XML_RSS object.

Here is a simple script that extracts the channel information and displays it as HTML.

```
require_once 'XML/RSS.php';

$rss = new XML_RSS('http://pear.php.net/feeds/cat_xml.rss');
$rss->parse();

$channel = $rss->getChannelInfo();

print "Channel data<br />\n";
printf("Title: %s<br />\n", $channel['title']);
printf("Description: %s<br />\n", $channel['description']);
printf("Link: <a href=\"%s\">%s</a><br />\n", $channel['link'],
                                              $channel['link']);
```

Open this script in your browser and you will see the following output:

Channel data

Title: PEAR: Latest releases in category xml

Description: The latest releases in the category xml

Link: http://pear.php.net/

To build a list with the latest releases of all XML-related packages in PEAR you only need to modify the script a bit:

```
require_once 'XML/RSS.php';

$rss = new XML_RSS('http://pear.php.net/feeds/cat_xml.rss');
$rss->parse();

$channel = $rss->getChannelInfo();

print 'Channel data<br />';
printf('Title: %s<br />', $channel['title']);
printf('Description: %s<br />', $channel['description']);
printf('Link: <a href="%s">%s</a><br />', $channel['link'],
                                          $channel['link']);
print '<ul>';
$items = $rss->getItems();
foreach ($items as $item) {
    $date = strtotime($item['dc:date']);
    printf('<li><a href="%s">%s</a> (%s)</li>', $item['link'],
                                               $item['title'],
                                               date('Y-m-d', $date));
}
print '</ul>';
```

This will print an unordered list of the latest ten packages below the general channel information. What's really great about this is that you can use exactly the same script to display the latest releases of any PEAR developer—just replace the URL of the feed with `http://pear.php.net/feeds/user_schst.rss`, for example. You can even use the same script to display a feed from any other website or blog. To display the latest news from `blog.php-tools.net`, just use the URL `http://blog.php-tools.net/feeds/index.rss2` and you will see news from the PAT web log. However you need to make a small adjustment to the script, as RSS version 2 uses `<pubDate/>` instead of the `<dc:date/>` tag. If you want to be able to read and display both RSS versions, just make this small modification to your script:

```
$items = $rss->getItems();
foreach ($items as $item) {
    if (isset($item['dc:date'])) {
        $date = strtotime($item['dc:date']);
    } elseif ($item['pubDate']) {
        $date = strtotime($item['pubDate']);
    }
  printf('<li><a href="%s">%s</a> (%s)</li>', $item['link'],
                                             $item['title'],
```

```
                                           date('Y-m-d', $date));
}
```

Although the PEAR feeds do not use this feature, it is possible to store information about images that should be displayed in conjunction with the feed. XML_RSS provides a method to extract this information from the feed:

```
$images = $rss->getImages();
foreach ($images as $image) {
  $size = getimagesize($image['url']);
  printf('<img src="%s" width="%d" height="%d" alt="%s" /><br />',
           $image['url'],
           $size[0],
           $size[1],
           $image['title']);
}
```

If you append this code snippet to your script you should see an image below the list of news entries in your browser.

As you have seen, integrating a news feed in your website is easy once you start working with the XML_RSS package in PEAR.

Summary

In this chapter, we have learned how to use several PEAR packages that can be used when working with XML. XML_Util, XML_FastCreate, and XML_Serializer can be used to easily create generic XML documents without having to worry about the rules of well-formed XML documents or tag indentation. XML_XUL allows us to create applications for Mozilla-based browsers like Firefox using PHP. This allows us to share the business logic with standard web applications but exchange the front end of our applications with an XUL-based interface.

In the second half of the chapter we have learned how to build a SAX-based parser to read an XML-based configuration file and automatically ignore the parts of the XML document that are not important to us. We have used XML_Unserializer to create arrays and objects from virtually any XML document. This allows us easy access to information stored in an XML document without needing to know anything about the parsing process itself. Last, we used the XML_RSS package to display the contents of an RSS feed in any PHP-based application.

4
Web Services

Web applications are moving closer to the center of today's infrastructures. While desktop applications have been the most important part of software development, more and more companies are moving their applications to the Web so they can be controlled from anywhere with any modern browser. This way, employees need not sit in front of their desktop computer in the office, but are able to use the applications from any place in the world.

Still, these applications often need to connect with other applications as nobody can afford a complete redesign and redevelopment of all the software components used by a company. So quite often these new web applications, often developed in PHP, have to live in a heterogeneous environment and communicate with various applications written in various programming languages like C/C++, Perl, Java, or even COBOL. In times past, developers often used CORBA or COM to enable communication between these applications, but the triumph of the Internet was also the dawn of modern day web services. These web services make use of proven protocols like HTTP, open standards like XML, and applications like web servers.

It all started with a very simple XML-based protocol: XML-RPC, short for XML Remote Procedure Call, was the first of the web service protocols that became popular and still is used by a lot of companies and applications. The evolution of XML-RPC led to SOAP, which takes lot of inspiration from XML-RPC but is a lot more flexible and also more complex. SOAP is now supported by almost every programming language, including PHP.

As these protocols were often too complex or too static for some companies, they developed their own proprietary protocols, usually based on XML. These protocols often have a lot in common with each other and the term REST (Representational State Transfer) has been coined to describe a web service that does not use one of the official protocols, but still is based on HTTP and XML.

In this chapter you will learn about the packages PEAR offers when it comes to working with various web services.

Consuming Web Services

When working with web services, most people start by consuming a service that is offered by somebody else. There are two different reasons why you might want to consume a web service:

1. You need to access customer data that cannot be accessed just by sending queries to the database. The reason for this might be security or the use of a data source not supported by PHP. Often the reason might be that you also want to access business logic that somebody else in your company has already implemented in Java, for example.
2. You want to use a service provided by another company. For example, if you want to integrate a search into your website, why would you bother writing a new search engine, if you could just as well use the search service offered by Google and pay for using this service. It will probably still be cheaper than implementing all the features Google has to offer. The same applies if you want to build an online auction, sell books, etc. There already are companies out there who offer top-notch solutions for a lot of web applications, and by using their services, you can rely on their business logic while maintaining your corporate identity.

In the first part of this chapter we will use web services that rely on the standard protocols XML-RPC and SOAP, using the respective PEAR packages. After that we will take a look at the `Services_Google` package, which makes working with the Google web service even easier, although Google is one of the companies that offer a SOAP-based web service. After working with all of those standard protocols, we will take a look at `Services_Ebay`, which offers an easy-to-use API for the proprietary eBay web services. This is unique, as it is a mixture of typical REST-based services and SOAP. Last, we will use two PEAR packages that are not part of PEAR's web services category to consume REST-based web services. With the help of these two packages you will be able to consume almost any REST-based services, even if there is no proxy implementation available in PEAR.

Consuming XML-RPC-Based Web Services

XML-RPC, the acronym for XML Remote Procedure Call, has been developed by Userland Software. It is a protocol to call functions on a different server using the HTTP protocol by encoding the function calls and the return value in XML. To use an XML-RPC service, you have to compose the XML containing the method name and all function arguments and send it to the server via an HTTP Post request. The server will parse the incoming XML, invoke the method, and create an XML document containing the result value, which will then be sent back to the original caller. Your script will then need to parse the XML it receives and extract the return value of the function.

Userland Software provides a very simple test service, which we will use in the following example. This service is able to return the name of a state of the USA, based on an integer value you pass to the service. The method offered by this service is `examples.getStateName()` and to call this method, you need to compose the following XML document:

```
<?xml version="1.0" encoding="UTF-8"?>
<methodCall>
    <methodName>examples.getStateName</methodName>
    <params>
        <param>
            <value><int>15</int></value>
        </param>
    </params>
</methodCall>
```

If the server receives this XML document, it will decode it and call the method `examples.getStateName()` and pass the integer value `15` as an argument to the method. After invoking the method, the XML-RPC service will create a new XML document containing information about the return value and send this document back to the client who sent the request:

```
<methodResponse>
    <params>
        <param>
            <value><string>Iowa</string></value>
        </param>
    </params>
</methodResponse>
```

So the state represented by the number 15 is Iowa.

This is all you need to know to work with the XML-RPC protocol. With the knowledge you gained about creating and processing XML documents in Chapter 3, you could probably already write your own XML-RPC client. But there is no need to do this as PEAR already provides an easy-to-use XML-RPC implementation. It is probably already installed, as PEAR has been using the XML-RPC protocol for communication between the PEAR installer and the PEAR repository since prior to PEAR version 1.4.0. So all you need to do is include it and use it in your applications.

A script accessing the Userland example service can be written with PEAR's `XML_RPC` package in less than ten lines (if you do not count documentation and error handling):

```
require_once 'XML/RPC.php';

// create a new client
$client = new XML_RPC_Client('/RPC2', 'betty.userland.com');

// encode the parameters for the message
$params = array(
             new XML_RPC_Value(15, 'int')
           );
// encode the method call in XML
$message = new XML_RPC_Message('examples.getStateName', $params);

// send the XML-RPC message
$response = $client->send($message);

// Check whether an error occured
if ($response->faultCode())
{
  echo "Could not use the XML-RPC service.\n";
  echo $response->faultString();
  exit();
}

// get the return value
$value = $response->value();

// decode the XML_RPC_Value object to a plain PHP variable
$stateName = XML_RPC_decode($value);

echo "The state is $stateName\n";
```

As with every script using PEAR, we start by including the package we want to use. Next, we create a new client for the service we plan to access. The constructor of the `XML_RPC_Client` class needs at least two parameters:

- The path of the service on the server (in this case, the service is located at `/RPC2`)
- The hostname of the service (in this case, `betty.userland.com`)

You could also pass more parameters to the constructor if the service is not located on port 80 or if you want to access the service through proxy. If you have to use a proxy with XML_RPC, the manual at http://pear.php.net/manual/en/package.webservices.xml-rpc.php will explain all the parameters you can use. After that we need to compose the XML for the method call we want to send to the server. To do this, we need to follow these steps:

1. First we create a numbered array containing the function arguments as XML_RPC_Value objects. For our simple example, we need only one argument, the integer value for which we want to retrieve the state name. The constructor of the XML_RPC_Value class accepts two parameters: the value to encode and the type of the value. If you omit the type, the type string will be assumed.
2. The newly created array will then be used to encode the actual method call, by creating a new instance of XML_RPC_Message. The constructor of this class requires two parameters: the name of the method to call and an array of XML_RPC_Value objects containing the arguments for the method call. To sum up, two lines of code are needed to create the complete XML document:

```
// encode the parameters for the message
$params = array(new XML_RPC_Value(15, 'int'));
// encode the method call in XML
$message = new XML_RPC_Message('examples.getStateName', $params);
```

To send this XML-RPC message to the service, call the send() method of the client and pass XML_RPC_Message as its sole argument. This method will return an instance of XML_RPC_Response, which represents the XML document that the server sent back.

This object provides an easy way to check whether an error occurred while invoking the remote procedure call. If the faultCode() method of the object does not return zero, it indicates that something has gone wrong. In this case, you can use the faultString() method to get a readable interpretation of the error that happened.

If no error occurred, you can use the value() method to extract the return value from the response. However, this is an instance of XML_RPC_Value, which contains the actual value as well as type information about the value. If you try to print it to the screen, you will not see the name of the state as expected, but something like **Object id #4**. You need to extract the actual value and convert it to a simple PHP value before you can use it. XML_RPC provides the XML_RPC_decode() function, which does this for you. The return value of this function now is the expected string containing the state name. So if you run the script, it will output:

```
The state is Iowa
```

With PEAR, using web services is a lot easier than you probably thought. As this example is of no use in real life, you probably aspire to use a complex web service built with XML-RPC. As the PEAR installer uses XML-RPC for communication with the PEAR website, you might think that you could use the same technique to communicate with the website. And yes, you are correct; this is easily possible with the `XML_RPC` package. If you have PEAR version 1.4.0 or higher installed, the installer is able to tell you which XML-RPC methods the PEAR service for any channel provides. All you need to do is run the command **`pear channel-info pear.php.net`** and you will see something like this:

```
Channel pear.php.net Information:
=================================
Name and Server         pear.php.net
Alias                   pear
Summary                 PHP Extension and Application Repository
Validation Package Name PEAR_Validate
Validation Package      default
Version
Server Capabilities
===================
Type   Version/REST type Function Name/REST base
xmlrpc 1.0               logintest
xmlrpc 1.0               package.listLatestReleases
xmlrpc 1.0               package.listAll
xmlrpc 1.0               package.info
xmlrpc 1.0               package.getDownloadURL
xmlrpc 1.1               package.getDownloadURL
xmlrpc 1.0               package.getDepDownloadURL
xmlrpc 1.1               package.getDepDownloadURL
xmlrpc 1.0               package.search
xmlrpc 1.0               channel.listAll
rest   REST1.0           http://pear.php.net/rest/
```

The highlighted lines list the XML-RPC methods provided by this service. All that you need to know is where the service is located so you can create a new client. For the PEAR website, the service is located at `http://pear.php.net/xmlrpc.php`. So if we want to search the PEAR website for a package that contains the term 'XML' in its name, all that is needed is the following script:

```
require_once 'XML/RPC.php';

$client = new XML_RPC_Client('/xmlrpc.php', 'pear.php.net');

$params = array(new XML_RPC_Value('XML', 'string'));
$message = new XML_RPC_Message('package.search', $params);

$response = $client->send($message);

if ($response->faultCode())
{
```

```
  echo "Could not use the XML-RPC service.\n";
  echo $response->faultString();
  exit();
}

$value = $response->value();
$packages = XML_RPC_decode($value);

foreach ($packages as $packageName => $packageInfo)
{
  echo "<h1>$packageName</h1>\n";
  echo "<p>{$packageInfo['summary']}<p>\n";
}
```

For this example we have used the `package.search()` method provided by the PEAR website service. This method returns an associative array over which we can easily iterate using a simple `foreach()` loop, as if the data had been delivered by any local source. Running this script will output:

```
XML_Beautifier: Class to format XML documents.
XML_CSSML: The PEAR::XML_CSSML package provides methods for creating
cascading style sheets (CSS) from an XML standard called CSSML.
XML_FastCreate: Fast creation of valid XML with DTD control.
XML_fo2pdf: Converts a xsl-fo file to pdf/ps/pcl/text/etc with the
help of apache-fop
XML_HTMLSax: A SAX parser for HTML and other badly formed XML
documents
XML_image2svg: Image to SVG conversion
XML_NITF: Parse NITF documents.
XML_Parser: XML parsing class based on PHP's bundled expat
XML_RPC: PHP implementation of the XML-RPC protocol
XML_RSS: RSS parser
XML_SVG: XML_SVG API
XML_Transformer: XML Transformations in PHP
XML_Tree: Represent XML data in a tree structure
XML_Util: XML utility class.
XML_Wddx: Wddx pretty serializer and deserializer
```

Of course the result might differ, as the packages provided by PEAR change frequently. This is what's really great about using web services; you always get the most current data.

Accessing the Google API

Google is one of the most popular sites to offer its functionality as a web service, and while the API is still labelled beta, it still is one of the most commonly used web services. You can learn more about the Google web service on its website at `http://www.google.com/apis/`. In order to access the Google API you will need to create a Google account. With this registration, you will receive a Google API key that you will have to supply with every request you send to the web service. This account entitles you to make 1,000 requests to the search API per day, free of charge.

As Google offers a SOAP-based service, you could easily use PHP 5's new SOAP extension to query the Google web service. For example, if you want to search for the phrase "Packt Publishing" using the Google API, the following code is required:

```
// Your personal API key
$myGoogleKey = 'YOURKEYHERE';

$google = new SoapClient('http://api.google.com/GoogleSearch.wsdl');
$result = $google->doGoogleSearch(
                $myGoogleKey,                // License key
                'Packt Publishing',          // search phrase
                0,                           // first result
                10,                          // Number of results to
                                                return
                false,                       // do not return similar
                                                results
                '',                          // restrict to topics
                true,                        // filter adult content
                '',                          // language filter
                '',                          // input encoding, ignored
                ''                           // output encoding,
                                                ignored
        );

// Display the titles of the first ten pages
$i = 1;
foreach ($result->resultElements as $entry)
{
  printf("%02d. %s\n", $i++, $entry->title);
}
```

The new SOAP extension is able to create proxy clients from any WSDL document you pass to the constructor. So you can easily call the methods provided by Google on this object. Nevertheless, using the client is not as simple as it could be, as you always have to specify all of the ten parameters although most times you do not even need them. That means you will have to remember the parameter order, otherwise the Google web service will react with a SOAP fault to your query. This is very annoying, as the last two parameters (input and output encoding) are not used by the web service but SOAP requires them to be passed.

With `Services_Google`, PEAR provides an easy-to-use wrapper around the SOAP extension, which makes dealing with the Google API a lot easier. The code required to send exactly the same query using `Services_Google` is a lot easier to read:

```
require_once 'Services/Google.php';

$myGoogleKey = 'GetYourOwnKey';
$google = new Services_Google($myGoogleKey);
$google->queryOptions['limit'] = 10;
$google->search('Packt Publishing');

$i = 1;
foreach($google as $entry)
{
    printf("%02d. %s\n", $i++, $entry->title);
}
```

After including the `Services_Google` class, you have to pass your API key and you can instantly start accessing the Google web service using the methods that `Services_Google` provides. You can easily set the limit for the search by accessing the `queryOptions` property of the newly created object. After that, you invoke the `search()` method and pass the search phrase as its sole argument. However, this will not automatically invoke the web service. The web service will only be used when you start accessing the results of the search. The `Services_Google` class implements the `Iterator` interface, which enables you to use the object like an array in a `foreach` loop as seen in the example. This means that the query will be sent just in time, when you need it.

So if you run this script, your result should look similar to this:

```
01. <b>Packt</b> <b>Publishing</b> Book Store
02. Asterisk
03. User Training for Busy Programmers
04. Building Websites with Mambo
05. Learning eZ publish 3
06. Building Websites with OpenCms
07. Content Management with Plone
08. BPEL
09. Building Online Stores with osCommerce: Beginner Edition
10. <b>Packt</b> <b>Publishing</b> | Gadgetopia
```

Besides the `limit` parameter, several other query options can be specified before using the `search()` method. The following table gives you an overview of the available options. If you are familiar with the Google web service, you will recognise that these are almost the same parameters that can be passed to the `doGoogleSearch()` method of the service.

Option name	Description	Default value
`start`	Number of the first result to fetch	`0`
`maxResults`	Maximum results to fetch at once	`10`
`limit`	Maximum results to fetch in total	`false`
`filter`	Whether to ignore similar results	`true`
`restricts`	Whether to restrict the search to any topics	empty string
`safeSearch`	Whether to ignore adult content	`true`
`language`	Language to restrict the search to	empty string

Still, there is one option that is not native to the Google web service. The limit option can be used to restrict the total number of search results that will be returned by `Services_Google`. The `doGoogleSearch()` method of the web service is only able to return 10 results per invocation. To retrieve the next 10 result pages, you will have to call the web service again.

When using `Services_Google`, this is done automatically for you when iterating over the result set. Just try it by increasing the value used for the `limit` option to 20. To process the results, still only one `foreach` loop is needed.

At the time of writing, Google also offers a spelling suggestion service and the ability to fetch the contents of a page from the Google cache. Of course, `Services_Google` also provides wrappers to access these services. Here is an example of how to access the spelling suggestions:

```
require_once 'Services/Google.php';

$myGoogleKey = 'GetYourOwnKey';

$google = new Services_Google($myGoogleKey);
$suggestion = $google->spellingSuggestion('HTTP portocrol');
echo $suggestion;
```

As expected, this simple script will output the correct spelling **HTTP protocol**. Retrieving a page from the Google cache is also this easy, as the following code shows:

```
require_once 'Services/Google.php';
```

```
$myGoogleKey = 'GetYourOwnKey';

$google = new Services_Google($myGoogleKey);
$html   = $google->getCachedPage('http://pear.php.net/');

echo $page;
```

If you run this script in your browser, you should see the typical output of the Google cache—the original page plus the Google cache page header, which provides information about the cached data.

As you have seen, working with the Google API gets even easier when using the `Services_Google` package.

Consuming REST-Based Web Services

As SOAP is an extremely complex protocol, a lot of the newer services are offered using a simpler protocol called REST. The next part of this chapter is devoted to consuming these services using PHP and PEAR.

Searching Blog Entries with Services_Technorati

While conventional search engines like Google allow you to search for specific keywords on any website, there are several search engines that focus on a smaller part of the Web. One of these specialized search engines is Technorati (`http://www.technorati.com`), a search engine that only searches for your keywords in web logs. Of course, Technorati also offers a web service API for you to use its service in your site; otherwise, we would not deal with it in this chapter. But before we take a deeper look at the API, let us first take a look at how Technorati works.

As a blog owner, you can easily register at for free at Technorati and *claim* your blog. By claiming your blog, you make it available to the Technorati index and Technorati will periodically index all of your blog entries. Apart from this, it will also try to detect links from your blog to other registered web logs and vice versa. This data will be used to calculate the ranking of your blog in the Technorati blog listing. Furthermore Technorati offers a JavaScript snippet that you can easily add to your web log, which adds useful Technorati-related links to your site. Technorati provides step-by-step instructions for claiming new blogs.

Now that we know what Technorati is, let us go back to the API offered by Technorati. When designing its API, it decided that it neither wanted to use XML-RPC nor SOAP for its web service, but defined a proprietary XML-based protocol. However, the transport layer for its protocol still is HTTP. The approach Technorati has been taking is called REST and is getting more and more popular, as it's easier to use than

XML-RPC and SOAP and in most cases provides all the features necessary for the web service API. We will deal with writing REST-based clients and servers later in this chapter. For now, we do not have to worry about the inner workings of REST, as PEAR already provides a client implementation for the Technorati web service. The package you need to install is `Services_Technorati` and you will need at least the packages `HTTP_Request` and `XML_Serializer`. You will probably already have them installed as both are common packages.

After installing the client, you will have to register for the Technorati developers' program at `http://www.technorati.com/developers/devprogram.html` in order to receive your personal API key. Registering at the developers' program is easy; if you already have a standard Technorati account you will have to answer some questions about your plans with the API and agree to the terms and conditions of the developers' program. Once your registration is complete you can access your API key on the website at `http://www.technorati.com/developers/apikey.html`. More information about the API and the developers' program can also be found at the developer wiki at `http://developers.technorati.com/wiki`. If you intend to access the API using `Services_Technorati`, you can skip the information in the wiki, as the package provides an intuitive way to access the service.

Using `Services_Technorati` in your scripts is nearly the same as any other PEAR package:

1. Include the package
2. Set up an instance of the class you want to use
3. Use the methods the object provides

Here is a very simple example that searches for the term "Packt publishing" in all registered web logs:

```
/**
 * Uses the Services_Technorati package
 */
require_once 'Services/Technorati.php';

// Replace this with your API key
$myApiKey = 'YOURKEYHERE';

// Create a new instance based on your key
$technorati = Services_Technorati::factory($myApiKey);

// Use the service, this will return an associative array
$result = $technorati->search('Packt Publishing');
```

```
// Iterate through the result set
$position = 1;
foreach ($result['document']['item'] as $entry)
{
  printf("%02d. %s\n%s\n\n", $position++, $entry['title'],
$entry['excerpt']);
}
```

If you run this script it will output something like this:

```
01. An Evening with Joomla's Mitch Pirtle
Last night BostonPHP hosted an evening with Mitch Pirtle of Joomla!
fame at our our Boston office ...  with the initiative.  <strong
class="keyword">Packt</strong> <strong class="keyword">publishing</
strong>, who sells Building Websites With Mambo, is planning on
<strong class="keyword">publishing</strong> a similar Joomla! book. I
have not recently talked to the Mambo team, which has reloaded

02. Permanent Link to
Building a Custom Module for DotNetNuke 3.0This sample chapter from
<strong class="keyword">Packt</strong> <strong class="keyword">Publ
ishing</strong> "Building Websites with VB.NET and DotNetNuke 3.0"
illustrates how to build and use a custom module

03. Packt Publishing December 2005 Newsletter
The latest <strong class="keyword">Packt</strong> <strong
class="keyword">Publishing</strong> newsletter is available online:
```

Of course the displayed results will differ as there surely will be new blog entries about Packt Publishing by the time you are reading this book.

This example has already demonstrated that you do not need to know anything about the internals of the API as this functionality is hidden inside the `Services_Technorati` package. Of course, searching for blog entries is not all that the package has to offer. If you know the name of any Technorati user, you can easily get information about this user from the Technorati service as the following example demonstrates:

```
/**
 * Uses the Services_Technorati package
 */
require_once 'Services/Technorati.php';

// Replace this with your API key
$myApiKey = 'YOURAPIKEY';

// Create a new instance based on your key
```

```
$technorati = Services_Technorati::factory($myApiKey);

// Get information about any technorati user
$result = $technorati->getInfo('schst');

print_r($result);
```

Just replace the username `schst` with the one you supplied when registering at the Technorati website and you should see information quite similar to this, but of course containing your name:

```
Array
(
    [version] => 1.0
    [document] => Array
        (
            [result] => Array
                (
                [username] => schst
                    [firstname] => Stephan
                    [lastname] => Schmidt
                    [thumbnailpicture] =>
                              http://www.technorati.com/progimages/
                                photo.jpg?uid=132607&amp;mood=default
                )
            [item] => Array
                (
                    [weblog] => Array
                        (
                            [name] => a programmer's best friend
                            [url] => http://blog.php-tools.net
                            [rssurl] =>
                            http://blog.php-tools.net/feeds/index.rss2
                            [atomurl] => http://blog.php-tools.net/
                                                   feeds/atom.xml
                            [inboundblogs] => 0
                            [inboundlinks] => 0
                            [lastupdate] => 2005-10-17 17:51:48 GMT
                            [rank] =>
                            [lat] => 0
                            [lon] => 0
                            [lang] => 26110
                        )
                )
        )
)
```

You could easily use this information to create a profile page with a listing for all blogs a user owns at your own website.

While registering for the developers' program is free, the number of API calls you are allowed to make per day is limited. However, you do not have to count the API calls you made per day to decide whether you still have some calls left, instead you can simply ask the API with a call to:

```
$result = $technorati->keyInfo();
$callsMade = (int)$result['document']['result']['apiqueries'];
$callsMax  = (int)$result['document']['result']['maxqueries'];
$callsLeft = $callsMax - $callsMade;
echo "You have made {$callsMade} of {$callsMax} allowed API calls
                  today. You still have {$callsLeft} API calls left";
```

This will output the number of queries you already made as well as the number of queries you are allowed to make per day. Calls to the `keyInfo()` method do not count as queries, so you may make as many of them as you like per day.

The Technorati Cosmos

The last functionality we will be dealing with is the Technorati cosmos. The cosmos tries to link the different blogs by analyzing all blog entries and extracting links from a blog to all other blogs and vice versa. The following example will explain how the cosmos can be accessed using the `Services_Technorati` API:

```
/**
 * Uses the Services_Technorati package
 */
require_once 'Services/Technorati.php';

// Replace this with your API key
$myApiKey = 'YOURAPIKEY';

// Create a new instance based on your key
$technorati = Services_Technorati::factory($myApiKey);

// Specify further options for the search
// We limit the result to ten links
$options = array('limit' => 10);

//Search blogs linking to the PEAR website
$result = $technorati->cosmos('http://pear.php.net', $options);

// Display some basic information
print "Searching for blogs that link to http://pear.php.net\n\n";
```

```
printf("Number of blogs found: %d\n", $result['document']['result']['i
nboundblogs']);
printf("Number of links found: %d\n", $result['document']['result']['i
nboundlinks']);

// Iterate through the found links
print "\nFirst ten links:\n\n";
foreach ($result['document']['item'] as $link)
{
  printf("Link on %s to %s\n",
         $link['weblog']['name'],
         $link['linkurl']);
}
```

If you execute this script it will output something similar to:

```
Searching for blogs that link to http://pear.php.net

Number of blogs found: 590
Number of links found: 1837

First ten links:

Link on satoru 120% to http://pear.php.net/manual/ja/
Link on satoru 120% to http://pear.php.net/
Link on minfish.jp/blog to http://pear.php.net/package/
Spreadsheet_Excel_Writer
...
Link on Ciro Feitosa | Desenvolvedor Web to http://pear.php.net/
                           packages.php?catpid=7&catname=Database
```

So if you are interested in a topic, Technorati helps you find pages that may provide more information on this topic by providing URLs of blog entries that link to your topic.

In this example we passed a second parameter to the `cosmos()` method to specify a limit for the search results. Most of the methods provided by `Services_Technorati` allow you to pass an additional associative array containing several options. You can find a list of all available methods and their respective options in the PEAR manual at `http://pear.php.net/manual/en/package.webservices.services-technorati.php`.

Accessing the Amazon Web Service

Another website that offers a web service based on a proprietary XML protocol is Amazon.com. Amazon tries to improve sales by offering an associates program where anybody may place links to products offered on the Amazon website. If any customer buys the product after being referred by the associate's website, the partner will receive a commission based on the price of the product.

To further improve sales triggered by the associates, Amazon offers a web service API to its partners so they can include several Amazon-related features on their website.

Setting up an Amazon Account

To use this web service, you need to start by registering as an Amazon associate at `http://www.amazon.com/gp/browse.html/?node=3435371`. After you finish registering as an Amazon associate you can start making money, but if you want to use the web service (and you will surely want to) you will have to create a web services account at `http://www.amazon.com/gp/browse.html/?node=3435361`. Amazon will then send you an email containing a subscription ID that will be used to identify your account when making web service calls. Make sure you save the token somewhere it will not get lost.

Now that you have a subscription ID all you need to do is install the `Services_Amazon` package and all of its dependencies and you can start using the Amazon web service. The package provides two classes that you may use to access the service:

- `Services_Amazon`
- `Services_AmazonECS4`

While `Services_Amazon` implements version 3.0 of the Amazon web service API, `Services_AmazonECS4` implements the new version 4.0 of the API, which is a lot more powerful. Furthermore, `Services_AmazonECS4` provides advanced features like integrated caching for the search results, which can help you improve the performance of your Amazon-based application. As the old version does not provide any features that are missing in the new version, we will focus completely on `Services_AmazonECS4`.

Setting up the package can be done in a few lines:

```
/**
 * Uses the Services_AmazonECS4 class
 */
require_once 'Services/AmazonECS4.php';

// Your subscription id
$subscriptionId = 'YOURAPIKEY';
```

```
// Your associates id
$accociateId = 'schstnet-20';

// create a new client by supplying
// subscription id and associates id
$amazon  = new Services_AmazonECS4($subscriptionId, $accociateId);
$amazon->setLocale('US');
```

Once you have included the class, instantiate a new instance and pass the web service subscription ID. As an optional parameter you may also pass your associate ID. If this ID has been passed, all returned URLs will automatically contain your associate ID so you can include them in your application. Any orders triggered by these links will be attached to your account and you will receive money for them. After the instance has been created, the `setLocale()` method will be used to set the website that will be used for the following API calls.

The following table lists all locales available and their respective Amazon shops.

Locale	Amazon website
US	amazon.com (USA)
UK	amazon.co.uk (United Kingdom)
DE	amazon.de (Germany)
JP	amazon.co.jp (Japan)
FR	amazon.fr (France)
CA	amazon.ca (Canada)

Now that the client is set up correctly, you can start calling the various methods.

Searching the Amazon.com Website

We will start with a very simple keyword-based search on the Amazon.com website with the following example:

```
$options = array();
$options['Keywords'] = 'PEAR';
$result = $amazon->ItemSearch('Books', $options);
```

To search for items we can use the `ItemSearch()` method, which accepts two parameters—the item index in which we want to search and an associative array containing options for the search. In this example we use this option only to supply the keyword we want to search for.

The `ItemSearch()` method will return a `PEAR_Error` object if the search failed or otherwise an array containing the search results as well as meta-information about the search. The following code snippet can be used to react on these two result types and display the data to the user:

```
if (PEAR::isError($result))
{
  print "An error occured\n";
  print $result->getMessage() . "\n";
  exit();
}

foreach ($result['Item'] as $book)
{
    $title  = $book['ItemAttributes']['Title'];
    $author = $book['ItemAttributes']['Author'];
    if (is_array($author))
    {
          $author = implode(', ', $author);
    }
    printf("%s by %s\n", $title, $author);
}
```

The output of the complete script is:

```
Behavior Modification: What It Is and How to Do It (7th Edition) by
Garry L. Martin, Joseph Pear
Web Database Applications with PHP & MySQL, 2nd Edition by
Hugh E. Williams
Learning PHP 5 by David Sklar
PHP Hacks : Tips & Tools For Creating Dynamic Websites (Hacks) by
Jack Herrington
An Instance of the Fingerpost by Iain Pears
The Portrait by Iain  Pears
The Prisoner Pear : Stories from the Lake by Elissa Minor Rust
Dream of Scipio by Iain  Pears
Apples & Pears : The Body Shape Solution for Weight Loss and Wellness
by Marie Savard, Carol Svec
Each Peach Pear Plum board book (Viking Kestrel Picture Books) by
Allan Ahlberg
```

While we expected to get books about the PHP Extension and Application Repository, we instead received several books written by authors named Pear. As we are only interested in books with the term PEAR in the book title, we modify the search request just a little bit:

```
$options = array();
$options['Title'] = 'PEAR';
$result = $amazon->ItemSearch('Books', $options);
```

Instead of using a keyword-based search, we set the key `Title` in the options array and resubmit the search.

The Amazon API documentation

Amazon provides in-depth documentation for all of its web services. This can be found at `http://www.amazon.com/gp/browse.html/?node=3487571`.

The `ItemSearch()` method allows you to supply a huge list of parameters to be passed in the option array and there are two ways of retrieving a complete list of the options for the method. The conventional way would be taking a look at the API documentation. The second way is using the API to get a list of all available parameters directly in your application. This can be done using the `Help()` method of `Services_AmazonECS4`:

```
// create a new client by supplying
// subscription id and associates id
$amazon  = new Services_AmazonECS4($subscriptionId, $accociateId);
$amazon->setLocale('US');

$result = $amazon->Help('Operation', 'ItemSearch');

print "Parameters for ItemSearch()\n";
foreach ($result['OperationInformation']['AvailableParameters']
                                                    ['Parameter']
                                                              as
$param)
{
  echo "* $param\n";
}
```

If you run this script, it will output a list of all parameters that can be set in the options array:

```
Parameters for ItemSearch()
* Actor
* Artist
* AssociateTag
* AudienceRating
```

```
* Author
* Availability
...
* Title
* Validate
* VariationPage
* Version
* XMLEscaping
```

The `Help()` method can be used to retrieve information about any of the methods that the API provides and can even be used to fetch documentation about the `Help()` method itself:

```
$result = $amazon->Help('Operation', 'Help');
print_r($result);
```

The `Help()` method not only provides documentation about the available parameters, but also about the required parameters as well as the possible responses:

```
Array
(
    [Request] => Array
        (
            [IsValid] => True
            [HelpRequest] => Array
                (
                    [About] => Help
                    [HelpType] => Operation
                )

        )
    [OperationInformation] => Array
        (
            [Name] => Help
            [RequiredParameters] => Array
                (
                    [Parameter] => Array
                        (
                            [0] => About
                            [1] => HelpType
                        )
                )
            [AvailableParameters] => Array
                (
                    [Parameter] => Array
```

```
                        (
                            [0] => AssociateTag
                            [1] => ContentType
                            [2] => Marketplace
                            [3] => Style
                            [4] => Validate
                            [5] => Version
                            [6] => XMLEscaping
                        )
                )
            [DefaultResponseGroups] => Array
                (
                    [ResponseGroup] => Array
                        (
                            [0] => Request
                            [1] => Help
                        )
                )
            [AvailableResponseGroups] => Array
                (
                    [ResponseGroup] => Array
                        (
                            [0] => Request
                            [1] => Help
                        )
                )
        )
)
```

If a parameter is in the list of required parameters you do not need to add it to the option array, as the `Services_AmazonECS4` client already requests you to pass the value for the parameter to the method as a separate argument like the `$about` and `$operation` parameters in the `getHelp()` method.

Controlling the Response

In the next example we will be using two more options of the `ItemSearch()` method call: the `Sort` option as well as the `ResponseGroup` option. While the first option is quite self-explanatory, the latter needs to be explained: Amazon stores a lot of information for every article in its range. If a call to `ItemSearch()` returned all available information on every item, the amount of data to be transmitted would grow extremely large. In most cases only parts of the item data is needed in response to a search request and the `ResponseGroup` option allows you to specify the item specific your application needs. This option accepts a comma-separated list of the XML nodes you want the service to return. `Services_AmazonECS4` will automatically convert the XML nodes into associative arrays so they can be accessed using the tag name.

Now let us take a look what can be achieved using the `ResponseGroup` option:

```
// create a new client by supplying
// subscription id and associates id
$amazon  = new Services_AmazonECS4($subscriptionId, $accociateId);
$amazon->setLocale('US');

$options = array();
$options['Publisher'] = 'Packt Publishing';
$options['Sort'] = 'salesrank';
$options['ResponseGroup'] = 'ItemIds,ItemAttributes,Images';
$result = $amazon->ItemSearch('Books', $options);

if (PEAR::isError($result))
{
  print "An error occured<br/>\n";
  print $result->getMessage() . "<br/>\n";
  exit();
}

foreach ($result['Item'] as $book)
{
    print '<div style="margin-bottom:20px; clear:both;">';
    printf('<a href="%s"><img src="%s"
             title="%s" style="float:left; padding-right: 10px;
             border: 0px;"/></a>',
            $book['DetailPageURL'],
            $book['SmallImage']['URL'],
            $book['ItemAttributes']['Title']);
    printf('<h3>%s</h3>', $book['ItemAttributes']['Title']);
    if (is_array($book['ItemAttributes']['Author']))
    {
      $book['ItemAttributes']['Author'] = implode(', ',
                                       $book['ItemAttributes']['Author']);
    }
    printf('<p>%s<br/>%s</p>',
            $book['ItemAttributes']['Author'],
            $book['ItemAttributes']['ListPrice']['FormattedPrice']);
    print '</div>';
}
```

Run this script in your browser and the result will be a listing of ten Packt Publishing books alphabetically sorted, including a small image of the cover as the following screenshot illustrates.

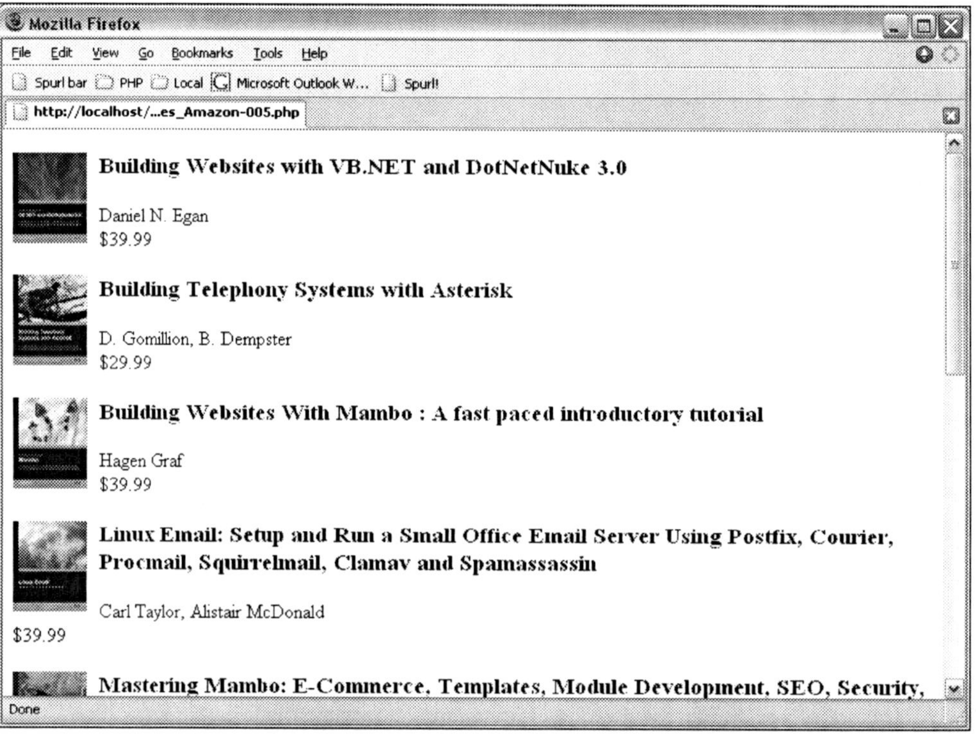

When clicking on the cover of a book you will be redirected to the Amazon website where you can directly order the book and your associate account will be credited for the purchase. This has been achieved by setting the `ResponseGroup` option to `ItemIds,ItemAttributes,Images`, which tells Amazon what kind of information should be returned for each item matching the search criteria.

Using this setting, the following information will be returned:

- `ItemAttributes` will contain an array of all attributes of each book, like its author, the manufacturer, the list price, etc.
- `SmallImage`, `MediumImage`, and `LargeImage` will contain URLs and sizes of cover images.
- `ASIN` will contain the unique ID of the item in the Amazon product catalog.

An easy way to see how the returned information can be accessed using PHP is to pass the return value of the `ItemSearch()` method to PHP's `print_r()` function.

Additional Services

Of course the Amazon web service provides a lot more methods you can use and most of the API calls are already supported by `Services_Amazon`. The range of features includes:

- Remotely controlled carts
- Search for and lookup product details
- Find similar items
- Access wish lists
- Access the Amazon marketplace
- Access customer reviews

All of these features can be accessed in the same manner as shown with the `ItemSearch()` functionality. If you are stuck with a method and are wondering which options you can pass to it, take a look at the excellent API documentation provided by Amazon. All XML tags can directly be mapped to associative arrays.

Finally we will use the `ItemLookup()` API call to illustrate how similar item lookups are to item searches. The `ItemLookup()` call will return information for one item based on its ASIN or ISBN. So if we wanted to get the authors for the excellent *Mastering Mambo* book, which has the ISBN 1-904811-51-5, the following code snippet is required:

```
// create a new client by supplying
// subscription id and associates id
$amazon  = new Services_AmazonECS4($subscriptionId, $accociateId);
$amazon->setLocale('US');

$options = array();
$options['ResponseGroup'] = 'ItemAttributes';
$result = $amazon->ItemLookup('1904811515', $options);

if (PEAR::isError($result))
{
   print "An error occured<br/>\n";
   print $result->getMessage() . "<br/>\n";
   exit();
}

print "The authors are ";
print implode(' and ', $result['Item'][0]['ItemAttributes']['Author']
);
```

If you run this script, it will output:

```
The authors are: Tobias Hauser and Christian Wenz
```

All that differs between the two API calls is the method name and the required arguments that have been passed to the methods. And that's how all methods of `Services_Amazon` work!

Consuming Custom REST Web Services

When using `Services_Technorati` or `Services_Amazon` you have already been using REST-based web services, but the client implementations hid all REST-related details from you. As REST is an emerging technology, you might want to access a service for which PEAR does not yet provide a client implementation. But there is no need to worry, as we will now take a closer look at how easy it is to implement a client for any REST-based web service using two other PEAR packages: `HTTP_Request` and `HTTP_Serializer`.

As an example web service, we will be using the Yahoo! web service for the following reasons:

- You already know Yahoo! and have probably used its web service in some of your applications.
- It is easy to register for the Yahoo! Web service.
- The Yahoo! web service is a typical REST service.
- The Yahoo! web service is well documented and easy to use.

Yahoo! offers most of the functionality it provides on its websites as a REST-based web service as well. In order to use any of its services, you need to get an application ID, which can be done for free at the Yahoo! developer center at `http://api.search.yahoo.com/webservices/register_application`. You need a Yahoo! ID in order to get an application ID, but registering at Yahoo! is free of charge as well. This application ID will be transmitted to the Yahoo! web service every time you use one of its services. This way it can keep track of the API calls you make.

The Yahoo! service is most famous for its search engine, so we will be using the search service as an example for REST-based services. However, it also provides access to the following services:

- `del.icio.us`, its social book marking system
- Flickr, its online photo gallery
- Yahoo! Maps
- The Yahoo! Music Engine

- The Yahoo! shopping catalog
- And many more...

Most of its services can be accessed in the exact same manner as the search web service.

How REST Services Work

Before we take a closer look at the Yahoo! web service, let's understand how REST services work in general. Like XML-RPC and SOAP, they use HTTP as their underlying protocol. However, they do not use HTTP POST to transmit XML data that contains the method call and its parameters; instead they simply use features provided by HTTP to wrap the name of the method and its arguments in the request. In most cases, the method of the API to call is embedded in the path of the URL that is requested and all arguments for the method call are transmitted in the query string. So a typical URL for a REST method call could look like this:

```
http://www.my-site.com/rest/search?query=PEAR&page=1
```

This URL contains all the information you need to access the web service, which is:

- The URL where the service is located (`http://www.my-site.com/rest/`)
- The method to call (`search`)
- The arguments for the method call (`query=PEAR` and `page=1`)

To call the same method using XML-RPC or even SOAP, you would have to create a complex XML document that would be sent to the web service. Still, using a web service the REST way has one disadvantage: all the arguments for the method calls do not contain type information and are transmitted as strings. However, this is not a real disadvantage as the service will know how to handle the arguments and convert them to their respective types. This is exactly how user input is treated in standard PHP applications.

After processing the method call, the service will respond similarly to a SOAP or XML-RPC service and return an XML document. The difference to the two other services is that there is no XML schema to describe the format of the resulting XML document. You may return an XML document that fits the result of the query best. You should check whether the vendor of the service provides a schema or documentation for the return format.

So the result for this query could be something along the lines of:

```
<?xml version="1.0" encoding="ISO-88591-"?>
<searchResult>
  <query>PEAR</query>
```

```
    <currentPage>1</currentPage>
    <results total="25" itemsPerPage="10" pages="3">
      <item ranking="1">
        <url>http://pear.php.net</url>
        <title>The PHP Extension and Application Repository</title>
      </item>
      <item ranking="2">
        <url>http://pear.php-tools.net</url>
        <title>The PAT PEAR Channel</title>
      </item>
      <item ranking="3">
        <url>http://www.pearadise.net</url>
        <title>The PEAR Channel directory</title>
      </item>
      ...
    </results>
  </searchResult>
```

The structure of the XML document is quite self-explanatory and can easily be interpreted by humans as well as an application. The document contains all the information you would expect from a method call to a search function:

- The total number of search results (25)
- The number of items per page (10)
- The number of pages (3)
- Detailed information about each search result

If you stuffed the same amount of information into a SOAP response, the data to construct, transmit, and parse would be a lot more, leading to longer response times for your search application. Again, the only disadvantage of using REST is the loss of type information for the return values but as PHP is a loosely-typed language this probably won't frighten you.

To call a REST-based web service you will have to follow these simple steps:

1. Construct the URL for the call including all arguments
2. Make an HTTP request and extract the XML document from the response
3. Parse the XML document and extract the information you need

Now that you know how REST basically works we will get back to the Yahoo! web service and learn how PEAR can aid you in performing these steps.

Accessing the Yahoo API

In our first example we will access Yahoo's web search, which probably is the most commonly used API. Documentation for the service is available at `http://developer.yahoo.net/search/web/V1/webSearch.html`. To access the service, we will have to make a HTTP request to `http://api.search.yahoo.com/WebSearchService/V1/webSearch`. If you open this URL in your browser, you will see the following XML document as a response:

```
<?xml version="1.0" encoding="UTF-8"?>
<Error xmlns="urn:yahoo:api">
  The following errors were detected:
  <Message>invalid value: appid</Message>
</Error>
<!-- ws02.search.re2.yahoo.com uncompressed/chunked Sun Jan  8
04:19:54 PST

 2006 -->
```

This error message reminds you to pass the application ID to every request you make to this service. So the request URL needs to be modified by appending it and now is `http://api.search.yahoo.com/WebSearchService/V1/webSearch?appid=YOURAPIKE Y`. However, this still results in an error:

```
<?xml version="1.0" encoding="UTF-8"?>
<Error xmlns="urn:yahoo:api">
  <Title>The following errors were detected:</Title>
  <Message>invalid value:   query</Message>
</Error>
<!-- ws02.search.re2.yahoo.com uncompressed/chunked Sun Jan  8
04:23:28 PST

 2006 -->
```

While you are now correctly accessing the search service, you did not tell the service what you want to search for and so it reacts with an error message. To finally get some useful results, you will have to append `&query=PEAR` to the URL to search the Yahoo! directory for the term PEAR. If you open the modified URL in your browser, it will return the following XML document:

```
<?xml version="1.0" encoding="UTF-8"?>
<ResultSet xmlns:xsi="http://www.w3.org/2001/XMLSchema-instance"
             xmlns="urn:yahoo:srch"
             xsi:schemaLocation="urn:yahoo:srch
               http://api.search.yahoo.com/WebSearchService/V1/
WebSearchResponse.xsd"
             totalResultsAvailable="1426310"
             totalResultsReturned="10"
```

```
    firstResultPosition="1">
     <Result>
       <Title>PEAR :: The PHP Extension and Application Repository</Title>
       <Summary>
         ... PEAR provides the above mentioned PHP components in the form
             of so called &quot;Packages&quot;. If you would like to
             download PEAR
         packages, you can browse the complete ...
       </Summary>
       <Url>http://pear.php.net/</Url>
       <ClickUrl>http://pear.php.net/</ClickUrl>
       <ModificationDate>1136534400</ModificationDate>
       <MimeType>text/html</MimeType>
     </Result>
     <Result>
       <Title>PEAR :: Package :: PEAR</Title>
       <Summary>
         ... The PEAR package contains: * the PEAR installer, for creating,
         distributing ...
       </Summary>
       <Url>http://pear.php.net/package/PEAR</Url>
       <ClickUrl>http://pear.php.net/package/PEAR</ClickUrl>
       <ModificationDate>1135065600</ModificationDate>
       <MimeType>text/html</MimeType>
       <Cache>
         <Url>http://216.109.125.130/...1&amp;.intl=us</Url>
         <Size>12366</Size>
       </Cache>
     </Result>
     <!-- More Result elements... -->
   </ResultSet>
   <!-- ws02.search.re2.yahoo.com compressed/chunked Sun Jan  8 04:27:41
   PST 2006

         -->
```

This XML document contains information about all websites contained in the Yahoo index that contain the term PEAR. For each of the items you will find a title, a short summary, a URL, and cache information if Yahoo! offers a cached version of the page.

Now let's try to implement a PHP script that sends the same API call to the service and extracts the title and summary from the result. For this we will follow the three steps we described before and construct the request URL. For this task, we will use the `HTTP_Request` package to execute the request:

```
/**
 * Use HTTP_Request to make the HTTP connection
 */
require_once 'HTTP/Request.php';

// Create a new request object based on the API URL
$request = new HTTP_Request('http://api.search.yahoo.com/
WebSearchService/V1/webSearch');

// append the request parameters
$request->addQueryString('appid', 'packt-pear-book');
$request->addQueryString('query', 'PEAR');

// Send the HTTP request and capture the response
$request->sendRequest();

// Check, whether the request was successful
if ($request->getResponseCode() == 200)
{

    // Display the resulting XML document
    echo $request->getResponseBody();
}
```

After instantiating a new `HTTP_Request` object, we can append as many GET parameters as we like and the class will automatically apply the URL encoding to the arguments so your URLs are valid. Then we use the `sendRequest()` method to actually send the request to the service and check the response code to determine whether the request was successful. The `getResponseBody()` method gives us access to the XML document returned from the service. As you can see, the `HTTP_Request` package helped us executing the first two steps in only six lines of code and we can now continue with parsing the XML document.

In Chapter 3 we got familiar with `XML_Unserializer`, a package that turns nearly every XML document into a PHP data structure. Here we will use `XML_Unserializer` to extract all available data from the service response to process it in our application.

```
/**
 * XML_Unserializer will parse the XML for us
 */
require_once 'XML/Unserializer.php';

$us = new XML_Unserializer();
// extract data from attributes
```

```
$us->setOption(XML_UNSERIALIZER_OPTION_ATTRIBUTES_PARSE, true);

// create arrays
$us->setOption(XML_UNSERIALIZER_OPTION_COMPLEXTYPE, 'array');

// decode UTF-8 to ISO-8859-1
$us->setOption(XML_UNSERIALIZER_OPTION_ENCODING_SOURCE, 'UTF-8');
$us->setOption(XML_UNSERIALIZER_OPTION_ENCODING_TARGET, 'ISO-8859-1');

// If only one result is returned still create an indexed array
$us->setOption(XML_UNSERIALIZER_OPTION_FORCE_ENUM, array('Result'));

// parse the XML document
$result = $us->unserialize($request->getResponseBody());

// check whether an error occured
if (PEAR::isError($result))
{
  echo "An error occured: ";
  echo $result->getMessage();
}

// fetch the result
$result = $us->getUnserializedData();
```

After instantiating the `XML_Unserializer` object we need to set several options to influence the parsing behaviors. First, we tell `XML_Unserializer` to process attributes, as the root node of the result document contains some attributes that might be important to us. Second, we decide that `XML_Unserializer` should create arrays instead of objects from nested tags. As Yahoo! returns UTF-8 encoded data and we prefer working with ISO-8859-1 encodings, we can use `XML_Unserializer` to decode all data in attributes and text nodes to ISO-8859-1 encoding. Last, we make sure that the `<Result/>` tag will always be stored in a numbered array no matter how often it occurs. This will make sure that there is an array to iterate over, irrespective of whether one or more pages have been found.

After setting all options, we pass the XML document to `XML_Unserializer` and let it work its magic. The return value of `unserialize()` could signal an error if the XML document contained any errors, so we check for a `PEAR_Error` prior to continuing. If no error occurred, we fetch the unserialized data, which is now an array with the following structure:

```
Array (
  [xmlns:xsi] => http://www.w3.org/2001/XMLSchema-instance
  [xmlns] => urn:yahoo:srch
```

```
    [xsi:schemaLocation] => urn:yahoo:srch
          http://api.search.yahoo.com/WebSearchService/V1/
  WebSearchResponse.xsd
    [totalResultsAvailable] => 1426310
    [totalResultsReturned] => 10
    [firstResultPosition] => 1
    [Result] => Array
      (
        [0] => Array
          (
            [Title] =>
              PEAR :: The PHP Extension and Application Repository
            [Summary] =>
              ... PEAR provides the above mentioned PHP components
                  in the form of so called "Packages". If you would
                  like to download PEAR packages, you can browse
                        the complete ...
            [Url] => http://pear.php.net/
            [ClickUrl] => http://pear.php.net/
            [ModificationDate] => 1136534400
            [MimeType] => text/html
          )
        [1] => Array
          (
            [Title] => PEAR :: Package :: PEAR
            [Summary] => ... The PEAR package contains:
             * the PEAR installer, for creating, distributing ...
            [Url] => http://pear.php.net/package/PEAR
            [ClickUrl] => http://pear.php.net/package/PEAR
            [ModificationDate] => 1135065600
            [MimeType] => text/html
            [Cache] => Array
              (
             [Url] => http://216.109.125.130/search/cache?appid=packt-
                    pear-book&query=PEAR&ei=UTF-8&u=pear.php.net/
                   package/PEAR&w=pear&d=aD-jIw0DMFBh&icp=1&.intl=us
                [Size] => 12366
              )
          )
        ...more results ...
  )
```

This array contains the exact same information as the XML document and can easily be traversed using a `foreach` loop:

```
// iterate over the result
```

```
foreach ($result['Result'] as $item)
{
    printf("%s\n", $item['Title']);
    printf("%s\n\n", $item['Summary']);
}
```

If you run the complete script, it will search for the term PEAR in the Yahoo! directory and display the results nicely formatted:

```
PEAR :: The PHP Extension and Application Repository
... PEAR provides the above mentioned PHP components in the form of so
called "Packages". If you would like to download PEAR packages, you
can browse the    complete ...

PEAR :: Package :: PEAR
... The PEAR package contains: * the PEAR installer, for creating,
distributing ...

Pear - Wikipedia, the free encyclopedia
From Wikipedia, the free encyclopedia. Pear. Genus: Pyrus. L. Pears
are trees of the genus Pyrus and the fruit of that tree, edible in
some species. ... are important for edible fruit production, the
European Pear Pyrus communis cultivated mainly in Europe and North ...
also known as Asian Pear or Apple Pear), both grown mainly in ...
```

`HTTP_Request` and `XML_Unserializer` may be used in exactly the same fashion to access nearly every REST-based web service. The only work left to you is to read the documentation of the service so you know which values to expect.

In the first half of this chapter, we learned how to access XML-RPC and SOAP-based web services as well as how to use some client implementations for proprietary web services offered by PEAR. In the second part of this chapter, we will take a closer look at offering services using several PEAR packages.

Offering a Web Service

Now that you have understood how to consume different types of web services with PHP and PEAR you are probably interested in learning how to offer a web service. So in the second part of this chapter we will use the `XML_RPC` package to offer a simple service that can easily be consumed by different clients and programming languages. Further we will offer the exact same functionality as a SOAP service and will see how intuitive working with SOAP and WSDL can be when using PHP 5 and `Services_Webservice`. Last we will offer a REST-based service using nothing more than a web server, PHP, and `XML_Serializer`.

Offering XML-RPC-Based Web Services

In the first part of this chapter we started our excursion into the field of web services by building an XML-RPC client. So what better way to start off the second part than by building our very first XML-RPC service that can be consumed by any XML-RPC client?

Creating an XML-RPC service is also quite easy using the same `XML_RPC` package we already used for building the client. This package not only provides functionality to build request messages and parse response messages, but it also provides the matching functionality needed to create a server:

- First, the server needs to extract the XML document sent by the client from the POST data of the HTTP Request.
- Second, the XML document must be parsed so that the name of the called function or method and the passed parameters can be extracted.
- Somehow this method needs to be invoked and the return value of the method must again be encoded in an XML-RPC-style XML document, which will be sent back to the client.

Before we get into the details of how to build an XML-RPC service, we need to implement some functionality that we will offer as a web service. As we will focus on the XML-RPC implementation, our example function should be as easy as possible. So let us go back to the record label we used in Chapter 3. All the classes required for the record label are stored in one file named `record-label.php`:

```
/**
 * List of available artists and the records
 * they released
 *
 * This list would surely be replaced by a database
 * if the web service were a real-life application
 */
$records = array('Elvis Presley' =>
            array('That\'s All Right (Mama) & Blue Moon Of Kentucky',
                  'Good Rockin\' Tonight',
                 ),
                'Carl Perkins'  => array(
                                    'Gone, Gone, Gone'
                                   )
               );

/**
 * get all records for an artist
```

```
 *
 * @access   public
 * @param    string          Name of the artist
 * @return   array|boolean   Array with all records, or false,
 *                           if the artist does not exist
 */
function getRecords($artist)
{
    // Replace this by a database query in real-life
    global $records;
    if (isset($records[$artist]))
    {
        return $records[$artist];
    }
    return false;
}
```

This is a very simple implementation of a function that returns all records that an artist recorded. The artists and their recorded albums are stored in a global array for the sake of simplicity. If you develop this application for an actual record label you would surely store this information in a database so that label owners can easily edit the data of the artists and their records. But for our example this code is sufficient. If we call the `getRecords()` function and pass the name of an artist (say Elvis Presley), we get the following result:

```
Array
(
    [0] => That's All Right (Mama) & Blue Moon Of Kentucky
    [1] => Good Rockin' Tonight
)
```

If we pass in the name of an artist that does not exist, the function will return `false`.

Now that we have finished implementing the business logic, we can start implementing the XML-RPC server. The `XML_RPC` package provides an `XML_RPC_Server` class, which does most of the work for us. This class will parse the XML message sent by the client and convert it to an `XML_RPC_Message` object (actually the same we created using the `XML_RPC` package on the client). It will then extract the name of the function to be called from the message and will check whether we registered a PHP function that matches this function name. If yes, it will call the PHP function and pass the `XML_RPC_Message` as an argument to this function.

This means that the function we implement has to be able to work with an `XML_RPC_Message` argument, but our `getRecords()` function expects a string to be passed.

In order to create a new service we will have to wrap our business logic with a new `getRecordsService()` function, which extracts the artist parameter from the `XML_RPC_Message` and calls the `getRecords()` function with this string:

```
function getRecordsService($args)
{
    $artist  = $args->getParam(0)->scalarval();
    $records = getRecords($artist);
}
```

After calling `getRecords()`, the `$records` variable should either contain an array or return `false` if the artist is unknown. We could try just returning this value and hope that the rest of the service will work automatically. But sadly enough, this will not work. Instead, we have to encode the return value of the function as an `XML_RPC_Value` and enclose this value in an `XML_RPC_Response`:

```
function getRecordsService($args)
{
    $artist  = $args->getParam(0)->scalarval();
    $records = getRecords($artist);
    $val = XML_RPC_encode($records);
    $response = new XML_RPC_Response($val);
    return $response;
}
```

This works exactly like encoding the values on the client and creating a new message. Now all that is left to do is create a new server and register this wrapper function as an XML-RPC function. Here is the code required for the complete server:

```
/**
 * Include the actual business logic
 */
require_once 'record-label.php';

/**
 * Include the XML-RPC server class
 */
require_once 'XML/RPC/Server.php';

/**
 * XML-RPC wrapper for this business logic
 *
 * @access  public
 * @param   XML_RPC_Message     The message send by the client
 * @return  XML_RPC_Response    The encoded server response
```

```
 */
function getRecordsService($args)
{
    $artist  = $args->getParam(0)->scalarval();
    $records = getRecords($artist);
    $val = XML_RPC_encode($records);
    $response = new XML_RPC_Response($val);
    return $response;
}

// map XML-RPC method names to PHP function
$map = array(
        'label.getRecords' => array(
                                   'function' => 'getRecordsService'
                                  )
            );

// create and start the service
$server = new XML_RPC_Server($map);
```

The `$map` array that is passed to the constructor of the `XML_RPC_Server` class is used to map the exposed RPC methods to the matching PHP function. The server will pass the `XML_RPC_Message` received as the sole argument to this PHP function.

After finishing our first server, we want to test whether it works as expected. But if you open the server URL in your browser, you will see the following error message:

```
faultCode 105 faultString XML error: Invalid document end at line 1
```

If you take a look at the source code of the page, you will see that this is actually an XML document, which has been treated as HTML by your browser:

```
<?xml version="1.0" encoding="UTF-8"?>
<methodResponse>
<fault>
  <value>
    <struct>
      <member>
        <name>faultCode</name>
        <value><int>105</int></value>
      </member>
      <member>
        <name>faultString</name>
        <value><string>XML error: Invalid document end at line 1
                                                  </string></value>
      </member>
```

```
      </struct>
    </value>
  </fault>
  </methodResponse>
```

This XML document signals that the XML-RPC server wants to send an error message to the client because it is not intended to be used by a browser, but an XML-RPC client. So to test our new service we will have to implement a client for it. As we have learned before, this is easy using the `XML_RPC` package:

```
require_once 'XML/RPC.php';

$client = new XML_RPC_Client('/record-label.php', 'localhost');

$params = array(
                  new XML_RPC_Value('Elvis Presley', 'string')
                );
$message = new XML_RPC_Message('label.getRecords', $params);

$response = $client->send($message);

if ($response->faultCode())
{
  echo "Could not use the XML-RPC service.\n";
  echo $response->faultString();
  exit();
}

$value = $response->value();
$records = XML_RPC_decode($value);

print_r($records);
```

Make sure that you adjusted the path and the hostname in the constructor of the `XML_RPC_Client` so it matches your local configuration. Now if you run this script, it will call the `getRecords()` method and pass `Elvis Presley` as a parameter to it. The script should now output:

```
Array
(
    [0] => That's All Right (Mama) & Blue Moon Of Kentucky
    [1] => Good Rockin' Tonight
)
```

Error Management

If you try to replace the method you are calling with any method you did not implement, the service will automatically trigger an error, which will be caught by the client and can be checked via the `faultCode()` method. So if we change one line in the client script to:

```
$message = new XML_RPC_Message('label.getArtists', $params);
```

The output of the script is:

```
Could not use the XML-RPC service. Unknown method
```

As we did not implement the method, the service will signal the error automatically without any intervention needed by the developer. But of course the user still could make some mistake while using the client, for example if there is a typo in the name of the artist that he or she passes in:

```
$params = array(
                    new XML_RPC_Value('Elvis Prely', 'string')
                 );
$message = new XML_RPC_Message('label.getRecords', $params);
```

If you run this script, the output is:

```
0
```

This happens because the original `getRecords()` method returns `false` when receiving an unknown artist and, as PHP is not type-safe, this results in the return value `0` on the client. Of course it would be better to signal an error in the XML-RPC server, which can be caught by the client as well. Signaling an error can be done by using a different signature for the `XML_RPC_Response` constructor. Instead of passing in an `XML_RPC_Value`, we pass `0` as the first parameter, followed by a fault code and a textual error message:

```
function getRecordsService($args)
{
    $artist  = $args->getParam(0)->scalarval();
    $records = getRecords($artist);
    if ($records === false)
    {
        $response = new XML_RPC_Response(0, 50,
                  'The artist "'.$artist.'" is not in our database.');
    } else
    {
       $val = XML_RPC_encode($records);
       $response = new XML_RPC_Response($val);
    }
```

```
        return $response;
    }
```

If we run the client script again after we have made this change, it will now output:

```
Could not use the XML-RPC service. The artist "Elvis Prely" is not in
our database.
```

This will tell the client a lot more about the problem that occurred than just returning `0`. Now there is only one problem left. Imagine a client calling the method without any parameters at all:

```
$message = new XML_RPC_Message('label.getRecords');
```

This will result in the following output:

```
Could not use the XML-RPC service. Invalid return payload: enable
debugging to examine incoming payload
```

If we enable debugging in the client using `$client->setDebug(1);` we will see the source of the problem:

```
<b>Fatal error</b>:  Call to undefined method XML_RPC_Response::
scalarval() in <b>/var/www/record-label.php</b> on line <b>21</b><br />
```

We tried to call the `scalarval()` method on an `XML_RPC_Value` that is not present in the actual request. We could easily solve this by checking whether a parameter has been passed in and signaling a fault otherwise, but there is an easier way to automate this. When creating the dispatch map for the XML-RPC service, besides defining a PHP function for each method of the service, it is also possible to specify the method signature for this method:

```
$map = array('label.getRecords' =>
             array(
                    'function'  => 'getRecordsService',
                    'signature' =>
                         array(
                                array('array', 'string'),
                              ),
                    'docstring' => 'Get all records of an artist.'
                  )
            );
```

The signature is an array as it is possible to overload the method and use it with different signatures. For each permutation you have to specify the return type (in this case an array) and the parameters the method accepts. As our method only accepts a string, we only define one method signature. Now if you run the client again, there will be a new error message, which is a lot more useful:

```
Could not use the XML-RPC service. Incorrect parameters passed to
method: Signature permits 1 parameters but the request had 0
```

You probably already noticed the additional entry `docstring` that we added to the dispatch map in the last example. This has been added to showcase another feature of the `XML_RPC_Server` class—it automatically adds to each XML-RPC service several methods that provide introspection features. This allows you to get a list of all supported methods of the service via any XML-RPC client:

```
require_once 'XML/RPC.php';

$client = new XML_RPC_Client('/record-label.php', 'localhost');

$message = new XML_RPC_Message('system.listMethods');

$response = $client->send($message);

$value = $response->value();
$methods = XML_RPC_decode($value);

print_r($methods);
```

If you run this script, it will display a list of all methods offered by the service:

```
Array
(
    [0] => label.getRecords
    [1] => system.listMethods
    [2] => system.methodHelp
    [3] => system.methodSignature
)
```

In the same way you can also get more information about one of the supported methods, which is why we added the `docstring` property to our dispatch map:

```
$message = new XML_RPC_Message('system.methodHelp',
                              array(new XML_RPC_Value(
                              'label.getRecords')));
$response = $client->send($message);

$value = $response->value();
$help = XML_RPC_decode($value);

echo $help;
```

Running this script will display the help text we added for the `label.getRecords()` method. Whenever you implement an XML-RPC based service, you should always add this information to the dispatch map to make it easier for service consumers to use your service.

Now you know everything that you need to offer your own XML-RPC-based web service with the `XML_RPC` package and you can start offering your services to a variety of users, applications, and programming languages.

Offering SOAP-Based Web Services

Since we have successfully offered an XML-RPC based service, we will now take the next step and offer a web service based on SOAP. Prior to PHP 5 this was extremely hard, but since version 5, PHP offers a new SOAP extension that does most of the work you need. We have already used this extension previously in this chapter, as `Services_Google` is only a wrapper around ext/soap that adds some convenience to it.

As the SOAP extension is already provided by PHP, you may wonder why a PHP package is still required. Well, one of the biggest drawbacks of the current SOAP extension is that it is not able to create WSDL documents from existing PHP code. WSDL is short for Web Service Description Language and is an XML format used to describe SOAP-based web services. A WSDL document contains information about the methods a web service provides and the signatures of these methods as well as information about the namespace that should be used and where to find the actual service. Writing WSDL documents manually is quite painful and error prone, as they contain a lot of information that is not very intuitive to guess and are often extremely long. For example, the WSDL document describing the Google web service is over 200 lines long, although Google only offers three methods in its current service.

All the information contained in the WSDL document could easily be extracted from the PHP code or the documentation of the PHP code and writing it by hand is often duplicate work. Most modern programming languages already support automatic WSDL generation and with the `Services_Webservice` package, PEAR finally brings this functionality to PHP. Although the package is relatively new, it makes implementing web services a piece of cake. `Services_Webservice` aims at automating web service generation and takes a driver-based approach, so it will eventually be possible to support not only SOAP, but also XML-RPC and possibly even REST. Currently only SOAP is supported.

Using `Services_Webservice`, you do not have to worry about the internals of SOAP at all; you only implement the business logic and pass this business logic to the package and it will automatically create the web service for you. As SOAP is mostly used in conjunction with object-oriented languages and PEAR is mainly OO-code as well, `Services_Webservice` expects you to wrap the business logic in classes. That means we have to start with a new implementation of the business logic and once again, we will be using our record label as an example. We can borrow a lot of code from the XML-RPC example, and wrap it all in one `RecordLabel` class, which should be saved in a file called `RecordLabel.php`:

```
/**
 * Offers various methods to access
 * the data of our record label.
 */
class RecordLabel
{
    /**
     * All our records.
     *
     * Again, in real-life we would fetch the data
     * from a database.
     */
    private $records =
         array(
                'Elvis Presley' =>
                  array(
                   'That\'s All Right (Mama) & Blue Moon Of Kentucky',
                          'Good Rockin\' Tonight',
                        ),
                'Carl Perkins'  => array(
                                          'Gone, Gone, Gone'
                                        )
              );

   /**
    * Get all records of an artist
    *
    * @param string
    * @return string[]
    */
    public function getRecords($artist)
    {
        $result = array();
        if (isset($this->records[$artist]))
        {
            $result = $this->records[$artist];
        }
        return $result;
```

```
    }

    /**
     * Get all artists we have under contract
     *
     * @return string[]
     */
    public function getArtists()
    {
        return array_keys($this->records);
    }
}
```

Again, we store the data in a simple array in a private property for the sake of simplicity. Our new class `RecordLabel` provides two methods, `getArtists()` and `getRecords()`. Both of them are quite self-explanatory. We also added `PHPDoc` comments to all the methods and the class itself, because those are evaluated by the `Services_Webservice` package. If you take a closer look, you will see a comment that will probably seem a bit strange to you. Both methods return a simple PHP array, but the doc block states `string[]` as the return type. This is because SOAP is intended to allow communication between various different programming languages and while PHP uses loose typing and an array in PHP could contain strings, integers, objects, and even arrays, this is not possible in typed languages like Java, where an array may only contain values of the same type. If you create an array in Java, you will have to tell the compiler what types the array will contain. In order to allow communication between these languages, SOAP establishes rules that must be fulfilled by all SOAP implementations and so the PHP implementation of `getRecords()` and `getArtists()` agrees that they will return arrays that only contain strings. The syntax of the doc comment is borrowed from Java, where you also just append `[]` behind a type to create an array of this type.

Apart from that, the code looks exactly like any standard PHP 5 OO code you are using everyday; there is no evidence of web services anywhere in it. Nevertheless, it can be used to create a new web service in less than ten lines of code, as the following example will prove:

```
// Include the business logic
require_once 'RecordLabel.php';
// Include the package
require_once 'Services/Webservice.php';

// Specify SOAP options
$options = array(
                 'uri' => 'http://www.my-record-label.com',
```

```
                    'encoding' => SOAP_ENCODED
                   );

// Create a new webservice
$service = Services_Webservice::factory('SOAP', 'RecordLabel',
                                        'http://www.my-record-label.com',
                                           $options);
$service->handle();
```

After including the business logic and the `Services_Webservice` class, all we need to do is specify two SOAP options:

- The namespace that uniquely identifies our web service
- The encoding we want to use for the web service

After that, we use the factory method of the `Services_Webservice` class to create a new web service by passing the following arguments:

- Type of the web service to create (currently only SOAP is supported)
- Name of the class that provides the methods (can also be an instance of this class)
- Namespace to use
- Array containing special options for the web service

The factory method will then return a new instance of `Services_Webservice_SOAP`, which can easily be started by calling the `handle()` method. If you open this script in your browser, it will automatically generate a help page that describes your web service, as the following image shows.

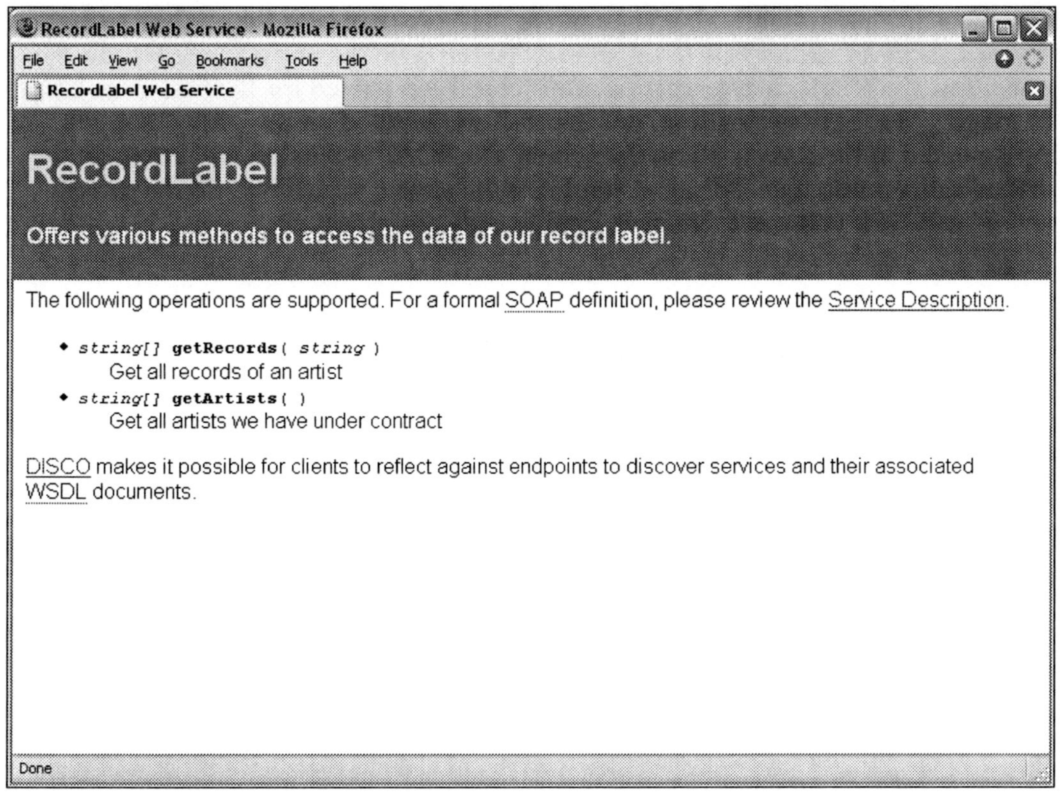

`Services_Webservice` automatically extracted the information from the doc blocks to display information about the web service itself (extracted from the class-level `docblock`) and each of the methods offered by the service. The help page also includes two links: one to the matching WSDL document and one to the matching DISCO document. A DISCO document is an XML document that contains information on where to find the WSDL documents that describe the web service.

`Services_Webservice` generates both these documents automatically and you can access them by appending `?wsdl` or `?DISCO` to the URL of your script. Now your web service can already easily be consumed by any client that supports SOAP-based web services. Of course we want to test it before making it public, but as `Services_Webservice` generates a WSDL document, this is extremely easy. Here is a test script that uses the SOAP extension of PHP 5:

```
$client = new SoapClient('http://localhost/record-label.php?wsdl');

$artists = $client->getArtists();
print_r($artists);
```

The new SOAP extension is able to generate PHP proxy objects for a SOAP web service directly from any WSDL document. To improve the performance of the proxy generation, the WSDL is even cached after it has been parsed for the first time. Using the magic `__call()` overloading, you can call any method on the proxy that you implemented in the class used on the server. The SOAP extension will intercept the method call, encode it in XML, and send it to the server, which will do the actual method call. So if you run this script, it will output as expected:

```
Array
(
    [0] => Elvis Presley
    [1] => Carl Perkins
)
```

You can call the second method that has been implemented in the same way:

```
$client = new SoapClient('http://localhost/record-label.php?wsdl');

$artists = $client->getArtists();
foreach ($artists as $artist)
{
    echo "$artist recorded:\n";
   $records = $client->getRecords($artist);
   foreach ($records as $record)
    {
          echo "...$record\n";
   }
}
```

In your scripts you do not need to worry about SOAP at all; just implement the logic on the server as if it were used locally and on the client you can access the data as if you were working with the `RecordLabel` object.

Error Management

Up to now we have not worried about signaling errors from the server, but as you will see, this is also extremely easy. Suppose we want to signal an error if someone tries to fetch all records by an artist that is not available in the database. All you need to do is change the business logic to throw an exception in this case:

```
/**
 * Get all records of an artist
 *
 * @param string
 * @return string[]
```

```
    */
    public function getRecords($artist)
    {
        if (isset($this->records[$artist]))
        {
            $result = $this->records[$artist];
            return $result;
        }
          else
        {
            throw new SoapFault(50,
                   'The artist "'.$artist.'" is not in our database.');
        }
    }
```

The `SoapFault` exception will be transported to the client, where you can easily catch the error:

```
try
{
    $records = $client->getRecords('Foo');
}
catch (SoapFault $f)
{
     echo "An error occured.\n";
     echo $f;
}
```

Besides extracting documentation and signatures, `Services_Webservice` is able to use further information from the doc blocks. If the use of a method is discouraged because there is a newer method that should be used instead, you just have to add `@deprecated` to the doc block:

```
   /**
    * Get all of Elvis' records.
    *
    * @return string[]
    * @deprecated Use getRecords() instead
    */
    public function getRecordsByElvis()
    {
        return $this->getRecords('Elvis Presley');
    }
```

This method will be marked as deprecated in the generated help page as well.

Last, it is also possible to hide some methods from the web service; this enables you to implement some helper methods that can only be called from the local server:

```
/**
 * This is a helper method and not visible by the web service.
 *
 * @webservice.hidden
 */
public function doSomeHelperStuff()
{
    // no code here, just a dummy method
}
```

With all these features of the new SOAP extension in PHP 5 and the `Services_Webservice` package, using SOAP-based web services is even easier than using XML-RPC.

Offering REST-Based Services using XML_Serializer

Now that you have used XML-RPC and SOAP to build standard web services to make your business logic accessible by anybody with an internet connection, you might wonder why you needed those standards in the first place. SOAP is extremely complex and leads to verbose XML, which in turn leads to more traffic and lower response rates of your service. A lot of companies have been asking these questions lately and REST has become more and more popular. So if you do not need the advantages of SOAP like interoperability and auto-generation of clients using WSDL, REST might be the best solution for your company.

REST makes use of the proven technologies HTTP and XML without adding a complicated syntax. Instead of encoding your request parameters in a complex XML document, it uses a feature that the HTTP standard already provides—parameters encoded in the URL. Calling a remote method in XML-RPC (which still is a lot simpler than SOAP) requires the following code:

```
<?xml version="1.0" encoding="UTF-8"?>
<methodCall>
    <methodName>label.getRecords</methodName>
    <params>
        <param>
            <value><string>Elvis Presley</string></value>
        </param>
    </params>
</methodCall>
```

Using REST, the same method call would just be represented by a URL similar to:

```
http://www.example.com/rest/label/getRecords?artist=Elvis+Presley
```

I have been using the term *similar* here because REST only describes the basic principle and does not enforce any strict rules on your web service. Any of the following URLs could be used to describe exactly the same method call:

```
http://www.example.com/index.php?method=label.getRecords&artist=El
vis+Presley
http://www.example.com/label/getRecords/Elvis+Presley
```

How the method call is encoded in the URL is left to the provider of the service.

Both method calls contain nearly the same information:

- The method to be called (`label.getRecords` or `/label/getRecords`)
- The parameter to be passed to the method call (`Elvis Presley`)

The only thing different is that the XML-RPC version transports type information for the parameter value, whereas the REST version only transports the value itself. However, since dynamically typed languages are getting increasingly popular this is not really a disadvantage.

Encoding the method call in a typical REST fashion has been a lot easier than using XML-RPC. Let's take a look at the responses. The response for the above XML-RPC call would be something along the lines of:

```
<?xml version="1.0" encoding="UTF-8"?>
<methodResponse>
  <params>
    <param>
       <value>
         <array>
           <data>
             <value>
               <string>
                 That's All Right (Mama) &amp; Blue Moon Of Kentucky
               </string>
             </value>
             <value><string>Good Rockin' Tonight</string></value>
           </data>
         </array>
      </value>
    </param>
  </params>
</methodResponse>
```

Again, a lot of XML code needs to be created, sent over the network, and parsed by the client. And all that just for transporting a simple numbered array containing two strings. Now let us take a look at the same response to the same method call, but this time using REST:

```
<?xml version="1.0" encoding="UTF-8"?>
<getRecordsResult>
    <record>That&apos;s All Right (Mama) &amp;
                                        Blue Moon Of Kentucky</record>
    <record>Good Rockin&apos; Tonight</record>
</getRecordsResult>
```

While again the response only contains the raw data without any type information it still carries the same information, saves bandwidth and resources, and is even easier to read and understand. As the XML document does not have to follow any rules you could as well just deliver this document:

```
<?xml version="1.0" encoding="UTF-8"?>
<label:records xmlns:label="http://www.example.com/my/label">
    <label:record title="That&apos;s All Right (Mama) &amp; Blue Moon
Of Kentucky"/>
    <label:record title="Good Rockin&apos; Tonight"/>
</getRecordsResult>
```

The only rules for REST results are that they are valid XML and that your users understand what your service is sending back as a response. Of course, you need to document the XML schema you are using so that your customers know how to interpret the returned XML.

Our Own REST Service

Let's try to implement our own REST service! And what better example than the record label that has accompanied us during the last two chapters. For our first REST service, we will be using exactly the same business logic we used in the `Services_Webservice` example. In case you have forgotten which methods the `RecordLabel` class provides and what their signatures looked like, here is a short reminder:

```
class RecordLabel
{
    public function getRecords($artist);
    public function getArtists()
}
```

The implementation of the class has been left out in this code snippet, as we have already used it in the last example and it is irrelevant for the REST web service. As the business logic provides two methods, our service should provide these two methods as well:

- `getArtists()` will return all artists our record label has contracted.
- `getRecords(string $artist)` will return all records an artist has recorded.

Before we can start we need to define the URL scheme the clients have to use to invoke these methods on our service. To avoid the annoyances `mod_rewrite` might bring into this, the easiest way is to encode the method name as a URL parameter so the requests can always use the same base URL. Other REST-based services (like Yahoo!) include the method name parameter as a part of the path and use Apache's `mod_rewrite` module to route the requests to the script that processes all requests. This way, there is no need to expose that you are using PHP for your web service.

All other parameters that the methods might accept will also be encoded in standard URL parameters. So typical URLs to access our service might be:

```
http://www.your-domain.com/REST/index.php?m=getArtists
http://www.your-domain.com/REST/index.php?m=getRecords&artist=
                                                      Elvis+Presley
```

We will now implement a new class that can be reached at `http://www.your-domain.com/REST/index.php` and which will evaluate all parameters passed to it. To handle these requests, the service will require at least the following data:

- The object that provides the business logic
- The name of the request parameter that contains the name of the method that should be invoked.

To make sure that this information is always available, we make it part of the constructor of our service:

```
/**
 * Generic REST server
 */
class REST_Server
{
   /**
    * object, that provides the business logic
    */
    private $handler;

   /**
    * name of the request parameter that contains the method name
    */
    private $methodVar;

   /**
```

```
     * Create new REST server
     *
     * @param    object      Object that provides the business logic
     * @param    string      Name of the request variable
     *                       that contains the method to call
     */
    public function __construct($handler, $methodVar = 'm')
    {
        $this->handler   = $handler;
        $this->methodVar = $methodVar;
    }
}
```

If we create a new service, it will not start automatically, so we have to add a new service method to handle the following tasks:

1. Check whether the client supplied a method to be invoked. If not, signal an error.
2. Check whether the business logic provides the method the client requested. If not, signal an error.
3. Check whether the client provided all arguments required to invoke the requested method. If not, signal an error.
4. Invoke the requested method. If it fails, signal an error. Otherwise create an XML representation of the result and send it to the client.

While the first task seems easy, you may wonder how tasks number two and three will be implemented. PHP 5 provides a new feature called **reflection**, which enables you to introspect classes, methods, and functions. In case of a generic REST service, we will be using reflection to check whether the business logic object provides the method the client wanted to call. Furthermore, reflection allows us to get the total number and names of arguments the method expects. This way, we can map the parameters sent with the HTTP request to the parameters of the method call. Using the reflection API is easy; the following code will check whether the passed object provides a method called `getRecords()` and will display the names of the parameters this method expects:

```
$label = new RecordLabel();

// Create a reflection object that is able to
// provide information about the object we passed
$reflect = new ReflectionObject($label);
try
{
    // get an object that provides information
```

```
        // about the getRecords() method
        $method = $reflect->getMethod('getRecords');
    }
    catch (ReflectionException $e)
    {
        echo "The method 'getRecords' does not exist.";
        exit();
    }

    echo "The method 'getRecords' exists.\n";
    echo "It accepts ".$method->getNumberOfParameters()." parameters\n";

    // get information about all parameters that
    // have to be passed to this method
    $parameters = $method->getParameters();

    foreach ($parameters as $parameter)
    {
        $name = $parameter->getName();
        echo " - $name\n";
    }
```

If you run this script, it will output:

```
The method 'getRecords' exists.
It accepts 1 parameters
 - artist
```

So the reflection API allows you to easily get information about methods at run time for any object you are using. We will use this feature to map the HTTP-request parameters to the method parameters in our generic REST service:

```
    /**
     * Start the REST service
     */
    public function service()
    {
        // We will send XML later
        header('Content-Type: text/xml');

        // get the name of the method that should be called
        if (!isset($_GET[$this->methodVar]))
        {
            $this->sendFault(1, 'No method requested.');
        }
```

```
        $method = $_GET[$this->methodVar];

        // Check whether the method exists
        $reflect = new ReflectionObject($this->handler);
        try
        {
            $method  = $reflect->getMethod($method);
        }
        catch (ReflectionException $e)
        {
            $this->sendFault(2, $e->getMessage());
        }

        // Check whether all parameters of the method
        // have been transmitted
        $parameters = $method->getParameters();
        $values = array();
        foreach ($parameters as $parameter)
        {
          $name = $parameter->getName();
          if (isset($_GET[$name]))
           {
            $values[] = $_GET[$name];
            continue;
           }
          if ($parameter->isDefaultValueAvailable())
           {
            $values[] = $parameter->getDefaultValue();
            continue;
           }
          $this->sendFault(3, 'Missing parameter ' . $name . '.');
        }

        // Call the actual method and send result to the client
        try
        {
            // This will work from PHP 5.1:
            // $method->invokeArgs($this->handler, $values);
            $result = call_user_func_array(
                  array($this->handler, $method->getName()), $values);
            $this->sendResult($method->getName(), $result);
        }
        catch (Exception $e)
        {
```

```
            $this->sendFault($e->getCode(), $e->getMessage());
        }
    }
```

This short method will handle almost all of the above mentioned tasks our service has to fulfill. First, it sends a `Content-Type` header, as the REST service will always deliver XML markup. Then it checks whether a method name has been sent with the request and whether the business logic object provides the specified method. If any on these checks fails, it will use the `sendFault()` method to signal an error. We will deal with the implementation of this method in few seconds. If the method exists, it will fetch the list of parameters it accepts and iterate over them. For each parameter it will either extract the parameter value from the request or use the default value. If a value has not been passed in the request and the implementation of the method does not provide a default value, another error will be signaled. The extracted values will be stored in the `$values` array. If all method parameters have successfully initialized, `call_user_func_array()` will be used to invoke the method. Until PHP 5.1 the reflection API did not provide the `invokeArgs()` method, which allows you to invoke any method by passing an array with the method arguments.

The result of the called method will be captured and sent as XML using the `sendResult()` method. In this code snippet, we already have used two methods without implementing them. So before we can test the service, we need to implement them. Here is the code required for the `sendFault()` implementation:

```
/**
 * Signal an error
 *
 * @param    integer     error code
 * @param    string      error message
 */
protected function sendFault($faultCode, $faultString)
{
    $serializer = new XML_Serializer();
    $serializer->setOption(XML_SERIALIZER_OPTION_ROOT_NAME,
                                                      'fault');
    $serializer->serialize(array('faultCode' => $faultCode,
                                 'faultString' => $faultString));
    echo $serializer->getSerializedData();
    exit();
}
```

If you have carefully read the chapter on XML processing with PEAR, you are already familiar with the package we are using here. `XML_Serializer` is able to create an XML document from just about any data. In this case, we are passing an array containing the fault code and the description of the error. These four lines of code will produce the following XML document:

```
<fault>
    <faultCode>1</faultCode>
    <faultString>No method requested.</faultString>
</fault>
```

If a client receives this XML document, it will easily recognize it as an error and process it accordingly. Our `sendFault()` method may now be called with any fault code and fault string to signal any kind of error to the client. The implementation of the `sendResult()` method is very similar to the `sendFault()` method:

```
/**
 * Send the result as XML to the client
 *
 * @param    string      name of the method that had been called
 * @param    mixed       result of the call to the business logic
 */
protected function sendResult($methodName, $result)
{
    $matches = array();
    if (preg_match('/^get([a-z]+)s$/i', $methodName, $matches))
    {
      $defaultTag = strtolower($matches[1]);
    }
    else
    {
        $defaultTag = 'item';
    }

    $serializer = new XML_Serializer();
    $serializer->setOption(XML_SERIALIZER_OPTION_ROOT_NAME,
                           $methodName.'Result');
    $serializer->setOption(XML_SERIALIZER_OPTION_DEFAULT_TAG,
                           $defaultTag);
    $serializer->serialize($result);
    echo $serializer->getSerializedData();
    exit();
}
```

However, it is a bit more intelligent as it uses the method name as the root tag and if the method starts with `get*`, it will use the rest of the name as a default tag for numbered arrays.

So if we call our new service with the example URLs mentioned above, we will receive the following XML documents from our server:

```
<getArtistsResult>
    <artist>Elvis Presley</artist>
    <artist>Carl Perkins</artist>
</getArtistsResult>

<getRecordsResult>
    <record>That&apos;s All Right (Mama) &amp; Blue Moon Of Kentucky
                                                                </record>
    <record>Good Rockin&apos; Tonight</record>
</getRecordsResult>
```

In the business logic classes, we can signal errors by throwing an exception, which is the standard way in object-oriented development. To add error management to the `getRecords()` method, we only need to modify the method a little:

```
/**
 * Get all records of an artist
 *
 * @param string
 * @return string[]
 */
public function getRecords($artist)
{
    if (isset($this->records[$artist]))
    {
        $result = $this->records[$artist];
        return $result;
    }
    throw new Exception('The artist "'.$artist.
                             '" is not in our database.', 50);
}
```

This exception will be automatically caught by the `REST_Server` class and transformed into an XML document, which will be sent to the client:

```
<fault>
    <faultCode>50</faultCode>
    <faultString>
        The artist &quot;P.Diddy&quot; is not in our database.
    </faultString>
</fault>
```

If you add new methods to the business logic, they will instantly become available through your new REST service. You may just as well pass in a completely different object that encapsulates business logic and you will be able to access it using the REST server. And as you are already quite familiar with the `XML_Serializer` package, you can easily tweak the format of the XML that is delivered.

Implementing a client for our newly created REST service will be left as an exercise.

Summary

In this chapter, we have worked with various web services. We learned about the concepts behind XML-RPC and SOAP as well as the principle of keeping it simple that REST-based services follow. This chapter covered consuming those services as well as offering your own services to the public.

We have used the `XML_RPC` package to access the web service offered by the PEAR website, which allows you to retrieve information about the offered packages. We have also used `Services_Google`, which acts as a wrapper around PHP's SOAP extension to access the Google search API. By using `Services_Amazon` and `Services_Technorati`, we accessed two REST-based services without having to worry about the transmitted XML documents. Using the Yahoo API as an example we also experienced how `HTTP_Request` and `XML_Unserializer` can be combined to consume any REST-based web-service, regardless of the returned XML format.

The second half of the chapter was devoted to offering web services. We learned how to use the `XML_RPC` package to offer an XML-RPC-based service that also allowed introspection. Using `Services_Webservice`, we automated the generation of a SOAP-based web service including WSDL generation from any class that needs to be exposed as a service. Last, we built a generic REST server that can be used to build a new service on top of any class that offers business logic.

PEAR's web service category is still growing and offers more and more clients for different web services. All of them follow one or more of the approaches showcased in this chapter.

5
Working with Dates

This chapter introduces PEAR's Date and Time section. It covers the packages `Date`, `Date_Holidays`, and `Calendar`. You will see what help they offer and learn how to use them to solve date- and time-related problems. You can visit the *Date and Time* section online at `http://pear.php.net/packages.php?catpid=8&catname=Date+and+Time`.

After reading the chapter, you will be able to use these packages as a replacement for PHP's native date and time functions. Knowledge of these three libraries will help you to program robust date-related applications.

Working with the Date Package

You may ask why you should use `PEAR::Date` instead of PHP's native Unix timestamp-based date and time functions. In fact, using `PEAR::Date` means a loss of performance because it is coded in PHP and not C. Additionally, you have to understand a new API and learn how to use it. But there are some advantages, the main one being that `PEAR::Date` is not based on Unix timestamps and does not suffer from their deficits.

A timestamp is used to assign a value in a certain format to a point in time. Unix timestamps count the seconds from 01/01/1970 00:00h GMT and today's computers store it in a signed 32-bit integer number, which means it can hold values from minus 2,147,483,648 to 2,147,483,648. This means 01/01/1970 00:00h GMT is represented by an integer value of 0 (zero). 01/01/1970 00:01h GMT would therefore be represented by an integer value of 60. The problem with Unix timestamps is that exactly on January 19, 2038, at 7 seconds past 3:14 AM GMT, the maximum possible integer value is reached. Imagine this as an event similar to the Y2K problem. One second later the counter will carry over and start from – 2,147,483,648. At this point many 32-bit programs all over the world will fail. Some people may say that computers in 2038 will be using at least 64-bit integers. That would be enough to store time representations that go far beyond the age of the universe. Certainly, that will be true for most applications. But what about legacy systems or programs that have to be downwards compatible to 32-bit software?

You will not suffer from the timestamp problem if you use `PEAR::Date`. Furthermore, `PEAR::Date` is object oriented, provides lots of helpful methods, and is timezone-aware. Also for instance a timespan of 1 hour does not have to be stated as 3600 seconds but can be represented as a `Date_Span` object like this:

```
$timespan = new Date_Span('1 hour')
```

`PEAR::Date` provides lots of really nice features and even if you develop software you do not plan to use in 2038 or later the package is definitely worth a try.

Date

The following sections will teach you how to create, query, and manipulate `Date` objects. You will also see how to compare different objects to each other and how to print the date and time these objects represent in whatever format a programmer's heart desires. Your journey starts now.

Creating a Date Object

When working with `PEAR::Date`, the first thing you need to know is how to create an object of the `Date` class. The constructor expects one optional parameter. If none is passed the object will be initialized with the current date/time. If you pass a parameter the object will be initialized with the specified time. Accepted formats for the parameter are ISO 8601, Unix timestamp, or another `Date` object:

```
require_once 'Date.php';

$now = new Date();

$iso8601 = new Date('2005-12-24 12:00:00');
$mysqlTS = new Date('20051224120000');
$unixTS  = new Date(mktime(12, 0, 0, 12, 24, 2005));
$dateObj = new Date($unixTS);
```

Once an object has been created you can use `setDate()` to modify its properties. Regardless of whether you use the constructor or `setDate()`, the object will be initialized with the system's default timezone.

Querying Information

`Date` objects have several methods that allow you to gather detailed information about their properties. For instance, there is a set of methods that provide information about an object's date and time properties, namely `getYear()`, `getMonth()`, `getDay()`, `getHour()`, `getMinute()`, and `getSecond()`.

If you want to access all the information by calling a single method you could use `getTime()` to retrieve an Unix timestamp or `getDate()` to get the date/time as a formatted string. The latter expects an optional parameter that defines the method's output format. The next table shows available output format constants and what the output would look like if you had the following object: `$date = new Date('2005-12-24 09:30:00')`.

Constant	Output format
DATE_FORMAT_ISO	2005-12-24 09:30:00 (YYYY-MM-DD hh:mm:ss)
DATE_FORMAT_ISO_BASIC	20051224T093000Z (YYYYMMDDThhmmssZ)
DATE_FORMAT_ISO_EXTENDED	2005-12-24T09:30:00Z (YYYY-MM-DDThh:mm:ssZ)
DATE_FORMAT_ISO_EXTENDED_MICROTIME	2005-12-24T09:30:0.000000Z (YYYY-MM-DDThh:mm:ss.s*Z)
DATE_FORMAT_TIMESTAMP	20051224093000 (YYYYMMDDhhmmss)
DATE_FORMAT_UNIXTIME	1135413000 (integer; seconds since 01/01/1970 00:00h GMT)

There is another set of methods that helps you find out information closely related to the date/time properties of a `Date` object. A description for some of these methods and the expected example output for the aforementioned `Date` object can be found in the following table:

Method	Description	Result (2005-12-24 09:30:00)
getDayName($abbr)	Returns the day's name. One optional parameter decides if it is abbreviated (false) or not (true)—default is false.	Saturday (string)
getDayOfWeek()	Returns the day of the week as an integer for the object's date: Sunday = 0, Monday = 1, ..., Saturday = 6	6 (integer)
getDaysInMonth()	Returns the number of days in the month for the object's date.	31 (integer)
getQuarterOfYear()	Returns the quarter of the year for the object's date.	4 (integer)

Method	Description	Result (2005-12-24 09:30:00)
`getWeekOfYear()`	Returns the number of the week for the object's date.	51 (integer)
`getWeeksInMonth()`	Returns the number of weeks in the month for the object's date.	5 (integer)
`isLeapYear()`	Determines whether the represented year is a leap year or not.	false (boolean)
`isPast()`	Determines whether the object's date is in the past.	true (boolean)
`isFuture()`	Determines whether the object's date is in the future.	false (boolean)

Having a `Date` object you can easily find out what comes next or what was before. This can be done using the methods `getNextDay()` or `getPrevDay()`. In the same way you can also find the next or previous weekday relative to your current `Date` object. See the following listing for an example:

```
$date   = new Date('2005-12-24 09:30:00');

$prev   = $date->getPrevDay();      // 2005-12-23 09:30:00
$prevWd = $date->getPrevWeekday(); // 2005-12-23 09:30:00

$next   = $date->getNextDay();      // 2005-12-25 09:30:00
$nextWd = $date->getNextWeekday(); // 2005-12-26 09:30:00
```

Each method returns a new `Date` object with the appropriate date information. The time information remains unchanged.

Do you need more date-related information?

If you still need to find out more information about any date or time, take a look at the `Date_Calc` class that ships with the `PEAR::Date` package. It is frequently used internally by the `Date` class and provides tons of helpful methods that you could look at if the `Date` class does not satisfy your needs.

Manipulating Date Objects

The `Date` object's properties can be set on construction and also by using setter methods during the object's lifetime. Setting all date/time properties at once can be done by calling `setDate()`. By default it expects an ISO 8601 date string as a parameter. Alternatively you can specify another format string by specifying the input format as the second parameter. It can be one of the constants described in the table showing output format constants for `getTime()` earlier in this chapter.

If you just want to precisely set a specific property of an object you can use one of the following setters: `setYear()`, `setMonth()`, `setDay()`, `setHour()`, `setMinute()`, and `setSecond()`. Each expects a single parameter representing the value to be set.

Another way to manipulate a `Date` object is to use `addSeconds()` or `subtractSeconds()`. You can specify an amount of seconds to be added or subtracted to an object's date/time. For example, if you call `$date->addSeconds(3600)`, the object's hour property would be increased by 1. As you will see in the section about `Date_Span`, there is another way to add or subtract timespans to an existing `Date` object.

If you have a `Date` object `$a` and want to apply its property values to another `Date` object `$b` you can do this by calling `copy()` on `$b` and providing `$a` as argument to the method. Afterwards `$b` will have the same date/time values as `$a`.

This listing shows you the methods to manipulate `Date` objects in action:

```
$date = new Date('2005-12-24 09:30:00');
$copy = new Date();        // $copy initialized with current date/time

$copy->copy($date);        // $copy => 2005-12-24 09:30:00

$copy->setHour(12);        // $copy => 2005-12-24 12:30:00
$copy->setMinute(0);       // $copy => 2005-12-24 12:00:00

$copy->addSeconds(30);     // $copy => 2005-12-24 12:00:30

$date->setDate($copy->getDate());  // $date => 2005-12-24 12:00:30
```

Comparing Dates

A typical task when working with dates is to compare them. `Date` objects provide methods to:

- Check whether an object's time lies ahead or is in the past for a specified date
- Check if two objects represent the same date and time
- Check if two `date` objects are equal or which is before or after the other one

If you have a `Date` object and want to find out how it relates to another `Date` object you can use one of the following three methods:

- `before()`
- `after()`
- `equals()`

They can be used to check whether two dates are equal or if one is before or after the other. The following code listing shows how to use them:

```
$d1 = new Date('2005-12-24');
$d2 = new Date('2005-12-30');

$equal        = $d1->equals($d2);   // false
$d1_Before_d2 = $d1->before($d2);   // true
$d1_After_d2  = $d1->after($d2);    // false
```

The `Date` class also provides a special method that comes in handy when having to compare dates to get them sorted. This method is `Date::compare()` and can be used statically. The method expects two parameters representing the `Date` objects to be compared. It returns `0` if they are equal, `-1` if the first is before the second, and `1` if the first is after the second. This behavior is perfect when you need to sort an array of `Date` objects as the method can be used as a user-defined method for PHP's array sorting functions. The following listing shows how `usort()` and `Date::compare()` can be utilized to sort an array of `Date` objects.

```
$dates   = array();
$dates[] = new Date('2005-12-24');
$dates[] = new Date('2005-11-14');
$dates[] = new Date('2006-01-04');
$dates[] = new Date('2003-02-12');

usort($dates, array('Date', 'compare'));
```

As `Date::compare()` is a static class method you need to pass an array consisting of two strings representing the class and method name.

Formatted Output

The properties of a `Date` object can be printed using the `format()` method. The returned string is localized according to the currently set locale. You can influence the locale setting with PHP's `setlocale()` method.

The following example shows how to use this function:

```
$date = new Date('2005-12-24 09:30:00');
echo $date->format('%A, %D %T'); // prints: Saturday, 12/24/2005
                                                  //09:30:00
```

As you see, the format of the returned string can be controlled by specifying placeholders. The following table shows a list of all valid placeholders you can use.

Placeholder	Description
`%a`	The abbreviated weekday name (Mon, Tue, Wed, ...)
`%A`	The full weekday name (Monday, Tuesday, Wednesday, ...)
`%b`	The abbreviated month name (Jan, Feb, Mar, ...)
`%B`	The full month name (January, February, March, ...)
`%C`	The century number (ranges from 00 to 99)
`%d`	The day of month (ranges from 01 to 31)
`%D`	Same as `%m/%d/%y`
`%e`	The day of month with single digit (ranges from 1 to 31)
`%E`	The number of days since Unix epoch (01/01/1970 00:00h GMT)
`%h`	The hour as a decimal number with single digit (0 to 23)
`%H`	The hour as decimal number (ranges from 00 to 23)
`%i`	The hour as decimal number on a 12-hour clock with single digit (ranges from 1 to 12)
`%I`	The hour as decimal number on a 12-hour clock (ranges from 01 to 12)
`%j`	The day of year (ranges from 001 to 366)
`%m`	The month as decimal number (ranges from 01 to 12)
`%M`	The minute as a decimal number (ranges from 00 to 59)
`%n`	The newline character (\n)
`%O`	The DST (daylight saving time)-corrected timezone offset expressed as '+/-HH:MM'
`%o`	The raw timezone offset expressed as '+/-HH:MM'
`%p`	Either 'am' or 'pm' depending on the time
`%P`	Either 'AM' or 'PM' depending on the time
`%r`	The time in am/pm notation, Same as '%I:%M:%S %p'
`%R`	The time in 24-hour notation, same as '%H:%M'
`%s`	The seconds including the decimal representation smaller than one second
`%S`	The seconds as a decimal number (ranges from 00 to 59)
`%t`	The tab character (\t)
`%T`	The current time, same as '%H:%M:%S'
`%w`	The weekday as decimal (Sunday = 0, Monday = 1, ..., Saturday = 6)
`%U`	The week number of the current year
`%y`	The year as decimal (ranges from 00 to 99)
`%Y`	The year as decimal including century (ranges from 0000 to 9999)
`%%`	The literal `%`

Creating a Date_Span Object

Besides the `Date` class `PEAR::Date` also provides the `Date_Span` class that is used to represent timespans with a precision of seconds. The constructor accepts a variety of different parameters. You can create a timespan from an array, a specially formatted string, or two date objects. There are some other possibilities but these are the most common. The following examples will show some ways to accomplish the creation of a `Date_Span` object that represents a timespan of 1 day, 6 hours, 30 minutes, and 15 seconds.

To create a timespan from an array it has to contain values for days, hours, minutes, and seconds:

```
$span = new Date_Span(array(1, 6, 30, 15));
```

If you specify two `Date` objects the timespan's value will be the difference between these two dates:

```
$span = new Date_Span(
  new Date('2005-01-01 00:00:00'),
  new Date('2005-01-02 06:30:15'));
```

When passing an integer value it will be taken as seconds:

```
$span = new Date_Span(109815);
```

The most flexible way is to pass a string as a parameter. By default this is expected in **Non Numeric Separated Values (NNSV)** input format. That means any character that is not a number is presumed to be a separator. The timespan's length depends on how many numeric values are found in the string. See the description from the API documentation:

"If no values are given, timespan is set to zero, if one value is given, it's used for hours, if two values are given it's used for hours and minutes, and if three values are given, it's used for hours, minutes, and seconds."

If you specify four values they are used for days, hours, minutes, and seconds respectively. See the following listing on how to create our desired timespan:

```
$span  = new Date_Span('1,6,30,15');
// thanks to NNSV input format you can use this one, too:
$span2 = new Date_Span('1,06:30:15');
```

The constructor is able to process very complex and specially formatted strings if you specify the input format. This can be done by using particular placeholders. Read more on this in the API documentation for `Date_Span::setFromString()`.

Manipulating Date_Span Objects

The properties of a `Date_Span` object can be influenced by using one of the various setter methods. A smart way to manipulate a timespan is using `set()`. It behaves exactly like the aforementioned constructor. In fact the constructor just delegates to this method when setting values for a newly created object. Another possibility is to use one of the following specific methods to set the timespan from hours, minutes, an array, or something else. The methods are `setFromArray()`, `setFromDateDiff()`. `setFromDays()`, `setFromHours()`, `setFromMinutes()`, `setFromSeconds()`, and `setFromString()`.

Further you can alter a timespan's value by adding or subtracting another timespan value. Use the methods `add()` or `subtract()` for this purpose:

```
$span1 = new Date_Span('1 hour');
$span2 = new Date_Span('2 hours');

$span1->add($span2); // $span1 is 3 hours now
```

`Date_Span` also provides a `copy()` method. It works like the `Date::copy()` method and you can use it to set the timespan from another `Date_Timespan` object.

Timespan Conversions

The `Date_Span` class provides four methods to get the timespan value as a numerical value. These are `toDays()`, `toHours()`, `toMinutes()`, and `toSeconds()`, each returning a value in the according unit:

```
$span = new Date_Span('1,06:30:15'); // 1 day, 6 hours, 30 min, 15 sec

$days    = $span->toDays();      // 1.27100694444
$hours   = $span->toHours();     // 30.5041666667
$minutes = $span->toMinutes();   // 1830.25
$seconds = $span->toSeconds();   // 109815
```

Comparisons

If you need to compare two `Date_Span` objects there are five relevant methods you can use: `equal()`, `greater()`, `greaterEqual()`, `lower()`, and `lowerEqual()`. Calling one of these methods on an object compares it to another one. Each method returns a Boolean value:

```
$span1 = new Date_Span('1,6:30:15');
$span2 = new Date_Span('2,12:30:15');

$span1->lower($span2);          // true
$span1->lowerEqual($span2);     // true
$span1->equal($span2);          // false
$span1->greater($span2);        // false
$span1->greaterEqual($span2);   // false
```

`Date_Span` also provides a `compare()` method that can be used to sort an array of `Date_Span` objects by their length. It expects two timespan objects as arguments and returns `0` if they are equal, `-1` if the first is shorter, and `1` if the second is shorter. The following code shows how to perform the sorting:

```
$tspans   = array();
$tspans[] = new Date_Span('1, 12:33:02');
$tspans[] = new Date_Span('1, 00:33:02');
$tspans[] = new Date_Span('3, 00:00:00');
$tspans[] = new Date_Span('1');

usort($tspans, array('Date_Span', 'compare'));
```

Another method that cannot be used for comparison purposes but is helpful anyway is `isEmpty()`. It returns true if the timespan is zero length or false otherwise:

```
$span  = new Date_Span('');
$empty = $span->isEmpty();    // true
```

Formatted Output

You can get a formatted string representation of a `Date_Span` object by using the `format()` method. Similar to the `Date::format()` method, it provides a handful of placeholders that can be used to achieve the desired output format and returns a string that is formatted accordingly. The following table shows some of the available placeholders. More can be found in the API documentation on the `Date_Span::format()` method.

Placeholder	Description
`%C`	Days with time, same as `%D, %H:%M:%S`
`%d`	Total days as a float number
`%D`	Days as a decimal number
`%h`	Hours as decimal number (ranges from 0 to 23)
`%H`	Hours as decimal number (ranges from 00 to 23)
`%m`	Minutes as a decimal number (ranges from 0 to 59)
`%M`	Minutes as a decimal number (ranges from 00 to 59)
`%R`	Time in 24-hour notation, same as `%H:%M`
`%s`	Seconds as a decimal number (ranges from 0 to 59)
`%S`	Seconds as a decimal number (ranges from 00 to 59)
`%T`	Current time equivalent, same as `%H:%M:%S`

Date Objects and Timespans

The `Date` class provides two methods that allow you to work with `Date_Span` objects. These allow you to do some arithmetic operations on date objects by adding or subtracting timespans. These methods are `addSpan()` and `subtractSpan()`, each expecting a `Date_Span` object as parameter. The following code shows how to increase a date by two days:

```
$date = new Date('2005-12-24 12:00:00');
$span = new Date_Span('2, 00:00:00');

$date->subtractSpan($span);
echo $date->getDate(); // 2005-12-22 12:00:00
```

This feature can be helpful in a lot of situations. Think about searching for the second Sunday in December 2005 for example. All you have to do is find the first Sunday and add a timespan of one week:

```
$date = new Date('2005-12-01');

// find first Sunday
while ($date->getDayOfWeek() != 0)
{
  $date = $date->getNextDay();
}

// advance to second Sunday
$date->addSpan(new Date_Span('7,00:00:00'));
echo $date->getDate();    // 2005-12-11 00:00:00
```

Dealing with Timezones using Date_Timezone

A timezone is an area of the earth that shares the same local time.

"*All timezones are defined relative to Coordinated Universal Time (UTC). The reference point for timezones is the Prime Meridian (longitude 0°) which passes through the Royal Greenwich Observatory in Greenwich, London, United Kingdom. For this reason the term Greenwich Mean Time (GMT) is still often used to denote the "base time" to which all other timezones are relative. UTC is, nevertheless, the official term for today's atomically measured time as distinct from time determined by astronomical observation as formerly carried out at Greenwich*" (`http://en.wikipedia.org/wiki/Timezone`).

Additionally, several countries all over the world change into another timezone during the summer (commonly called daylight savings time (DST)). The central European states share the CET (UTC+1) in the winter and the CEST (UTC+2) during the summer months.

Luckily `PEAR::Date` bundles the `Date_Timezone` class that can ease your pain when working with timezones.

Creating a Date_Timezone object

The class constructor expects a single argument, which is the ID of the timezone to create. If the timezone ID is valid you will get a corresponding `Date_Timezone` object, otherwise the created timezone object will represent UTC.

You can get a `Date_Timezone` object representing the system's default timezone by calling the static method `getDefault()`. If you prefer another default timezone you can reset it with `setDefault()`, which can be statically used, too.

When in doubt what timezone IDs you can pass to the constructor or `setDefault()` you can find out all the supported timezones by calling `Date_Timezone::getAvailableIDs()` or check an ID by using `Date_Timezone::isValidID()`. The following listing shows an example demonstrating some of these methods:

```
require_once 'Date/TimeZone.php'; // TimeZone.php with
                                  // uppercase 'Z'

$validIDs = Date_Timezone::getAvailableIDs(); // array with
                                              // about 550 IDs

$tz1 = new Date_Timezone('Europe/London');
echo $tz1->getID();          // Europe/London

// invalid TZ
$tz2 = new Date_Timezone('Something/Invalid');
echo $tz2->getID();          // UTC

// system's default TZ
$default = Date_Timezone::getDefault();
echo $default->getID();      // UTC
```

Querying Information about a Timezone

The `Date_Timezone` class provides a set of methods that allow you to query a timezone's ID, short and long name, whether it has a daylight savings time, and more. The following table shows these methods and a description for each one:

Method	Description
`getID()`	Returns the ID for the timezone.
`getLongName()`	Returns the long name for the timezone.
`getShortName()`	Returns the short name for the timezone.
`getDSTLongName()`	Returns the DST long name for the timezone.
`getDSTShortName()`	Returns the DST short name for the timezone.

Method	Description
`hasDaylightTime()`	Returns true if the timezone observes daylight savings time, otherwise false.
`getDSTSavings()`	Get the DST offset for this timezone (Note: this is currently hard-coded to one hour! The DST offset for some timezones may differ from that value, which means the returned value would be incorrect). Returns zero if the timezone does not observe daylight savings time.
`getRawOffset()`	Returns the raw offset (non-DST-corrected) from UTC for the timezone.

Comparing Timezone Objects

As you may have guessed, there are some methods that allow you to do comparisons between `Date_Timezone` objects. In fact there are two methods—`isEqual()` and `isEquivalent()`. `isEqual()` checks whether two objects represent an identical timezone meaning that 'Europe/London' is only equal to 'Europe/London' and no other timezone. Whereas `isEquivalent()` can be used to test whether two timezones have the same offset to UTC and both observe daylight savings time or not. The following example will show these methods in action:

```
$london    = new Date_Timezone('Europe/London');    // UTC
$london2   = new Date_Timezone('Europe/London');    // UTC
$berlin    = new Date_Timezone('Europe/Berlin');    // UTC+1
$amsterdam = new Date_Timezone('Europe/Amsterdam'); // UTC+1

$london->isEqual($london2);            // true
$london->isEqual($berlin);             // false

$london->isEquivalent($berlin);        // false
$berlin->isEquivalent($amsterdam);     // true
```

Date Objects and Timezones

Objects of both the `Date` class and the `Date_Timezone` class provide methods for interaction with each other. For instance you can change the timezone of a `Date` object with or without converting its date/time properties. Furthermore you can check whether a date object's current date/time is in daylight savings time or calculate the offset from one timezone to UTC considering a certain date/time. The next table shows methods provided by the `Date` class that enable you to work with timezones.

Method	Description
`setTZ($tzObj)`	Sets the specified timezone object for the Date object.
`setTZByID($id)`	Sets the timezone for the Date object from the specified timezone ID.
`convertTZ($tzObj)`	Converts the date object's date/time to a new timezone using the specified timezone object.
`convertTZbyID($id)`	Converts the date object's date/time to a new timezone using the specified timezone ID.
`toUTC()`	Converts the date object's date/time to UTC and accordingly sets the timezone to UTC.
`inDaylightTime()`	Tests whether the object's date/time is in DST.

Nobody is perfect, not even PEAR::Date

When it comes to timezones, `PEAR::Date` relies on functions that are dependent on the operating system and not safe to use on every computer. For example, this affects the methods `Date_Timezone::inDaylightTime()` and `Date_Timezone::getOffset()`. The following short excerpt indicates these problems:

"WARNINGS: This basically attempts to "trick" the system into telling us if we're in DST for a given timezone. This uses `putenv()`, which may not work in safe mode, and relies on Unix time, which is only valid for dates from 1970 to ~2038. This relies on the underlying OS calls, so it may not work on Windows or on a system where `zoneinfo` is not installed or configured properly."

The next listing demonstrates how to use some of these methods. It shows how a `Date` object's time is converted from the 'Europe/Berlin' timezone to the 'Europe/London' timezone.

```
$date = new Date('2005-12-24 12:00:00');
$date->setTZbyID('Europe/Berlin');
echo $date->getDate();                  // 2005-12-24   12:00:00

$date->convertTZbyID('Europe/London');
echo $date->getDate();                  // 2005-12-24 11:00:00
```

Earlier you saw that `Date_Timezone` provides the `getRawOffset()` method to determine the offset of a specific timezone to UTC. This does not consider a specific date and whether it is in DST. If you want to check the offset to UTC for a specific date and timezone you can call `getOffset()` on a `Date_Timezone` object with a `Date` object as argument. This method will take into account whether the timezone is in DST for the specified date and return the DST-corrected offset.

Conclusion on the PEAR::Date Package

As you have seen `PEAR::Date` is a powerful package that can really bail you out of a mess when working with dates, doing arithmetic operations with them, or when having to work with timezones. When looking for a comfortable object-oriented API or a solution for the year 2038 problem it is definitely worth a test run.

The downside is that especially when working with timezones it relies on OS-dependent methods and may therefore not work on every system.

Nevertheless it is a great package! You will find no better solution until PHP 5.1 and its date extension. So if you use PHP < 5.1 stick with the `PEAR::Date` package.

Date_Holidays

If you develop an application that needs to calculate holidays, `PEAR::Date_Holidays` is certainly a helpful solution. Its main job is calculating holidays (or other special days) and checking whether dates represent holidays. It hides the complexity of calculating non-static holidays like Easter or Whitsun. Additionally it allows for easy filtering of holidays and is I18N aware, in so far as it provides information about holidays in different languages.

Checking if your birthday in 2005 is a holiday is as easy as:

```
require_once 'Date/Holidays.php';

$driver = Date_Holidays::factory('Christian', 2005);

// actually this checks my date of birth ;-)
if($driver->isHoliday(new Date('2005-09-09')))
{
  echo 'Oh happy day! Holiday and birthday all at once.';
} else {
  echo 'Jay, it is my birthday.';
}
```

So, if you do not want to reinvent the wheel for a library calculating holidays that occur on different dates in different religions/countries, use `Date_Holidays`.

Before we start coding there are some concepts you should understand. But do not fear—we will keep it short.

Instantiating a Driver

`Date_Holidays` utilizes special classes that perform the calculation of holidays for specific religions, countries, or regions. These classes are called drivers. That means you tell `Date_Holidays` the year and country you want the holidays to be calculated for and it gives you a driver that you can use to query further information. It will tell you about the holidays it knows, you can ask it whether a date is a holiday, and much more.

The driver is instantiated via the `Date_Holidays` class. It provides a static factory method that expects the driver ID, year, and locale to be used as arguments and returns a driver object:

```
$driver = Date_Holidays::factory($driverId, $year, $locale);
if (Date_Holidays::isError($driver))
{
  die('Creation of driver failed: ' . $driver->getMessage());
} else
{
  // ... go on
  echo 'Driver successfully created!';
}
```

In this example the method `Date_Holidays::factory()` take three arguments, of which only the driver ID is mandatory. The driver ID is the name of the calculation driver to create. Currently the package ships with the following seven drivers (as of package version 0.16.1) (driver IDs are formatted in **bold**):

- **Christian** (Christian holidays)
- **Composite** (Special driver to combine one or more real drivers. It behaves like a "normal" driver. Read more on this in the section *Combining Holiday Drivers.*)
- **Germany** (German holidays)
- **PHPdotNet** (Dates of birth of several PHP community members)
- **Sweden** (Swedish holidays)
- **UNO** (United Nations Organization holidays)
- **USA** (U.S. American holidays)

To find out which drivers your version of `Date_Holidays` provides you can simply call the `Date_Holidays::getInstalledDrivers()` method, which will return an array holding the information about installed drivers.

The second argument is the year for which you want the holidays to be calculated.

The third argument is an optional string that represents the locale that will be used by the driver. The locale you pass in here affects any driver method that returns a holiday object, holiday title, or other localized information. A locale string can be an ISO 639 two-letter language code or a composition of a two-letter language code and an ISO 3166 two-letter code for a specific country. For instance you would use `"en_GB"` for *English/United Kingdom*. If no locale setting is specified the driver will use English default translations.

You should always check if the factory method successfully returned a driver object or produced an error. `Date_Holidays` utilizes PEAR's default error handling mechanisms so this can be statically checked with `Date_Holidays::isError()`.

If you want to reset the year for which holidays have been calculated you can use the `setYear()` method. It expects one argument representing the new year that holidays shall be calculated for. Whenever you call this method the driver has to recalculate the dates of all its holidays, which means that this method is somewhat computationally expensive.

Creating drivers by country codes instead of driver IDs

The ISO 3166 standard (`http://www.iso.org/iso/en/prods-services/iso3166ma/index.html`) defines codes for the names of countries and dependent areas, which may consist of two or three letters as well as three digits. `Date_Holidays` provides an additional factory method to create a driver by specifying such a two- or three-letter code instead of a driver ID. For instance to create a driver for Sweden you just need to call `Date_Holidays::factoryISO3166('se')` or `Date_Holidays::factoryISO3166('swe')` instead of `Date_Holidays::factory('Sweden')`.
View `http://www.unc.edu/~rowlett/units/codes/country.htm` to see a list of valid ISO 3166 codes.

Identifying Holidays

To identify a holiday it must have an ID that can be used to refer to it. Think about it as a primary key in database systems. In the context of `Date_Holidays` such an identifier is called an **internal name**. To get information about a specific holiday you have to tell a driver the holiday's internal name. To find out which internal names/holidays it supports, each driver provides a method called `getInternalHolidayNames()`. You can see it in the following listing:

```
$driver        = Date_Holidays::factory($driverId, $year, $locale);
$internalNames = $driver->getInternalHolidayNames();
```

This method returns an indexed array that contains the internal holiday names of the driver:

Array

(

[0] => jesusCircumcision

[1] => epiphany

[2] => mariaCleaning

...

[43] => newYearsEve

)

Knowing all the internal names of the holidays the driver supports gives you a better overview about which holidays a driver is able to calculate. You will need this when using the `getHoliday()` method for instance. More on that later.

The Date_Holidays_Holiday Class

Some methods of a driver return objects of the `Date_Holidays_Holiday` class. An object of this type gives you information about a single holiday. See the table below for the methods that offer information you may need.

Method	Description
`getDate()`	Returns a Date object representing the holiday's date.
`getInternalName()`	Returns the holiday's internal name.
`getTitle()`	Returns the holiday's localized title.
`toArray()`	Returns the holiday's data as an associative array. It contains the keys `"date"`, `"internalName"`, and `"title"`.

Calculating Holidays

After this short introduction you know how to create driver objects. Now it is time to find out how we can use drivers to find out some information about holidays.

Getting Holiday Information

If you are interested in all holidays a driver can provide you should use the `getHolidays()` method. It will return an associative array with internal holiday names as keys and the corresponding `Date_Holidays_Holiday` objects as values.

A `Date_Holidays_Holiday` object contains complete information about a holiday, including its internal name, title, and date. If you are only interested in the title or date you can use `getHolidayTitles()` or `getHolidayDates()`. Both return the same associative array having internal names as keys and titles or `PEAR::Date` objects as values.

The following listing shows these methods in action:

```
$driver   = Date_Holidays::factory('Christian', 2005);
$holidays = $driver->getHolidays();      // returns associative array
$titles   = $driver->getHolidayTitles(); // returns associative array
$dates    = $driver->getHolidayDates();  // returns associative array
```

Date_Holidays and dates

`PEAR::Date_Holidays` uses `PEAR::Date` objects to represent the dates of holidays. The hour, minute, and second properties of these objects are always zero. Additionally the timezone used by the objects is UTC.

When you do not want information about all holidays a driver provides but only about a specific holiday you can use `getHoliday()`. It expects the holiday's internal name as the first argument. Assuming we want to get information on Easter Sunday we have to pass `"easter"` because it is the internal name used for this holiday.

Some methods do not return a complete holiday object but only the title or date information. These are `getHolidayTitle()` and `getHolidayDate()`. Just like `getHoliday()` each one expects the internal holiday name as the first argument. On success you get the specified holiday's title or its date as a `PEAR::Date` object.

The next listing demonstrates the usage of the methods mentioned above:

```
$driver  = Date_Holidays::factory('Christian', 2005);
$holiday = $driver->getHoliday('easter');
                                    // Date_Holidays_Holiday object
$title   = $driver->getHolidayTitle('easter');
                                    // string(13) "Easter Sunday"
$date    = $driver->getHolidayDate('easter');
                                    // Date object: 2005-03-27
```

Filtering Results

Some methods introduced in the previous section provided information about multiple holidays by using arrays as return values. By default, a driver returns information about all holidays it knows. Sometimes this is more information than you need. To enable you to restrict the amount of returned data, these methods allow the use of filters.

A filter is an object that contains internal names of holidays. When you pass it to functions that return a list/array of holidays as result, it decides which ones are included in the return value.

`Date_Holidays` supports different types of filters:

- **Blacklist Filters:** Elements of a blacklist filter are excluded from a method's return value. Filter class: `Date_Holidays_Filter_Blacklist`.
- **Whitelist Filters:** If specified, only elements of a whitelist filter are included in a method's return value. Filter class: `Date_Holidays_Filter_Whitelist`.
- **Composite Filters:** A composite filter allows you to combine several filters into a single one. It behaves just like a normal filter. The single filters are combined in an OR relation.
- **Predefined Filters:** Predefined filters are available for various purposes. For instance there are filters that only accept official holidays. Currently there are only a few predefined filters included in the `Date_Holidays` package.

To find out which filters your version of `Date_Holidays` provides you can simply call the `Date_Holidays::getInstalledFilters()` method, which will return an array holding the information about installed filters.

Blacklist and whitelist filters are created by using their one-argument constructor, whose argument has to be an array containing internal holiday names. The following example shows how to create and use these filter types:

```
$driver     = Date_Holidays::factory('Christian', 2005);

echo count($driver->getHolidays());   // prints: 44

$whitelist  = new Date_Holidays_Filter_Whitelist(
    array('goodFriday', 'easter', 'easterMonday'));
$wlHolidays = $driver->getHolidays($whitelist);
echo count($wlHolidays);              // prints: 3
```

```
$blacklist  = new Date_Holidays_Filter_Blacklist(
    array('goodFriday', 'easter', 'easterMonday'));
$blHolidays = $driver->getHolidays($blacklist);
echo count($blHolidays);              // prints: 41
```

As the example shows, the driver knows 44 holidays. If you use the whitelist filter `getHolidays()` returns an array containing exactly three elements (`goodFriday`, `easter`, and `easterMonday`). When using a blacklist filter that contains these elements, they are not included in the return value. Thus the returned array contains only 41 elements. Using these two filter types you can decide for yourself which holidays you are interested in.

Predefined filters are blacklist or whitelist filters that have internal knowledge about which holidays are accepted or denied. This means you can instantiate them by using an argument-less constructor. All necessary internal holiday names are already defined in the classes themselves. You can instantiate a predefined filter using the `new` operator and pass it to any function accepting filters.

If you want to use a combination of two or more filters, this can be done by using the `Date_Holidays_Filter_Composite` class. This is primarily useful to combine predefined filters but of course you can use any class that extends `Date_Holidays_Filter`. All you need to do is create a composite filter object and add (`addFilter()`) or remove (`removeFilter()`) filter objects. Afterwards you can start using the filter. See the following listing:

```
require_once 'Date/Holidays.php';
require_once 'Date/Holidays/Filter/Composite.php';

$driver    = Date_Holidays::factory('Christian', 2005);

$filter1   = new Date_Holidays_Filter_Whitelist(
    array('goodFriday', 'easter'));
$filter2   = new Date_Holidays_Filter_Whitelist(
    array('easterMonday'));

$composite = new Date_Holidays_Filter_Composite();
$composite->addFilter($filter1);
$composite->addFilter($filter2);

$holidays  = $driver->getHolidays($composite);
echo count($holidays);    // prints: 3
```

Note that you have to explicitly include the file containing the `Date_Holidays_Filter_Composite` class. It is rarely used in `Date_Holidays` and therefore not included by default.

Combining Holiday Drivers

As mentioned in the previous section, it is possible to combine several filters and treat them like a normal filter. This works just as well for driver objects. To do so, you first need to instantiate an object of `Date_Holidays_Driver_Composite` class via the `Date_Holidays::factory()` method. Afterwards you can use `addDriver()` to add a driver object to the compound and `removeDriver()` to remove one. Both methods expect the affected driver object as argument. See the following listing for an example. If you add together the internal names of the two standalone drivers you will see that the composite driver is indeed a combination of both of them.

```
$driver1   = Date_Holidays::factory('Christian', 2005);
echo count($driver1->getInternalHolidayNames()); // prints: 44

$driver2   = Date_Holidays::factory('UNO', 2005);
echo count($driver2->getInternalHolidayNames()); // prints: 67

$composite = Date_Holidays::factory('Composite');
$composite->addDriver($driver1);
$composite->addDriver($driver2);

$holidays  = $composite->getInternalHolidayNames();
echo count($holidays);                           // prints: 111
```

Is Today a Holiday?

`Date_Holidays` provides two ways to check whether a certain date represents a holiday.

Use `isHoliday()` to determine whether a certain date represents a holiday. It expects a Unix timestamp, ISO 8601 date string, or a `Date` object as the first argument. Optionally you can pass a filter object as the second argument. The method always returns a Boolean value. Let us see if 5th May, 2005 is a holiday:

```
$driver   = Date_Holidays::factory('Christian', 2005);

if ($driver->isHoliday('2005-05-05'))
{
  echo 'It is a holiday!';
} else
{
  echo 'It is not a holiday!';
}
```

If you want to get information about a specific date's holiday(s) you can use `getHolidayForDate()`. Like `isHoliday()` it expects a variable identifying a date as first argument. By default the method returns a `Date_Holidays_Holiday` object if it finds a holiday for this date or `null` if none was found. In the real world it is possible that there are multiple holidays on the same date. If you are using composite drivers the possibility is even higher. To address this issue you can use the third argument to define whether you accept multiple matches. If you pass a Boolean `true` the return value of the method will be an array containing holiday objects, even if it only finds a single match.

For the sake of completeness the second argument has to be mentioned here too. It can be used to specify a locale. If passed, it forces the method to use the specified locale instead of the global one set for the driver. We will talk about that later in the section *Multi-Lingual Translations*.

The next listing is an example on how to use `getHolidayForDate()`:

```
$driver    = Date_Holidays::factory('Christian', 2005);
$date      = '2005-05-05';

// no multiple return-values
$holiday   = $driver->getHolidayForDate($date);
if (! is_null($holiday))
{
  echo $holiday->getTitle();
}

// uses multiple return-values
$holidays = $driver->getHolidayForDate($date, null, true);
if (! is_null($holidays))
{
  foreach ($holidays as $holiday)
  {
    echo $holiday->getTitle();
  }
}
```

The example shows how the method's return value changes depending on the setting of the third argument. One time you get a holiday object and the other time an array is returned.

Using these methods you could also retrieve all holidays within a certain timespan by using a loop. Fortunately `Date_Holidays` provides the `getHolidaysForTimespan()` method, which makes this a lot easier for you. Additionally it is faster because internally it uses a hashed structure where holidays are already indexed by their date. The method expects two arguments that specify the start and end date of the timespan. The method returns an array that contains `Date_Holidays_Holiday` objects of all holidays within the given timespan. Like several other methods you already know, it additionally allows you to specify a filter and locale as the third and fourth arguments.

Multi-Lingual Translations

It was mentioned that `Date_Holidays` provides internationalization (I18N) features. This means that it provides holiday information in different languages. It uses language files in XML format, each containing a set of translations for a certain driver's holidays. These XML files contain information that allows you to assign localized titles to holidays. The next listing shows an excerpt of the French translations for the Christian driver:

```
<?xml version="1.0" encoding="ISO-8859-1" standalone="yes" ?>
<driver-data>
  <holidays>
    <holiday>
      <internal-name>jesusCircumcision</internal-name>
      <translation>Circoncision de Jésus</translation>
    </holiday>

    <holiday>
      <internal-name>epiphany</internal-name>
      <translation>'épiphanie</translation>
    </holiday>

  [...]

  </holidays>
</driver-data>
```

When you want to use the I18N features you have to tell `Date_Holidays` where it can find the necessary language files and set the driver's locale according to the translation you desire. The bundled language files will be installed in the `data` directory of your PEAR installation.

The language files allow you to specify translations for holiday titles and also define additional information about holidays. Using the `<property>` tag you can specify as much information as you desire. Each property has a unique ID (in the scope of a single holiday) and character data value. The XML markup could look like the following:

```
<holiday>
  <internal-name>jesusCircumcision</internal-name>
  <translation>Circoncision de Jésus</translation>
```

```
    <properties>
      <property id="type">static</property>
      <property id="since">4th century</property>
    </properties>
  </holiday>
```

There are no predefined values you should use as ID; this is completely up to you. You can store any information you desire. You could use the properties to state if a holiday occurs statically, you could provide a detailed description, etc. There are two ways to access the property information for a holiday. You can use `Date_Holidays_Holiday::getProperties()` if you have a holiday object or the `getHolidayProperties()` method of a `Date_Holidays_Driver` object. It expects the internal holiday name and the locale identifier as arguments.

Adding a Language File

To add a language file, driver classes provide the methods `addTranslationFile()` and `addCompiledTranslationFile()`. The first method allows you to add a translation file containing XML data; the second expects a file with serialized data. The second method works a lot faster because it does not need to parse the XML anymore. Both methods expect two arguments—the absolute path to of the file and the locale of the translations contained by the file respectively.

```
$driver = Date_Holidays::factory('Christian', 2005);

$file   = '/var/lib/pear/data/Date_Holidays/lang/Christian/fr_FR.xml';
$driver->addTranslationFile($file, 'fr_FR');
```

After adding translations this way a driver will be able to provide localized information.

Compiled language files use the `.ser` file extension and reside in the same directory as the normal XML language files.

You can even build your own language files and put them into whatever directory you like. If they are valid and `Date_Holidays` has the necessary rights to access them it will be able to use them. To compile your custom XML language files you can use the `pear-dh-compile-translationfile` CLI script that comes with `Date_Holidays`. It expects the name of the file to be converted (it can also handle multiple filenames) and writes the compiled data to a file using the same base name and the `.ser` file extension. You can type **`pear-dh-compile-translationfile --help`** on your PHP-CLI prompt to get detailed information about the script and its options:

```
$ pear-dh-compile-translationfile --help
Date_Holidays language-file compiler
--
```

```
Usage: pear-dh-compile-translationfile [options] filename(s)

-d --outputdir=<value>       Directory where compiled files are saved. Defaults
                                                to the current working directory.
-v --verbose                 Enable verbose mode.
--parameters values(1-...)   Input file(s)
```

Getting Localized Output

You can control the output language of driver methods by defining a locale. This setting can affect an entire driver object or a single method call.

Setting the locale for an entire driver object can be done in two different ways:

1. On construction of the driver object via the `Date_Holidays::factory()` method. The third argument can be used to pass a string identifying the locale to be used.
2. After construction of the driver object using the `setLocale()` method, which expects the locale string as argument.

Several driver methods also support setting a locale that is used during the method call: `getHoliday()`, `getHolidayForDate()`, `getHolidays()`, `getHolidayTitle()`, and `getHolidayTitles()`. Each of these methods expects the locale as one of its arguments.

The next listing shows how the per-driver and per-method localization settings affect the output.

```
// driver uses Italian translations by default
$driver  = Date_Holidays::factory('Christian', 2005, 'it_IT');

$driver->addCompiledTranslationFile(
     '/var/lib/pear/data/Date_Holidays/lang/Christian/it_IT.ser',
                                                             'it_IT');
$driver->addCompiledTranslationFile(
     '/var/lib/pear/data/Date_Holidays/lang/Christian/fr_FR.ser',
                                                             'fr_FR');

// uses default translations
echo $driver->getHolidayTitle('easter') . "\n";

// per-method French translation
echo $driver->getHolidayTitle('easter', 'fr_FR') . "\n";

// set fr_FR as default locale
$driver->setLocale('fr_FR');
```

```
// uses default translations. now French
echo $driver->getHolidayTitle('easter') . "\n";
```

When executed the script prints:

Domenica di Pasqua della Risurrezione

dimanche de Pâques

dimanche de Pâques

Note that not all translation files are complete. That means it is possible that you add a language file (e.g. French), set an according locale (e.g. `fr_FR`), but do not get the right translation of a holiday title. This can happen when a language file does not contain the required translation. By default the method called will raise an error when it encounters this problem. But you can modify this behavior by using the `Date_Holidays::staticSetProperty()` method. It expects the name of the property to be modified as first argument and its value as the second. The property you need to set is called `"DIE_ON_MISSING_LOCALE"`. If you set it to `false`, you will get the driver's English default translation when no localized value can be found. You can decide which way you prefer. The following example shows how to handle the static properties:

```
$driver = Date_Holidays::factory('Christian', 2005, 'fr_FR');
$driver->addCompiledTranslationFile(
    '/var/lib/pear5/data/Date_Holidays/lang/Christian/fr_FR.ser',
                                                          'fr_FR');

// default setting, no need to explicitly set this
Date_Holidays::staticSetProperty('DIE_ON_MISSING_LOCALE', true);

$title = $driver->getHolidayTitle('whitMonday');
if (Date_Holidays::isError($title))
{
  echo $title->getMessage();
} else
{
  echo $title;
}
echo "\n---\n";

// default setting, no need to explicitly set this
Date_Holidays::staticSetProperty('DIE_ON_MISSING_LOCALE', false);

// no need to check for an error but title may not be correctly
// localized
echo $driver->getHolidayTitle('whitMonday') . "\n";
```

The script will produce the following output:

The internal name (whitMonday) for the holiday was correct but no localized title could be found

---

Whit Monday

Help appreciated

If you write a custom driver for `Date_Holidays` that could be included in the distribution, feel free to contact the package maintainers or open a feature request at the package homepage on the PEAR website to attach a patch in the bug tracking tool.

Conclusion on Date_Holidays

`Date_Holidays` eases the task of calculation and internationalization of holidays or other special events. Currently it supports six drivers. Most language files are available in English and German, and some in French and Italian. The amount of this bundled data could be larger and will hopefully increase in future releases.

Nevertheless the package provides a well thought-out architecture you can easily extend by writing your own drivers, filters, and language files.

Working with the Calendar Package

If you search for PHP-based calendar utilities on the Web you will find lots of solutions. Some are good, others are not. However, in most cases you will experience some constraints. Several libraries have month/day names hard-coded or are tied to a specific output format.

`PEAR::Calendar` helps you generate calendar structures without forcing you to generate a certain type of output or depending on a special data store as back end. It simplifies the task of generating tabular calendars and allows you to render whatever output you like (e.g. HTML, WML, ASCII).

The package provides classes representing all important date entities like year, month, week, day, hour, minute, and second. Each date class can build subordinated entities. For instance an object representing a month is able to build contained day objects. Try the following script to build and fetch objects for each day in December 2005:

```
// Switch to PEAR::Date engine
define('CALENDAR_ENGINE', 'PearDate');

require_once 'Calendar/Month.php';
require_once 'Calendar/Day.php';

$month = new Calendar_Month(2005, 12); // December 2005
$month->build(); // builds the contained day objects

// iterate over the fetched day objects
while ($day = $month->fetch())
{
  echo $day->getTimestamp() . "\n";
}
```

As a result it prints the timestamps for each day in a single line:

2005-12-01 00:00:00

2005-12-02 00:00:00

...

2005-12-31 00:00:00

Most methods return numeric values, which is a great benefit when trying to build language-independent applications. You can localize date formats and names by directly using PHP's native functions or the `PEAR::Date` functions.

`PEAR::Calendar` supports different calculation engines. It bundles a Unix timestamp and a `PEAR::Date`-based engine. You could even build a calendar engine for more complex calendars like the Chinese one.

Whenever you lack a feature you can easily add it by using decorators. `PEAR::Calendar` already provides a decorator base you can rely on when building your own decorators. This way your modifications will not necessarily be overwritten by future releases of the Calendar package.

The following sections introduce the `PEAR::Calendar` package and show how to benefit from the possibilities it provides.

Calendar engines

`PEAR::Calendar` uses calendar engines to perform date and time calculations. These classes implementing the `Calendar_Engine` interface are exchangeable. Currently there is an engine based on Unix timestamps (used by default) and one based on `PEAR::Date`. You can choose which one to use by redefining the `'CALENDAR_ENGINE'` constant. The possibilities are: `define('CALENDAR_ENGINE','UnixTs')` or `define('CALENDAR_ENGINE','UnixTs')`.

Introduction to Basic Classes and Concepts

`PEAR::Calendar` provides a lot of public classes you can use to solve different problems. Each of those classes falls into one of four categories. These are date classes, tabular date classes, decorators, and validation classes. First you will get to know the basic calendar date and tabular date classes.

Each date class represents one of the basic date entities: year, month, day, hour, minute, and second. Tabular date classes are mainly designed for building table-based calendars. Classes of both categories are descendants of the `Calendar` class and they inherit its methods. A UML diagram of the `Calendar` class is shown in the figure opposite.

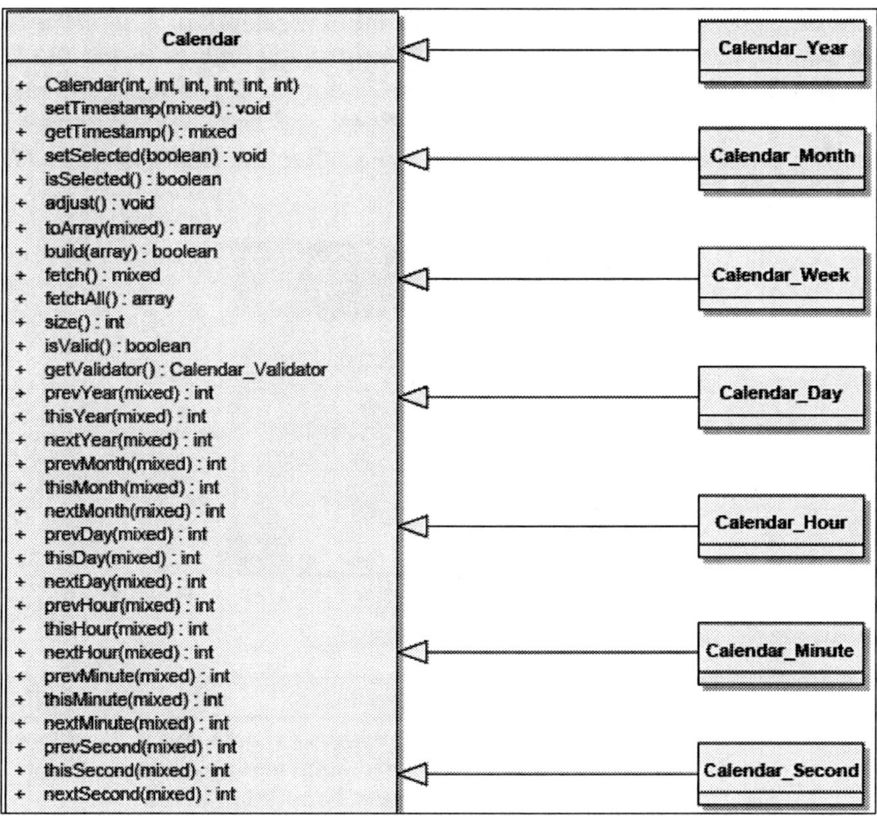

The following table lists the date classes, their include path, a short description for each, and the names of entities the class is able to build.

Class	require/include	Description	Builds
`Calendar_Year`	`Calendar/Year.php`	Represents a year.	`Calendar_Month`, `Calendar_Month_Weekdays`, `Calendar_Month_Weeks`
`Calendar_Month`	`Calendar/Month.php`	Represents a month.	`Calendar_Day`
`Calendar_Day`	`Calendar/Day.php`	Represents a day.	`Calendar_Hour`
`Calendar_Hour`	`Calendar/Hour.php`	Represents a hour.	`Calendar_Minute`
`Calendar_Minute`	`Calendar/Minute.php`	Represents a minute.	`Calendar_Second`
`Calendar_Second`	`Calendar/Second.php`	Represents a second.	-

The tabular date classes make it easy to render tabular calendars. Therefore these classes set information about whether a day is empty, the first, or last in the tabular representation. The figure showing a tabular calendar for September 2005 makes this clear. Empty days are gray, first days are green, and last days are orange. The corresponding `Calendar_Day` objects return `true` when the `isEmpty()`, `isFirst()`, or `isLast()` method is invoked.

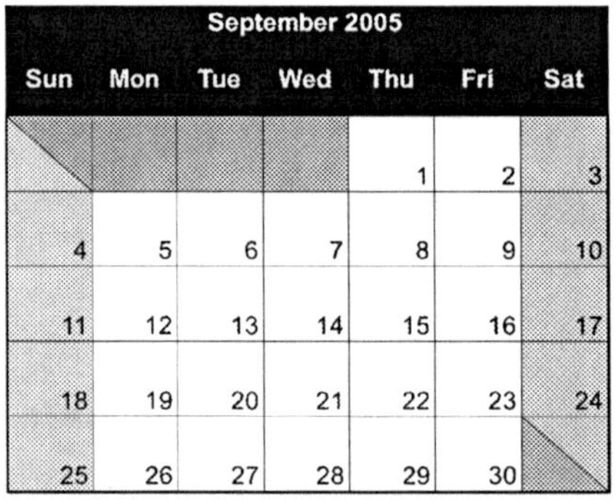

September 2005						
Sun	Mon	Tue	Wed	Thu	Fri	Sat
				1	2	3
4	5	6	7	8	9	10
11	12	13	14	15	16	17
18	19	20	21	22	23	24
25	26	27	28	29	30	

The following table shows the tabular date classes:

Class	require/include	Description	Builds
`Calendar_Month_Weekdays`	`Calendar/Month/Weekdays.php`	Represents a month and is able to build contained day objects. In addition to the `Calendar_Month` class it sets the information for the `isFirst()`, `isLast()`, and `isEmpty()` states for each day being built. This can be used when building tabular output for a calendar's month view.	`Calendar_Day`
`Calendar_Month_Weeks`	`Calendar/Month/Weeks.php`	Represents a month and is able to build week objects.	`Calendar_Week`
`Calendar_Week`	`Calendar/Week.php`	Represents a tabular week in a month. It is able to build day objects and sets the `isEmpty()` status if necessary.	`Calendar_Day`

Object Creation

The constructor of each basic date class accepts integer values as arguments. The number of arguments you need to pass on construction depends on what kind of date object you want to create. In general you need to define just as many arguments are as needed to exactly locate a certain date entity. A year would need one argument to be sufficiently accurately specified, but you have to specify three arguments when creating a `Calendar_Day` object. The following listing shows the construction of every single basic calendar class.

```
// date classes
$year   = new Calendar_Year(2005);
$month  = new Calendar_Month(2005, 12);
$day    = new Calendar_Day(2005, 12, 24);
$hour   = new Calendar_Hour(2005, 12, 24, 20);
$minute = new Calendar_Minute(2005, 12, 24, 20, 30);
$second = new Calendar_Second(2005, 12, 24, 20, 30, 40);

// tabular date classes
$firstDay = 0; // Sunday is the first day in the tabular
                 // representation
$monthWkD = new Calendar_Month_Weekdays(2005, 12, $firstDay);
$monthWk  = new Calendar_Month_Weeks(2005, 12, $firstDay);
$week     = new Calendar_Week(2005, 12, 24, $firstDay);
```

The tabular date classes allow you to specify a third argument representing the first day. This can be a number from 0 to 6 (Sunday = 0, Monday = 1, ..., Saturday = 6). This example already shows a nice feature of the Calendar package: `$week` would be the week that contains 24th December 2005. You just had to call `$week->thisWeek('n_in_month')` to get the week number within the month and `$week->thisWeek('n_in_year')` to get the week number within the current year.

Querying Information

The basic calendar classes provide several methods for retrieving information from a certain object. There are methods that allow you to determine what date/time an object represents or which dates come before or after. The methods are `this*()`, `prev*()`, and `next*()`. The asterisk stands for a certain date unit. It can be Year, Month, Day, Hour, Minute, or Second. The `Calendar_Week` class additionally provides the methods `thisWeek()`, `prevWeek()`, and `nextWeek()`. The following example shows how these methods are called on a `Calendar_Day` object.

```
$day = new Calendar_Day(2005, 12, 24);

echo $day->thisYear();      // prints: 2005
```

```
echo $day->thisMonth();      // prints: 12
echo $day->thisDay();        // prints: 24
echo $day->thisHour();       // prints: 0
echo $day->thisMinute();     // prints: 0
echo $day->thisSecond();     // prints: 0
```

The `this*()`, `prev*()`, and `next*()` methods accept an optional argument that allows you to influence the returned value. This is achieved by passing a string that determines the return value format. Possible values for the string argument are:

- `"int"`: The integer value of the specific unit; this is the default setting if no argument is specified.
- `"timestamp"`: Returns the timestamp for the specific calendar date unit.
- `"object"`: Returns a calendar date object; this is useful in combination with the methods `next*()` and `prev*()`.
- `"array"`: Returns the date unit's value as an array.

Possible arguments for the methods `thisWeek()`, `prevWeek()`, and `nextWeek()` of `Calendar_Week` are `"timestamp"`, `"array"`, `"n_in_month"`, and `"n_in_year"`. The next listing shows how to use the preceding arguments to influence the return value of the methods.

```
$second = new Calendar_Second(2005, 12, 24, 20, 30, 40);

echo $second->nextDay('int') . "\n";
echo $second->nextDay('timestamp') . "\n";
print_r( $second->nextDay('object') );
print_r( $second->nextDay('array') );
```

The example prints the following output:

25

2005-12-25 00:00:00

Calendar_Day Object

(

! contents omitted for brevity !

)

Array

(

```
    [year] => 2005
    [month] => 12
    [day] => 25
    [hour] => 0
    [minute] => 0
    [second] => 0
)
```

The `Calendar` class provides two more methods: `getTimestamp()` and `setTimestamp()`. As the name suggests, `getTimestamp()` returns the timestamp value of the calendar date object and `setTimestamp()` allows you to modify an object's date/time. The value returned by `getTimestamp()` depends on the calendar engine used. If you use the Unix timestamp-based engine it will return a Unix timestamp. If you use the `PEAR::Date`-based engine it will return a string of the format YYYY-MM-DD hh:mm:ss. Note that calling `$day->getTimestamp()` has the same effect as `$day->thisDay('timestamp')`.

Building and Fetching

As mentioned in the introduction to the Calendar package, the date classes and tabular date classes are able to build contained date entities. They provide the `build()` method that can be used to generate the "children" of the current date object.

Once the `build()` method has been called you can access one child after the other or all together. To access the children in a row you can use the `fetch()` method, which utilizes the iterator concept. Each call returns one child of the series. A subsequent call will return the next child and when the end of the series is reached `fetch()` returns `false`. This way you can comfortably iterate over all children in a `while` loop. The following code listing shows how to use the iterator concept. It should look familiar to you, as you have already seen it in the introduction.

```
$month = new Calendar_Month(2005, 12); // December 2005
$month->build();

while ($day = $month->fetch())
{
  echo $day->getTimestamp() . "\n";
}
```

The script builds the contained days of December 2005 and prints a formatted date for each day:

2005-12-01 00:00:00

2005-12-02 00:00:00

...

2005-12-31 00:00:00

To get all children at once you can use the `fetchAll()` method, which will return an indexed array containing the date objects representing the children. Depending on the date class, the returned array starts with an index equal to `0` or `1`. For `Calendar_Year`, `Calendar_Month`, `Calendar_Month_Weekdays`, `Calendar_Month_Weeks`, and `Calendar_Week` the array's first index is `1`. For `Calendar_Day`, `Calendar_Hour`, `Calendar_Minute`, and `Calendar_Second` it is `0`. If you wonder why, have a look at the tables for the date and tabular date classes and consider what type of children a class builds. The ones that build hours, minutes, and seconds return arrays starting with a `0` index.

The concept of building and fetching introduced in this section makes the creation of calendar date objects a non-computationally-expensive operation. Children are never built on construction but only when you really request them and explicitly call the `build()` method.

Make a Selection

The `build()` method can specially mark items when it builds them. This is done when you specify an indexed array of date objects that will be taken as a selection. When the `build()` method generates the children, it compares them to the items of the array and when it finds an equal match the generated child is selected. After selection, calling the `isSelected()` method on the child returns `true`. You could use this feature to mark days that should look special in a generated output of a calendar. The next listing shows how the selection feature works.

```
$month = new Calendar_Month(2005, 12);

$stNicholas = new Calendar_Day(2005, 12, 6);
$xmasEve    = new Calendar_Day(2005, 12, 24);

$selection  = array($stNicholas, $xmasEve);
$month->build($selection);

while ($day = $month->fetch())
{
  if ($day->isSelected())
  {
    echo $day->getTimestamp() . "\n";
```

```
    }
}
```

The script prints:

2005-12-06 00:00:00

2005-12-24 00:00:00

The objects in the `$selection` array matching the children that are being built will replace them. That means `fetch()` or `fetchAll()` will return the object you put into the selection array. This way you can insert your own special objects. Normally you will accomplish this by extending the `Calendar_Decorator` base class for decorators. You will find out more about decorators in the section *Adjusting the Standard Classes' Behavior*.

Validating Calendar Date Objects

`PEAR::Calendar` provides validation classes that are used to validate calendar dates. For a simple validation you can call the `isValid()` method on every subclass of `Calendar`. This method returns `true` if the date is valid or `false` otherwise. To allow more fine-grained validation, each of the basic calendar classes can return a `Calendar_Validator` object via the `getValidator()` method. The validator object provides a handful of methods that help you identify an error more precisely. The methods of the `Calendar_Validator` class are described in the next table.

Method	Description
`fetch()`	Iterates over all validation errors.
`isValid()`	Tests whether the calendar object is valid. This calls all the `isValid*()` methods.
`isValidDay()`	Tests whether the calendar object's day unit is valid.
`isValidHour()`	Tests whether the calendar object's hour unit is valid.
`isValidMinute()`	Tests whether the calendar object's minute unit is valid.
`isValidMonth()`	Tests whether the calendar object's month unit is valid.
`isValidSecond()`	Tests whether the calendar object's second unit is valid.
`isValidYear()`	Tests whether the calendar object's year unit is valid.

The following listing is an example of how to validate calendar date objects:

```
$day = new Calendar_Day(2005, 13, 32);

if (! $day->isValid()) {
  echo "Day's date is invalid! \n";
```

```
    // finer grained validation
    $validator = $day->getValidator();

    if (! $validator->isValidDay())
    {
      echo "Invalid day unit: " . $day->thisDay() . "\n";
    }
    if (! $validator->isValidMonth())
    {
      echo "Invalid month unit: " . $day->thisMonth() . "\n";
    }
    if (! $validator->isValidYear())
    {
      echo "Invalid year unit: " . $day->thisYear() . "\n";
    }
  }
```

The example will print:

Day's date is invalid!

Invalid day unit: 32

Invalid month unit: 13

Validation Versus Adjustment

Instead of validating date objects you can also adjust them to represent valid dates. All you have to do is call the `adjust()` method. It will transmogrify the invalid date into a valid one. For instance 32 December 2005 would be adjusted to 2006-02-01:

```
$day = new Calendar_Day(2005, 13, 32);
$day->adjust();

echo $day->getTimestamp();    // prints: 2006-02-01 00:00:00
```

Dealing with Validation Errors

The `Calendar_Validator` class allows you to iterate over existent errors using the `fetch()` method. It returns `Calendar_Validation_Error` objects or `false` if there are no errors. Such an error object provides four methods: `getMessage()`, `getUnit()`, `getValue()`, and `toString()`.

See their descriptions in the following table.

Method	Description
`getMessage()`	Returns the validation error message. These validation error messages are in English but can be modified by redefining the constants `CALENDAR_VALUE_TOOSMALL` and `CALENDAR_VALUE_TOOLARGE`.
`getUnit()`	Returns the invalid date unit. The unit is one of the following: `"Year"`, `"Month"`, `"Day"`, `"Hour"`, `"Minute"`, `"Second"`.
`getValue()`	Returns the value of the invalid date unit. This is the same integer that would be returned by calling `thisYear()`, `thisMonth()`, etc.
`toString()`	Returns a string containing the error message, unit, and the unit's value. Actually it is a combination of the first three methods.

Using these methods you can exactly locate the reason for the invalidity. See the next listing for an example on how to iterate over existent validation errors and display them.

```
$day = new Calendar_Day(2005, 13, 32);

if (! $day->isValid())
{
  $validator = $day->getValidator();
  while ($error = $validator->fetch())
  {
    echo sprintf("Invalid date: unit is %s, value is %s. Reason: %s
\n",
          $error->getUnit(),
          $error->getValue(),
          $error->getMessage());
  }
}
```

The output of the script looks like the following:

Invalid date: unit is Month, value is 13. Reason: Too large: max = 12

Invalid date: unit is Day, value is 32. Reason: Too large: max = 31

Adjusting the Standard Classes' Behavior

Decorators allow you to add custom functionality to the main calendar objects. The benefit of using a decorator is that you do not directly need to extend one of the main calendar classes.

What are Decorators?

Decorators allow you to dynamically broaden the functionality of an object. A decorator achieves this by wrapping the object to be modified instead of extending it. The benefit is that this way you can choose which objects should be decorated instead of influencing all objects of a certain class.

A decorator normally expects the object to be decorated as an argument on construction and provides the same API as the wrapped object or offers even more methods. Set up this way, a decorator can decide on its own whether method calls are routed through to the decorated object with or without modifying the return value.

The Common Decorator Base Class

`PEAR::Calendar` comes with a decorator base class—`Calendar_Decorator`. This provides the combined API of all subclasses of the `Calendar` class. `Calendar_Decorator` expects an object of type `Calendar` as an argument in the constructor. It does not decorate anything but only passes all method calls to the decorated `Calendar` object that was passed on construction. This saves you a lot of work when building your own decorators as you just have to extend `Calendar_Decorator` without the need to implement any delegation method.

As mentioned in the section *Make a Selection* you can inject objects with custom functionality by passing an array of these to the `build()` method of a calendar date object. Each object in the array has to implement the public API of the `Calendar` class. The best way to make your custom classes meet these requirements is letting them extend the `Calendar_Decorator` class.

Bundled Decorators

`PEAR::Calendar` ships with a few decorators that may come in handy in some situations. To use one of these classes you have to explicitly include them in your script. See a list of the bundled decorators in the following table:

Decorator	Description
`Calendar_Decorator_Textual`	Helps you with fetching textual representations of months and weekdays. If performance matters you should use the `Calendar_Util_Textual` class unless you have an important reason for using a decorator.
`Calendar_Decorator_Uri`	Helps you with building HTML links for navigating the calendar. If performance matters you should use the `Calendar_Util_Uri` class unless you have an important reason for using a decorator.

Decorator	Description
Calendar_Decorator_ Weekday	Helps you with fetching the day of the week.
Calendar_Decorator_ Wrapper	Helps you wrap built children in another decorator. Decorates the fetch() and fetchAll() methods and allows you to specify the name of a decorator that will wrap the fetched object.

Generating Graphical Output

When talking about calendars in websites most people think about tabular formatted widgets that allow you to navigate through the months, weeks, and days of a year. PEAR::Calendar has some nice features that help you build calendars like that. Theoretically you could build a calendar so detailed that it allows you to browse a year from a monthly to minutely perspective.

The methods isFirst(), isLast(), and isEmpty() of the Calendar_Day class help you build up the tabular structure. You would need the following few lines of code to render a tabular calendar output for September 2005:

```
// September 2005, first day is Monday
$month = new Calendar_Month_Weekdays(2005, 9, $firstDay = 1);
$month->build();

// localized text for the calendar headline
$header = strftime('%B %Y', $month->thisMonth('timestamp'));

echo <<<EOQ
<table width="250">
    <!-- calendar headline -->
    <tr><td colspan="7" align="center">$header</td></tr>
    <tr>
        <td align="center">Mon</td>
        <td align="center">Tue</td>
        <td align="center">Wed</td>
        <td align="center">Thu</td>
        <td align="center">Fri</td>
        <td align="center">Sat</td>
        <td align="center">Sun</td>
     </tr>

    <!-- calendar data -->
```

```
    <tr>
EOQ;

// iterate over the built weekdays and display them
while ($Day = & $month->fetch())
{
    if ($Day->isFirst())
    {
        echo '<tr>';
    }

    if ($Day->isEmpty())
    {
        echo '<td><div> </div></td>';
    }
      else
    {
        echo '<td align="center"><div>'.$Day->thisDay().'</div></td>';
    }

    if ($Day->isLast())
    {
        echo "</tr>\n";
    }
}
echo '</table>';
```

When a `Calendar_Day` object indicates that it is the first (`isFirst()` returns `true`) a new row is started. Empty days (`isEmpty()` returns `true`) are rendered as table cells with a non-breaking space entity (` `) and after days that indicate they are the last (`isLast()` returns `true`) a table row is ended. The resulting output in the browser is shown in the following screenshot:

September 2005						
Mon	Tue	Wed	Thu	Fri	Sat	Sun
			1	2	3	4
5	6	7	8	9	10	11
12	13	14	15	16	17	18
19	20	21	22	23	24	25
26	27	28	29	30		

Navigable Tabular Calendars

Normally you will not only render a static calendar but also one that allows the user to browse different months/weeks/days or more. `PEAR::Calendar` comes with two classes that help you to render links for navigation: `Calendar_Util_Uri` and `Calendar_Decorator_Uri`, which both solve the same problems. If you care about performance you should stick to the `Calendar_Util_Uri` class. The constructor expects at least one and up to six arguments. You can use them to specify the names of request parameters used for year, month, day, hour, minute, and second. An object created with `$foo = new Calendar_Util_Uri('y', 'm', 'd')` would generate URI strings looking like this: `"y=2005&m=9&d=9"`. The more fragment names you specify, more the parameters are contained in the URI string. The class provides three methods `prev()`, `next()`, and `this()`, which return the URI string for the previous, next, or current date unit. Each of these methods expects a subclass of `Calendar` as the first argument and a string identifying the affected date unit as the second argument. This string must be one of `"year"`, `"month"`, `"week"`, `"day"`, `"hour"`, `"minute"`, or `"second"`. The following listing shows an extended version of the preceding example. This one has added arrows in the calendar header that allow you to step one month back and forward.

```
// get date information from request or use current date
$y = isset($_GET['year']) ? $_GET['year'] : date('Y');
$m = isset($_GET['month']) ? $_GET['month'] : date('m');

$month = new Calendar_Month_Weekdays($y, $m, $firstDay = 1);
$month->build();

// Localized text for the calendar headline
$header = strftime('%B %Y', $month->thisMonth('timestamp'));

// URI Util for generation of navigation links
$uriUtil = new Calendar_Util_Uri('year', 'month');
$nextM = $uriUtil->next($month, 'month');
$prevM = $uriUtil->prev($month, 'month');

echo <<<EOQ
<table width="250">
    <!-- calendar headline -->
    <tr>
        <td align="left"><a href="{
                                $_SERVER['PHP_SELF']}?$prevM">&lt;</a></td>
        <td colspan="5" align="center">$header</td>
        <td align="right"><a href="{
                                $_SERVER['PHP_SELF']}?$nextM">&gt;</td>
    </tr>
    <tr>
```

```
            <td align="center">Mon</td>
            <td align="center">Tue</td>
            <td align="center">Wed</td>
            <td align="center">Thu</td>
            <td align="center">Fri</td>
            <td align="center">Sat</td>
            <td align="center">Sun</td>
        </tr>

        <!-- calendar data -->
        <tr>
EOQ;

// from this point the code is similar to the preceding listing
```

In the next step we will extend the previous example to make the script highlight empty days and holidays. Additionally the `title` attribute of the `div` element will be used to display a holiday's name when the mouse moves over it in the calendar output. To determine when to highlight a holiday we will use the selection feature of the `Calendar::build()` method. Therefore we first need to build a decorator that can be used in the selection array of the `build()` method and provides access to a `Date_Holidays_Holiday` object:

```
if (!defined('CALENDAR_ROOT'))
{
  define('CALENDAR_ROOT', 'Calendar'.DIRECTORY_SEPARATOR);
}
require_once CALENDAR_ROOT.'Decorator.php';

class Calendar_Decorator_Holiday extends Calendar_Decorator
{
  private $holiday;

  public function __construct($Calendar, $holiday)
  {
    parent::Calendar_Decorator($Calendar);
    $this->holiday = $holiday;
  }

  public function getHoliday()
  {
    return $this->holiday;
  }
}
```

Using this decorator in the script that produces the tabular calendar output, we can now retrieve the holidays of the month to be displayed with the `Date_Holidays_Driver::getHolidaysForDateSpan()` method. For each holiday object in the resulting array a corresponding `Calendar_Decorator_Holiday` object will be created. Each decorator object gets passed a `Calendar_Day` and a `Date_Holidays_Holiday` object that share the same date. The decorator objects are put into the `$selection` array and passed to the `build()` method. If the method encounters a match, the corresponding decorated object will replace the built `Calendar_Day` object and get returned by the `fetch()` method.

Later in the script we iterate over the built `Calendar_Day` objects to generate the HTML markup for the calendar. The code is very similar to that in the previous example. This time, when a day is indicated to be empty we use the HTML `class` attribute to assign a CSS class (`div.empty`) to the surrounding `div` container. If a day is not empty we test whether it was selected or not. Non-selected days are displayed normally and selected days are marked as holidays using the `div.holiday` class for the `div` container. The whole script follows:

```
require_once 'Calendar/Month/Weekdays.php';
require_once 'Calendar/Util/Uri.php';
require_once 'Calendar/Day.php';
require_once 'Date.php';
require_once 'Date/Holidays.php';
require_once 'Calendar_Decorator_Holiday.php';

setlocale(LC_ALL, $locale= 'en_US');

// get date information from request or use current date
$y = sprintf('%04d', isset($_GET['year']) ? $_GET['year'] :
date('Y'));
$m = sprintf('%02d', isset($_GET['month']) ? $_GET['month'] :
date('m'));

// get holidays for the displayed month
$startDate = new Date($y .'-'. $m . '-01 00:00:00');
$endDate   = new Date($y .'-'. $m . '-01 00:00:00');
$endDate->setDay($endDate->getDaysInMonth());
$driver = Date_Holidays::factory('Christian', $y, $locale);
if (Date_Holidays::isError($driver))
{
  die('Creation of driver failed: ' . $driver->getMessage());
}
$holidays = $driver->getHolidaysForDatespan($startDate, $endDate);
if (Date_Holidays::isError($holidays))
{
  die('Error while retrieving holidays: ' . $holidays->getMessage());
}
```

```
// create selection-array with decorated objects for the build()
// method
$selection = array();
foreach ($holidays as $holiday)
{
  $date = $holiday->getDate();
  $day  = new Calendar_Day($date->getYear(), $date->getMonth(),
                                             $date->getDay());
  $selection[] = new Calendar_Decorator_Holiday($day, $holiday);
}

$month = new Calendar_Month_Weekdays($y, $m, $firstDay = 1);
$month->build($selection);

// Localized text for the calendar headline
$header = strftime('%B %Y', $month->thisMonth('timestamp'));

// URI Util for generation of navigation links
$uriUtil = new Calendar_Util_Uri('year', 'month');
$nextM = $uriUtil->next($month, 'month');
$prevM = $uriUtil->prev($month, 'month');

echo <<<EOQ
<style type="text/css">
  div.empty {background-color: #bfbfbf;}
  div.holiday {background-color: #b8ffa4;}
</style>

<table width="250" cellpadding="0" cellspacing="0">
  <!-- calendar headline -->
  <tr>
    <td align="left"><a href="{$_SERVER['PHP_SELF']}?
                              $prevM">&lt;</a></td>
    <td colspan="5" align="center">$header</td>
    <td align="right"><a href="{$_SERVER['PHP_SELF']}?
                               $nextM">&gt;</td>
  </tr>
  <tr>
    <td align="center">Mon</td>
    <td align="center">Tue</td>
    <td align="center">Wed</td>
    <td align="center">Thu</td>
    <td align="center">Fri</td>
    <td align="center">Sat</td>
    <td align="center">Sun</td>
   </tr>
```

```
    <!-- calendar data -->
    <tr>
  EOQ;

  // iterate over the built weekdays and display them
  while ($day = & $month->fetch())
  {
    if ($day->isFirst())
    {
        echo '<tr>';
    }

    if ($day->isEmpty())
    {
      echo '<td><div class="empty"> </div></td>';
    }
      else
    {
      if ($day->isSelected())
      {
        echo '<td align="center"><div class="holiday" '
            . 'title="' . $day->getHoliday()->getTitle() . '">'.
                                                $day->thisDay()
            . '</div></td>';
      }
        else
      {
        echo '<td align="center"><div>'.$day->thisDay().'</div></td>';
      }
    }

    if ($day->isLast())
    {
      echo "</tr>\n";
    }
  }
  echo '</table>';
```

The whole listing is not even a hundred lines of code but produces a tabular calendar that is navigable and highlights holidays. When cleanly separating CSS, HTML, and PHP code it would be far more concise. The combination of the PEAR Date and Time section makes it possible! You can see the output it produces in the following screenshot. With a few more lines of CSS code it would look even more beautiful.

<			October 2005			>
Mon	Tue	Wed	Thu	Fri	Sat	Sun
					1	2
3	4	5	6	7	8	9
10	11	12	13	14	15	16
17	18	19	20	21	22	23
24	25	26	27	28	29	30
31						

Summary

PEAR's date and time section provides three very powerful packages. Each package is well designed and helps you develop applications that are fast and effective. A big advantage of the three packages is that you can use them in combination with each other without fearing incompatibilities. Both the `PEAR::Calendar` and `Date_Holidays` packages are able to use `PEAR::Date` classes. PHP's native date and time functions are certainly faster but if you want an object-oriented API that is comfortable and powerful at the same time, the date packages are a very good solution.

Index

E

F

G

H

M

P

Y

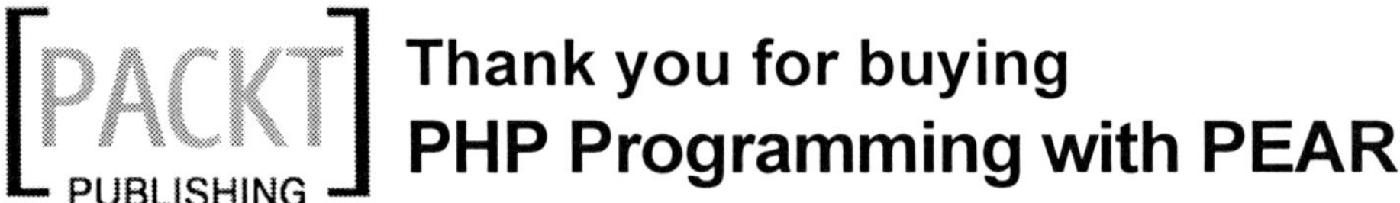

Packt Open Source Project Royalties

When we sell a book written on an Open Source project, we pay a royalty directly to that project. Therefore by purchasing PHP Programming with PEAR, Packt will have given some of the money received to the PEAR project.

In the long term, we see ourselves and you—customers and readers of our books—as part of the Open Source ecosystem, providing sustainable revenue for the projects we publish on. Our aim at Packt is to establish publishing royalties as an essential part of the service and support a business model that sustains Open Source.

If you're working with an Open Source project that you would like us to publish on, and subsequently pay royalties to, please get in touch with us.

Writing for Packt

We welcome all inquiries from people who are interested in authoring. Book proposals should be sent to `authors@packtpub.com`. If your book idea is still at an early stage and you would like to discuss it first before writing a formal book proposal, contact us; one of our commissioning editors will get in touch with you.

We're not just looking for published authors; if you have strong technical skills but no writing experience, our experienced editors can help you develop a writing career, or simply get some additional reward for your expertise.

About Packt Publishing

Packt, pronounced 'packed', published its first book "Mastering phpMyAdmin for Effective MySQL Management" in April 2004 and subsequently continued to specialize in publishing highly focused books on specific technologies and solutions.

Our books and publications share the experiences of your fellow IT professionals in adapting and customizing today's systems, applications, and frameworks. Our solution-based books give you the knowledge and power to customize the software and technologies you're using to get the job done. Packt books are more specific and less general than the IT books you have seen in the past. Our unique business model allows us to bring you more focused information, giving you more of what you need to know, and less of what you don't.

Packt is a modern, yet unique publishing company, which focuses on producing quality, cutting-edge books for communities of developers, administrators, and newbies alike. For more information, please visit our website: `www.PacktPub.com`.

Printed in the United States
97857LV00005B/93-96/A

9 781904 811794